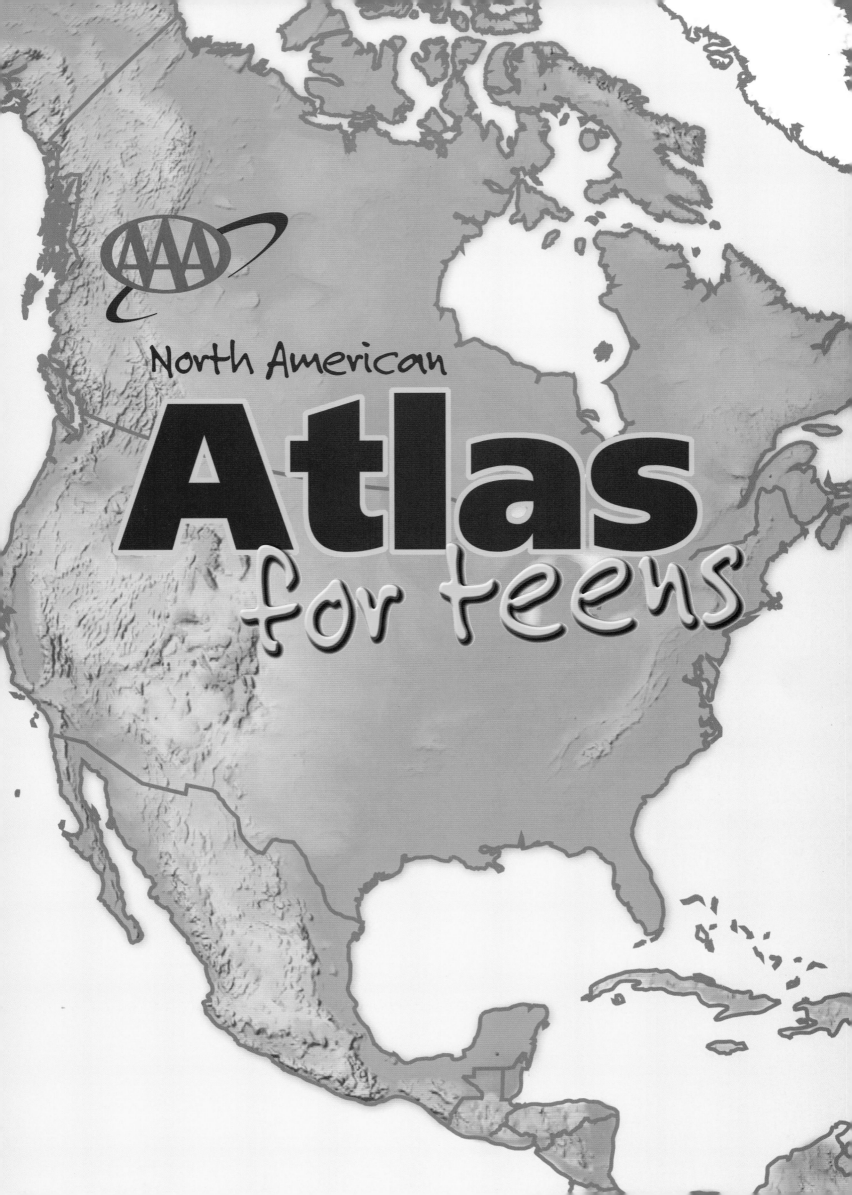

North American

Atlas
for teens

President & CEO	**Robert Darbelnet**
Executive Vice President, Publishing & Administration	**Rick Rinner**
Managing Director, Travel Information	**Bob Hopkins**
Director, Product Development	**Bill Wood**
Director, Sales & Marketing	**John Coerper**
Director, Purchasing & Corporate Services	**Becky Barrett**
Director, Business Development	**Gary Sisco**
Director, Tourism Information Development (TID)	**Michael Petrone**
Director, Travel Information	**Jeff Zimmerman**
Director, Publishing Operations	**Susan Sears**
Director, GIS/Cartography	**Jan Coyne**
Director, Publishing/GIS Systems & Development	**Ramin Kalhor**
Product Manager	**Beverly Donovan**
Managing Editor, Product Development	**Margaret Cavanaugh**
Marketing Manager	**Bart Peluso**
AAA Travel Store & e-store Manager	**Sharon Edwards**
Manager, Business Line Publicity	**Janie Graziani**
Print Buyer	**Laura Cox**
Managing Editor, GEM Points of Interest	**Suzanne Lemon**
Manager, Product Support	**Linda Indolfi**
Manager, Electronic Media Design	**Mike McCrary**
Manager, Pre-Press & Quality Services	**Tim Johnson**
Manager, GIS/Cartography	**Mike Mouser**
Art Director (Cover)	**Barbra Natali**
Cover Design	**Michele Trimble**
Map Design / Production	**Bill Hagerty and Laura Myers**
Publishing Systems & Development	**James White**
Research (Seminole County Teacher Interns)	**Kathryn Myers and Gemara Goodwin**

AAA Publishing wishes to acknowledge the following for their assistance:
Robin Abrams, Bob Crooks, Mary McNeal, Jane Palmer, Sheryl Pennington, Stan Shave and Mary Ann Venezia from Seminole County Florida Public Schools. Kristen Cortese, Matthew Jones, Hallie Nimrichter, Brittney Schonk and Cory Woods for participating in the teen focus group. Bob Sellers' Sanford Middle School Social Studies class for input on the cover design.

BOOKMARK ASSOCIATES, INC.

Editorial Director	**Sharon Yates**
Research Editor	**Hildegard Anderson**
Spanish Research Editor	**Joseph Gonzalez**
Copy Editor	**Norm Goldstein**

MEDIA PROJECTS INCORPORATED

Project Director	**Carter Smith**
Art Director & Production Coordinator	**Laura Smyth**
Cartographers	**Arlene Goldberg, Alex Ferrari**
Photo Researcher	**James Burmester**
Indexer	**Aaron Murray**
Editorial Interns	**Celine Geiger, Kathryn Briggs**

Published by AAA Publishing, 1000 AAA Drive, Heathrow, Florida 32746

Printed in Hong Kong through Asia Pacific Offset, Inc.

ISBN 1-56251-744-9 / AAA Stock No.: 200202

For information about other titles published by AAA, visit our e-store at www.aaa.com

Maps derived from Map Images maps © 2001, Map Images, Lambertville, New Jersey 08530 www.mapresources.com

Table of Contents

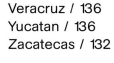

Arctic Ocean

GREENLAND

Denmark Strait

ICELAND

Davis Strait ★
NUUK
(Godthab)

Hudson Strait

Hudson

Bay

C A N A D A

*Gulf of
St. Lawrence*

OTTAWA ★

U N I T E D   S T A T E S

★ WASHINGTON D. C.

Pacific Ocean

Golfo de California

M E X I C O

Atlantic Ocean

Gulf of Mexico

BAHAMAS ★

HAVANA ★

CUBA

SANTO
DOMINGO ★

SAN JUAN ★

PORT-AU-PRINCE ★

PUERTO
RICO

★ MÉXICO
CITY

JAMAICA ★
KINGSTON

HAITI

BELIZE
★ BELMOPAN

Caribbean Sea

GUATAMALA
GUATEMALA

HONDURAS
TEGUCIGALPA

SAN SALVADOR
EL SALVADOR

NICARAGUA
MANAGUA

SAN JOSE ★
COSTA RICA

PANAMA
PANAMA

SOUTH   AMERICA

0		500 Miles
0	500 Kilometers	

The winter months in the Caribbean are usually hot and dry, making the beaches like this one in Barbados a popular vacation spot.

TIMELINE

13,000 B.C. **Ancestors of the American Indians cross a temporary land bridge from Asia to North America.**

986 **Led by Eric the Red, Vikings from Norway settle on the island of Greenland.**

200 B.C. to A.D. 900 **Mayan Indian civilization develops in Central America and southern Mexico.**

Introduction

North America is the third largest continent in the world, after Asia and Africa. It encompasses Greenland, Canada, the United States, Mexico, Central America, and the Caribbean Islands. It includes nearly every type of environment — from frozen tundra and flowering meadows to deserts, steamy rain forests, and coral reefs. An almost unbroken line of mountains runs down North America's western side. You can trace it with your finger on the map shown on the opposite page. There are oceans, seas, lakes, and rivers. Such variety in habitats creates homes for animals ranging from whales and polar bears to macaws, monarch butterflies, and mosquitoes.

The ancestors of North Americans first came from Asia across a land bridge that existed temporarily between the two continents. Then, centuries later, Europeans sailed across the ocean. Africans were first brought as slaves to the Caribbean and Central America and later to the United States. Waves of colonists and immigrants have since come from almost every country on Earth to begin new lives. The collective skills and talents of all these people have built the continent into what it is today. You will determine its future.

About this book

In the pages that follow, you'll find topographical maps with major geographical features identified, such as mountains, lakes, and rivers. Main highways and cities are also indicated as well as must-see tourist sites. The special triangular **AAA GEM** symbol indicates a site that is a Great Experience for AAA Members, and you'll find descriptions of these on the page under **Selected Must-See Points of Interest**. Other Must-See Points of Interest are also located for you on the maps.

Fresh Facts offers basic information about each country, state, or province, and the **Timeline** gives a very brief historical overview. The **Inside Scoop** box highlights fun facts and trivia about the country, state, or province.

In the back of the book, the **Fresh Facts Extremes** page lists highs and lows, firsts and lasts, biggests and smallests and much more about places, people, and things across the continent.

We hope you will find this book about our fabulous North American continent informative, useful, and entertaining.

AREA 9,347,000 square miles (24,208,000 square kilometers)

POPULATION 481,000,000

HIGHEST POINT Mount McKinley, Alaska, 20,320 feet (6,194 meters)

LOWEST POINT Death Valley, Calif., 282 feet (86 meters) below sea level

OTHER MAINLAND POINTS Boothia Peninsula, Northwest Territories, Canada (northernmost); Peninsula de Azuero/Darien National Park, Panama (southernmost); Cape Prince of Wales, Alaska (westernmost); Cape Spear, Newfoundland, Canada (easternmost).

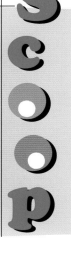

Snow-capped mountains like Oregon's Mount Hood run throughout North America, from northern Canada all the way to southern Panama.

Inside Scoop

CANADA IS the second largest country in the world after Russia.
NORTH AMERICA has a longer total coastline than any other continent.
THE SHORES OF the North American continent border three oceans, the Pacific, Arctic, and Atlantic.
GREENLAND IS the world's largest island.
THE GULF OF MEXICO is the largest gulf in the world.

Icebergs float off the coast of Greenland. Because most of North America's largest island is frozen under the polar ice cap, Greenland's only towns are along the coast.

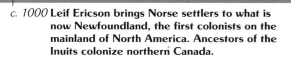

_c. 1000_ Ancestors of today's Pueblo Indians build large multistory dwellings, similar to apartment buildings, into the cliffs of New Mexico, Arizona, Colorado, and Utah.

_c. 1000_ Leif Ericson brings Norse settlers to what is now Newfoundland, the first colonists on the mainland of North America. Ancestors of the Inuits colonize northern Canada.

_1325–1519_ The Aztec empire flourishes in Mexico until Spanish conquistadors conquer it.

_1492_ Christopher Columbus discovers the West Indies (the Caribbean Islands).

Greenland

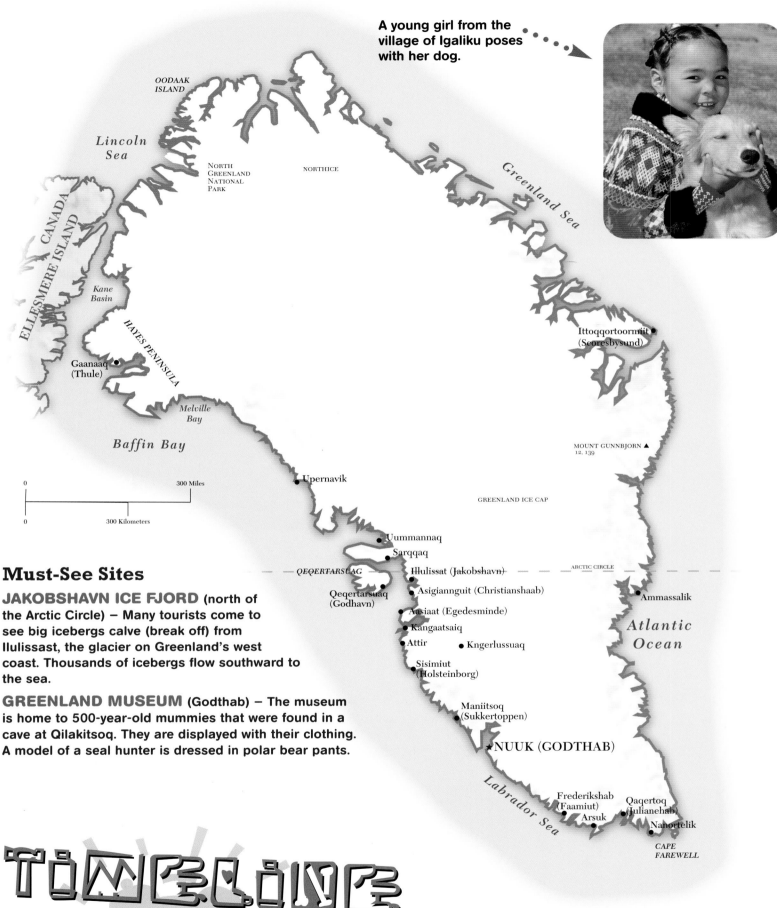

A young girl from the village of Igaliku poses with her dog.

OODAAK ISLAND

Lincoln Sea

NORTH GREENLAND NATIONAL PARK

NORTHICE

Greenland Sea

CANADA

ELLESMERE ISLAND

Kane Basin

HAYES PENINSULA

Gaanaaq (Thule)

Ittoqqortoormiit (Scoresbysund)

Melville Bay

Baffin Bay

MOUNT GUNNBJORN ▲ 12, 139

0   300 Miles

0   300 Kilometers

Upernavik

GREENLAND ICE CAP

Uummannaq

Sarqqaq

QEQERTARSUAG

ARCTIC CIRCLE

Ilulissat (Jakobshavn)

Qeqertarsuaq (Godhavn)

Asigiannguit (Christianshaab)

Ammassalik

Aasiaat (Egedesminde)

Kangaatsiaq

Attir

Kngerlussuaq

Atlantic Ocean

Sisimiut (Holsteinborg)

Maniitsoq (Sukkertoppen)

★ NUUK (GODTHAB)

Labrador Sea

Frederikshab (Faamiut)

Qaqertoq (Julianehab)

Arsuk

Nanortelik

CAPE FAREWELL

Must-See Sites

JAKOBSHAVN ICE FJORD (north of the Arctic Circle) – Many tourists come to see big icebergs calve (break off) from Ilulissast, the glacier on Greenland's west coast. Thousands of icebergs flow southward to the sea.

GREENLAND MUSEUM (Godthab) – The museum is home to 500-year-old mummies that were found in a cave at Qilakitsoq. They are displayed with their clothing. A model of a seal hunter is dressed in polar bear pants.

TIMELINE

c. 982 Eric the Red, a Viking from Norway, discovers Greenland. Some four years later, he brings the first colonists from Norway to the island.

1380 When Norway and Denmark are united, Greenland is ruled by Denmark.

1261 The inhabitants vote for union with Norway.

1400s The population declines due to the severe climate and possibly because of attacks from the Inuits (people living in the North).

1721 A Norwegian missionary, Hans Egede, sets up a mission and trading center near present-day Godthab.

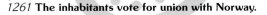

FRESH FACTS

NAME Eric the Red gave the island its name to encourage the Norse to settle there. In fact, only the areas along the coast are green.

CAPITAL Godthab (Nuuk)

AREA 836,330 square miles, (2,166,095 square kilometers)

POPULATION 56,000

INDEPENDENCE None (province of Denmark)

HIGHEST POINT Mount Gunnbjorn (12,139 feet; 3,700 meters)

LOWEST POINT Sea level

AGRICULTURE Hay, potatoes, seafood, sheep, vegetables

FLAG The flag's colors are the same as those of the Danish flag, representing Greenland's ties to Denmark. The red sun rising over the white polar ice symbolizes the return of light and heat in midsummer. The flag was adopted in 1985.

Greenland celebrated the history of Viking exploration and settlement in 2000, with a visit from ships modeled on those sailed 1,000 years before by Eric the Red and his son Leif Ericson.

In Greenland, you can see the Northern Lights year-round, but they are easiest to see in the fall months. The Northern Lights, also known as the Aurora Borealis, are caused by tiny energy particles, called electrons and protons, colliding with the upper atmosphere.

Inside Scoop

GREENLAND is the world's largest island.
FOR PART OF the summer, the sun never sets and for part of the winter, it never shines.
THE WORLD'S TALLEST ICEBERG rises off Greenland's western coast. It is 550 feet (168 meters) high — about 5 feet (1.5 meters) shorter than the Washington Monument — and was measured by a U.S. Coast Guard ice cutter in 1958.

1814 After Denmark and Norway end their union, Greenland stays with Denmark.

1979 Greenland is given home rule but remains a province of Denmark.

1800s Scientific expeditions explore and map Greenland.

2000 Greenland celebrates the 1,000-year anniversary of Leif Ericson's voyage to Vinland in North America.

Canada

The Canadian Rockies are home to beautiful Banff National Park's Payton Lake.

Arctic Ocean

Beaufort Sea

0 ——— 500 Miles
0 ——— 500 Kilometers

Patrick Island

Ellesmere Island

Axel Heiberg Island

Sverdrup Islands

Queen Elizabeth Islands

Banks Island

Melville Island

Devon Island

Baffin Bay

Tuktoyaktuk

Prince of Wales Island

Baffin Island

Davis Strait

ALASKA

Yukon R.

YUKON TERRITORY

Mt Logan

WHITEHORSE

Great Bear Lake

Port Radium

Victoria Island

Boothia Pen.

Melville Pen.

Gulf of Alaska

Mackenzie Mountains

Mackenzie R.

NORTHWEST TERRITORIES

★YELLOWKNIFE

Great Slave Lake

NUNAVUT

Baker Lake

Rankin Inlet

Hudson Strait

Cape Howe

Pacific Ocean

Bear Lake

Rocky Mountains

Dawson Creek

Peace River

Lake Athabasca

Fort Chipewyan

Ungava Bay

Queen Charlotte Islands

Prince Rupert

Prince George

Grande Prairie

Fort McMurray

SASKATCHEWAN

Churchill

Inukjuak

Hudson Bay

BRITISH COLUMBIA

ALBERTA

Athabasca River

Churchill R.

Nelson River

QUEBEC

Vancouver Island

Kamloops

Red Deer

Prince Albert

Flin Flon

Thompson

MANITOBA

Labrad C

★VANCOUVER

Kelowna

CALGARY

North Battleford

Saskatchewan River

Lake Winnipeg

ONTARIO

Trail

Lethbridge

SASKATOON

Swift Current

Moosonee

QUEBEC

WASHINGTON

★WINNIPEG

Brandon

Lake Nipigon

Timmins

Amos

IDAHO

MONTANA

NORTH DAKOTA

Thunder Bay

L. Superior

Trois-rivieres

MINNESOTA

Sudbury

North Bay

Montreal

L. Nipigon

OTTAWA★

St. Lawrence R.

L. Michigan

L. Huron

Kingston

TORONTO

L. Ontario

NEW YORK

E R M O N T

MICHIGAN

L. Erie

PENNSYLVANIA

OHIO

July 1 is Canada Day, a national holiday celebrating the anniversary of the day in 1867 when Canada first became a self-governing dominion of Great Britain.

TIMELINE

c.1000 The Vikings are the first known Europeans to settle in Canada, at L'Anse aux Meadows, Newfoundland. Ancestors of the Inuit migrate into Canada.

1534 French navigator Jacques Cartier claims Canada for France.

1608 The French colony of Québec is founded by Samuel de Champlain.

1763 France and Britain end their conflict over Canada. The Treaty of Paris gives Britain control of Canada.

1497 John Cabot, exploring for England, reaches the Canadian coast, near present-day Newfoundland or Nova Scotia.

1604 The French colony of Acadia is founded in present-day Nova Scotia.

1670 English King Charles II grants a charter to the Hudson's Bay Company for land in the Hudson Bay region.

Inside Scoop

CANADA IS the second largest country in the world after Russia.

ENGLISH AND FRENCH are Canada's official languages.

THE FIRST organized game of hockey was played in 1873 in Montreal. Today, ice hockey is the most popular sport in Canada. About 500,000 Canadian children belong to hockey leagues.

CANADA AND THE United States have the world's longest undefended border, 5,600 miles (9,010 kilometers).

NAME From the Huron-Iroquois word "kanata," meaning "village" or "settlement."

CAPITAL Ottawa

ABBREVIATION Can.

AREA 3,556,000 square miles (9,220,970 square kilometers)

POPULATION 31,592,805

INDEPENDENCE July 1, 1931 (from the United Kingdom)

HIGHEST POINT Mount Logan, Yukon (19,525 feet; 5,951 meters)

LOWEST POINT Sea level

INDUSTRIES Chemicals, electrical and electronic equipment, food products, metals and metal products, mining, natural gas, oil, paper products, transportation equipment, wood products

AGRICULTURE Barley, canola, cattle, chickens, dairy products, fruits, hogs, oats, seafood, tobacco, vegetables, wheat

MOTTO From sea to sea.

FLAG Canada's official colors are red and white—red represents the Atlantic and Pacific oceans, and white stands for the nation's snow-filled northern lands. The maple leaf is one of Canada's national symbols. The flag was adopted in 1965.

NATIONAL SYMBOLS The **maple leaf** was officially adopted as a national symbol in 1996. Maple trees have been of economic importance to Canada because of their valuable wood and their sap, which is made into maple syrup. The **beaver**, which became an official symbol in 1975, attracted fur traders to Canada in the 1600s and 1700s, when Europeans prized its fur for hats.

NATIONAL ANTHEM "O Canada!" (words by Judge Adolphe-Basile Routhier; music by Calixa Lavallee)

ROYAL ANTHEM "God Save the Queen" (words and music attributed to English composer Henry Carey in the mid-1700s)

Although the beaver is one of Canada's official national symbols, to many people the moose is also a symbol of the country. This one was photographed in Ontario's Puhaskwa National Park.

Labrador Sea

Smallwood Res.

NEWFOUNDLAND

Newfoundland

Corner Brook

Gulf of St. Lawrence

ST. JOHN'S

PRINCE EDWARD ISLAND — Sydney

NEW BRUNSWICK

Moncton

Nova Scotia

HALIFAX

AINE

NOVA SCOTIA

Atlantic Ocean

1867 The British Parliament creates the Dominion of Canada, a confederation including the Province of Canada, Nova Scotia, and New Brunswick. Over time, more provinces and territories are added.

1931 Canada gains independence from Great Britain.

1999 The province of Nunavut, whose population is mostly Inuit, is created from the Northwest Territories. It is Canada's third territory after the Northwest and Yukon Territories.

1791 Canada is divided into two territories: Upper (English-speaking, present-day Ontario) and Lower (French-speaking, present-day Québec). They are reunited in 1841 as the Province of Canada.

1885 The Canadian Pacific Railway connects the country's east and west coasts with a transcontinental railroad.

1993 Canada signs the North American Free Trade Agreement with Mexico and the United States, lowering trade barriers between the countries.

Alberta

NAME For Louise Caroline Alberta, fourth daughter of Queen Victoria and the wife of the Marquis of Lorne, a Canadian governor general in 1882.

CAPITAL Edmonton

AREA 255,287 square miles (661,200 square kilometers)

POPULATION 2,974,807

PROVINCE Sept.1, 1905 (8th province)

HIGHEST POINT Mount Columbia (12,294 feet; 3,747 meters)

LOWEST POINT Slave River (557 feet; 170 meters)

INDUSTRIES Chemical products, food products, forest products, mining, natural gas, oil, petroleum products, printed materials, ranching, tourism

AGRICULTURE Barley, canola, cattle, chickens, hogs, rye, sugar beets, wheat, whitefish

MOTTO Strong and free.

FLAG Alberta's shield of arms appears in the center. The red St. George's Cross shows the province's ties to England. The snow-capped mountains, hills, prairie, and wheat field represent Alberta's landscape. The flag became official in 1968.

BIRD The **great horned owl** became the official bird after children of the province voted for it. The owl lives in Alberta year-round and was adopted in 1977.

FLOWER The **wild rose,** adopted in 1930, grows throughout Alberta.

TREE The **lodgepole pine** was adopted in 1984, thanks to the efforts of the Junior Forest Warden Association of Alberta. First used for railroad ties, the tree is now used for plywood, pulp, and other wood products.

AAA GEMS:
Selected Must-See Points of Interest

BANFF NATIONAL PARK – Canada's oldest national park is famous for its mountains, glaciers, wildlife refuge, and summer and winter sports.

CALGARY ZOO, BOTANICAL GARDEN AND PREHISTORIC PARK – More than 1,000 animals and 10,000 plants live here. Check out the Asian elephant that can paint and the life-size dinosaur replicas.

CANADA OLYMPIC PARK (Calgary) – Test your strength, speed, and accuracy in simulated athletic competitions in this park where the 1988 Winter Olympic Games were held.

Banff National Park has been chosen by the United Nations as a World Heritage Site.

Inside Scoop

THE PROVINCE is called "Sunny Alberta" because it gets 2,000 hours of sunlight a year, more than any other province.

THE CALGARY STAMPEDE, held each July since 1925, features a chuck-wagon race, a parade by Alberta Indians, square dancing, and a state-of-the-art rodeo.

WOOD BUFFALO NATIONAL PARK is home to the world's biggest free-roaming buffalo herd.

TIMELINE

1778 American Peter Pond builds the first trading post on the Athabasca River.

1914 Oil is discovered in the Turner Valley.

1883 The Canadian Pacific Railway connects Calgary to Canadian cities in the East.

1988 Calgary hosts the Winter Olympic Games.

1998 The world's largest shopping mall is completed at West Edmonton. It has 800 shops, an amusement park, 20 theaters, an ice arena, and other attractions.

British Columbia

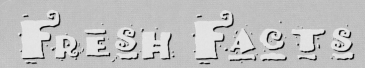

NAME Queen Victoria named the colony in 1858 after the Columbia River. The river had been named by American explorer Capt. Robert Gray for his ship "Columbia."

CAPITAL Victoria

AREA 365,948 square miles (947,805 square kilometers)

POPULATION 3,907,738

PROVINCE July 20, 1871 (6th province)

HIGHEST POINT Mount Fairweather (15,300 feet; 4,663 meters)

LOWEST POINT Sea level

INDUSTRIES Finance, food products, mining, paper products, refined fuel, wood products

AGRICULTURE Cattle, chickens, dairy products, fruits, grain, hogs, salmon, vegetables

MOTTO Splendor without diminishment.

FLAG The British flag at the top shows the province's ties to Great Britain. The wavy blue and white bars represent the Pacific Ocean. The setting sun symbolizes British Columbia as Canada's westernmost province.

BIRD The noisy **Steller's jay** was voted the most popular bird by British Columbians and was adopted in 1987. It is North America's largest jay.

FLOWER The flowers of the **Pacific dogwood tree** bloom in April and May. The flower was adopted in 1956.

TREE The **Western red cedar,** adopted in 1988, has been a valuable source of beautiful and long-lasting wood. Native people used it for canoes and totem poles, pioneers used it for log cabins, and today, it is prized for shingles and decks.

Kitwanga, where this peaceful hayfield is located, was the site of a famous battle between Indian nations in which the local Gitwangak warriors rolled logs downhill to stop attackers from other tribes. The battle took place in about 1600.

Inside Scoop

VANCOUVER'S Nine O'Clock Gun booms so dependably every night that people use it to make sure their own timepieces are accurate.

THE LAST SPIKE of the Canadian Pacific Railway was pounded in at Craigellachie on Nov. 7, 1885, linking Vancouver on the Pacific coast with Montreal on the Atlantic coast.

AAA GEMS:
Selected Must-See Points of Interest

MINIATURE WORLD (Victoria) – Animation, lighting, and sound effects bring to life 80 detailed miniature scenes, including a circus, dollhouses, fairy tales, and such classic books as "Gulliver's Travels."

ROYAL BRITISH COLUMBIA MUSEUM (Victoria) – Come here to see a frontier town with silent movies, an Indian village, a pioneer settlement, a rain forest, and more.

VANCOUVER AQUARIUM MARINE SCIENCE CENTER – Among the 8,000 marine animals are octopuses, jellyfish, whales, and giant fish from the Amazon River.

TIMELINE

1792–94 George Vancouver, English explorer, maps the coast and names many of the places he sees.

1858 Gold is discovered along the Fraser River, attracting thousands of prospectors.

1825 Hudson's Bay Company builds Fort Vancouver.

1846 Great Britain and the United States set the national boundary at the 49th parallel.

1943 The Alaska-Canada Highway is completed, linking Dawson Creek with Delta Junction, Alaska. It is 1,397 miles (2,248 kilometers) long.

1993 Kim Campbell from British Columbia becomes Canada's first female prime minister.

Manitoba

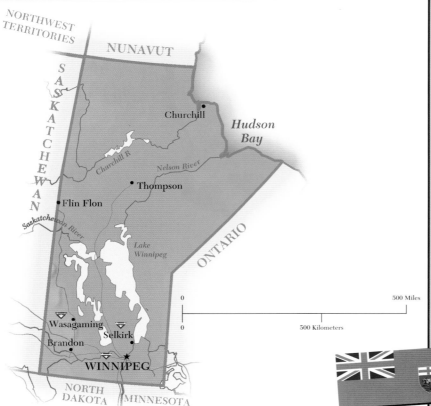

NAME From the Aboriginal words "Manito waba," meaning "place where the Great Spirit (Manito) whispers."

CAPITAL Winnipeg

AREA 250,947 square miles (649,950 square kilometers)

POPULATION 1,119,583

PROVINCE July 15,1870 (5th province)

HIGHEST POINT Baldy Mountain (2,729 feet; 832 meters)

LOWEST POINT Sea level along Hudson Bay

INDUSTRY Electrical equipment and power, food products, mining, printed materials, transportation equipment

AGRICULTURE Barley, canola, cattle, dairy products, hay, hogs, sugar beets, sunflowers, wheat

MOTTO Glorious and free.

FLAG Adopted in 1966, the flag shows the British Union Jack in the left-hand corner, symbolizing the province's ties to England. The seal shows a buffalo, an important animal in Manitoba's early days.

BIRD The **great gray owl** is the largest owl in North America and lives in Manitoba year-round. It was selected by school groups and adopted in 1987.

FLOWER The **prairie crocus,** adopted in 1906, is the first flower to bloom in spring, sometimes while snow is still on the ground.

TREE The **white spruce,** adopted in 1991, was used widely by natives and early settlers.

AAA GEMS:
Selected Must-See Points of Interest

LOWER FORT GARRY NATIONAL HISTORIC SITE (Selkirk) — Costumed interpreters lead you through restored buildings of an 1850s fur trading post and tell you what it was like to live there during its heyday.

RIDING MOUNTAIN NATIONAL PARK (Wasagaming) — The park's meadows, forests, and lakes are home to bison, bears, beavers, and a wide variety of waterfowl and other birds.

ROYAL CANADIAN MINT (Winnipeg) — Take a guided tour through the building where all circulating Canadian coins and many foreign coins are made. The Mint's other building is in Ottawa.

A grain tower stands out against the sky in Manitoba. Some of the world's richest farmland is in Manitoba.

Inside Scoop

THE INTERNATIONAL PEACE GARDEN, located partly in Manitoba and partly in North Dakota, honors the friendship between Canada and the United States. A landmark made of rocks from both countries indicates the border between the two countries.

CHURCHILL is called the "Polar Bear Capital of the World." Thousands of polar bears gather there each fall to hunt for seals.

WINNIE THE POOH® was named after a bear who lived in a London zoo. His owner came from Winnipeg and was so homesick that he called his pet Winnie.

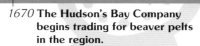

TIMELINE

1612 Sir Thomas Button of England leads the first European explorers along the west coast of Hudson Bay.

1738 Fort Rouge, a fur trading post, is established on the present-day site of Winnipeg.

1670 The Hudson's Bay Company begins trading for beaver pelts in the region.

1876 Manitoba begins exporting wheat, and it soon becomes the province's most important product.

1916 Manitoba grants women the right to vote, the first province to do so.

1999 The Pan American Games are held in Winnipeg.

New Brunswick

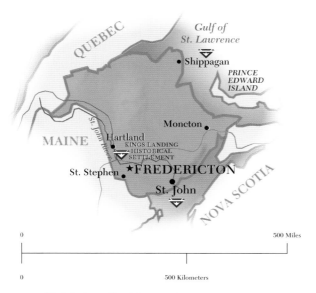

 ## AAA GEMS:
Selected Must-See Points of Interest

AQUARIUM & MARINE CENTRE (Shippagan) –
Exhibits tell the story of the region's fishermen and their ships from the 1500s to the present. The aquarium has 125 kinds of marine life.

KINGS LANDING HISTORICAL SETTLEMENT –
Tour this re-created village from the 1800s with its forge, sawmill, school, store, theater, and other buildings. Take the wagon ride around the site.

NEW BRUNSWICK MUSEUM (St. John) – View skeletons of the rare North Atlantic right whale and an Ice Age mastodon at this museum. Travel millions of years as you walk the geological trail.

Inside Scoop

THE WORLD'S LONGEST covered bridge spans the St. John River at Hartland. It extends 1,282 feet (390 meters), about the length of four football fields.

WHEN ARTHUR GAGNON of St. Stephen took chocolate on his fishing trips, it melted and left his pockets gooey. In 1910 he wrapped his treats in foil and sold them as the world's first chocolate bars.

KING STREET in St. John is Canada's steepest main street. It rises 80 feet (24 meters) in two blocks, about the height of an eight-story building.

Fresh Facts

NAME In honor of King George III, who was also Duke of Brunswick.

CAPITAL Fredericton

AREA 28,355 square miles (73,440 square kilometers)

POPULATION 729,498

PROVINCE July 1, 1867 (one of the original four provinces)

HIGHEST POINT Mount Carleton (2,690 feet; 820 meters)

LOWEST POINT Sea level

INDUSTRIES Finance, food products, insurance, mining, paper products, tourism, wood products

AGRICULTURE Cattle, chickens, dairy products, fish, hogs, milk, potatoes

MOTTO Hope was restored.

FLAG Adopted in 1965, the flag is patterned after the province's coat of arms. The lion represents New Brunswick's ties to England. The ship symbolizes the importance of the sea and shipbuilding in the province's early days.

BIRD The **black-capped chickadee** won most of the votes in a contest sponsored by The New Brunswick Federation of Naturalists. The bird was adopted in 1983.

FLOWER School children and the Women's Institute promoted the **purple violet** because it grows throughout the province. It was chosen in 1936.

TREE The **balsam fir,** adopted in 1987, is a tall evergreen that is often used as a Christmas tree.

The Bay of Fundy is home to all kinds of unusual wildlife. Whales are attracted to the giant blooms of plankton in the area. Dolphins, seals, and hundreds of thousands of shorebirds can also be found here.

Timeline

1534 Jacques Cartier, a French explorer, sights the coast of New Brunswick.

1763 France cedes the region to England

1785 St. John becomes the first incorporated Canadian city.

1969 New Brunswick requires teachers and government workers to be equally bilingual in English and French, the first province to do so.

1997 Confederation Bridge, linking New Brunswick and Prince Edward Island, opens.

Newfoundland and Labrador

Ungava Bay
Labrador Sea
NEWFOUNDLAND
LABRADOR
Labrador City
QUEBEC
L'Anse aux Meadows
GROS MORNE NATIONAL PARK
Rocky Harbour
ISLAND OF NEWFOUNDLAND
Corner Brook
Gulf of St. Lawrence
THE GRAND BANKS
Atlantic Ocean
★ST. JOHN'S
NOVA SCOTIA

0   500 Miles
0   500 Kilometers

FRESH FACTS

NAME The island of Newfoundland was named by King Henry VII after John Cabot's discovery of the "New Found Land." The peninsula of Labrador was named by Gaspar Corte-Real, a Portuguese explorer who called the mainland "Terra del Lavrador," meaning "land of the farmer."

CAPITAL St. John's

AREA 156,649 square miles (405,720 square kilometers)

POPULATION 512,930

PROVINCE March 31, 1949 (10th province)

HIGHEST POINT Mount Caubvick (5,420 feet; 1,652 meters)

LOWEST POINT Sea level

INDUSTRIES Lumber, mining, paper products, tourism

AGRICULTURE Cabbage, cattle, chickens, corn, dairy products, fish, hay, potatoes, turnips, wheat

MOTTO Seek ye first the kingdom of God.

FLAG The white is for snow and ice, the blue for the sea and Great Britain. The two red triangles stand for the mainland and the province's islands. The golden arrow points to a bright future. The trident stands for fishing. The flag was adopted in 1980.

BIRD The **Atlantic puffin** was selected in 1991. Newfoundland is home to the largest colony of puffins in North America. About 95 percent of North American puffins breed here.

FLOWER The **pitcher plant** traps insects in its pitcher-shaped leaves, then dissolves and absorbs them for nourishment. The plant was adopted in 1954.

TREE The **black spruce,** chosen in 1993, is the most common tree in Labrador. It is also called the bog spruce because it lives in swamps and other wet places.

AAA GEMS: Selected Must-See Points of Interest

GROS MORNE NATIONAL PARK (Rocky Harbour) – This park has lakes, fjords, mountains, sand dunes, and is the home of more than 230 kinds of birds as well as moose, bears, and foxes.

Inside Scoop

THE FIRST LABRADOR retriever came from Newfoundland.

THE IDEA FOR packaged frozen food came to Clarence Birdseye, a native of Brooklyn, N.Y., when he observed that fish caught by the Inuit and other native peoples of Labrador froze immediately and remained edible and tasty when it was thawed months later.

MOST NEWFOUNDLANDERS live closer to Ireland than they do to Manitoba or Florida.

Quidi Vidi Village, a 17th-century fishing village, hosts a rowing and sailing event each August called the Royal St. John's Regatta. It is thought to be the oldest annual sporting event in North America.

TIMELINE

c.1000 The Vikings are the first known Europeans to settle in North America, at L'Anse aux Meadows.

1497 John Cabot, an Italian navigator working for England, discovers Newfoundland and the Grand Banks.

1824 Newfoundland becomes a British colony.

1992 Cod fishing is banned due to overfishing in coastal waters.

2001 Canada's Parliament officially changes the name of the province to Newfoundland and Labrador when it unites the two.

Northwest Territories and Nunavut Territory

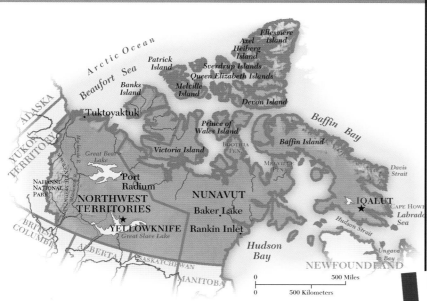

Selected Must-See Points of Interest

WAGER BAY NATIONAL PARK (South Central Nunavut) – Glaciers formed the park's ridges, lakes and valleys. In summertime, beluga whales and their young can be seen here. Other animals that live here include seals, polar bears, caribou, wolves, and foxes. Forty species of birds nest at Wager Bay. Visitors to the park can take boat excursions, hike or visit historic and prehistoric sites.

NAHANNI NATIONAL PARK RESERVE (Northwest Territories) – The park has many unique features: hot springs, steep waterfalls, deep canyons, and caves. Many forms of wildlife make their home here: Dall's sheep, mountain goats, caribou, wolves, bears, and trumpeter swans. In 1978 this reserve became the world's first site to be given World Heritage status by UNESCO (United Nations Educational, Scientific and Cultural Organization).

Inside Scoop

THE NORTHWEST TERRITORIES lie so far north that the sky does not turn dark through most of the summer.

THERE ARE EIGHT OFFICIAL LANGUAGES in the Northwest Territories: Inuktitut, English, French, Slavey, Dogrib, Chipewayan, Cree, and Gwich'in.

VIRGINIA FALLS in Nahanni National Park in the Northwest Territories are twice the height of Niagara Falls.

Fresh Facts

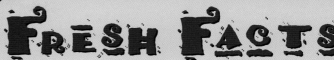

NORTHWEST TERRITORIES

NAME For its location in Canada.
CAPITAL Yellowknife
AREA 1,322,910 square miles (3,426,337 square kilometers)
POPULATION 37,360
TERRITORY July 15, 1870 (1st territory)
HIGHEST POINT Mount Sir James MacBrien (9,062 feet; 2,762 meters)
LOWEST POINT Sea level
INDUSTRY Food products, mining, petroleum products, wood products
AGRICULTURE Cattle, chickens, eggs, vegetables
MOTTO None.
FLAG The blue bands symbolize lakes and other waters; the white background represents ice and snow. The coat of arms appears in the center. The flag was adopted in 1969.
BIRD The **gyrfalcon**, chosen in 1990, is the biggest of the falcons. It is an expert hunter and a fast flier.
FLOWER Chosen in 1957, **mountain avens** grow close to the ground in areas that are too cold and windy for trees to survive.
TREE The **tamarack** was adopted in 1999. Its wood is used for houses and tools.

NUNAVUT TERRITORY

NAME In Inuktitut, the language of the Inuit, "nunavut" means "our land."
CAPITAL Iqalut
AREA 770,000 square miles (1,994,300 square kilometers)
POPULATION 26,745
TERRITORY April 1, 1999 (3rd territory)
HIGHEST POINT Mount Barbeau (8,583 feet; 2,615 meters)
LOWEST POINT Sea level
INDUSTRY Crafts, mining, natural gas, packaged fish and meat
AGRICULTURE Caribou, fish
MOTTO Our strength.
FLAG In the center is a red "Inuksuk," an Inuit monument made of stones and used as a landmark. The blue star stands for the North Star. The flag was adopted in 1999.
BIRD The **rock ptarmigan**, selected in 2000, lives much of the year on Arctic mountain slopes. In the winter, the bird is white; in the summer, the female's feathers turn brown and the male's head and back feathers turn brown.
FLOWER The **purple saxifrage**, adopted in 2000, grows throughout the Arctic region. Its lilac flowers were used by the Inuit for dyes.
TREE None.

Timeline

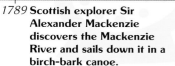

1576 English mariner Martin Frobisher reaches Baffin Island.

1789 Scottish explorer Sir Alexander Mackenzie discovers the Mackenzie River and sails down it in a birch-bark canoe.

1934 Gold is discovered on the eastern shore of Yellowknife Bay.

1982 Residents of the Northwest Territories vote to divide the region into two territories, East and West. The Eastern territory, where more than 80 percent of the people are Inuit, becomes Nunavut.

1991 Miners find diamonds near Lac de Grace.

1999 Nunavut officially joins the Canadian Confederation.

Nova Scotia

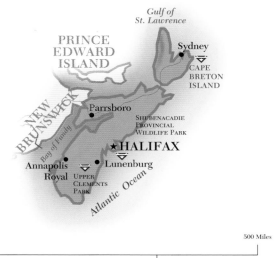

NEWFOUNDLAND

Gulf of St. Lawrence

PRINCE EDWARD ISLAND

Sydney

CAPE BRETON ISLAND

NEW BRUNSWICK

Parrsboro

SHUBENACADIE PROVINCIAL WILDLIFE PARK

★HALIFAX

Annapolis Royal

Lunenburg

UPPER CLEMENTS PARK

Bay of Fundy

Atlantic Ocean

0   500 Miles

0   500 Kilometers

 ## AAA GEMS:
Selected Must-See Points of Interest

FISHERIES MUSEUM OF THE ATLANTIC
(Lunenburg) — Inspect the decks and gear aboard an old fishing schooner and a steel-hulled trawler. Stop by the aquarium and the room full of boat models.

FORTRESS OF LOUISBOURG NATIONAL HISTORIC SITE (Cape Breton Island) — Stroll through this reconstructed French fort and town where costumed guides will entertain you with stories, dances, music, and demonstrations.

UPPER CLEMENTS PARK — This family park offers rides on a carousel, a roller coaster, and a train. You can also play miniature golf and watch craft demonstrations.

To mark the Scottish heritage of many of Nova Scotia's early settlers, the International Gathering of the Clans, featuring traditional music, dance, games, parades, picnics, and more, takes place in Nova Scotia every four years.

NAME From the Latin for "New Scotland," representing the many Scottish immigrants who settled in the province.

CAPITAL Halifax

AREA 21,425 square miles (55,490 square kilometers)

POPULATION 908,007

PROVINCE July 1, 1867 (one of the original four provinces)

HIGHEST POINT White Hill, Cape Breton Island (1,747 feet; 532 meters)

LOWEST POINT Sea level

INDUSTRIES Food products, lumber, mining, paper products, transportation equipment

AGRICULTURE Apples, chickens, dairy products, fish, hogs, milk

MOTTO One defends and the other conquers.

FLAG The flag, authorized in 1625, shows the Cross of St. Andrew and the arms of Scotland, symbolizing the province's close ties to Scotland.

BIRD The **osprey** is a bird of prey that dives into the water feet first, grasps fish in its talons, and then flies off with its catch. The bird was adopted in 1994.

FLOWER The fragrant **mayflower** was considered a symbol of achievement by early colonists because it blooms in the early spring, even when snow is on the ground. It was adopted in 1901.

TREE Pioneers steeped and fermented the twigs of the **red spruce** in water to treat scurvy. The tree, adopted in 1987, was also used for building ships.

Inside Scoop

THE BAY OF FUNDY, which separates Nova Scotia and New Brunswick, has the world's highest tides — 56 feet (17 meters). The world's average tidal height is 2.5 feet (0.8 meters).

SOME OF THE WORLD'S smallest dinosaur footprints can be seen at the Fundy Geological Museum in Parrsboro. The tiny footprints (half-inch; 1.3-centimeter) were made by a creature the size of a robin that lived more than 200 million years ago.

NOVA SCOTIANS are often called "Bluenoses," after the fishermen whose noses turned blue when working in cold, coastal waters.

THE FAMOUS Sable Island horses live in Shubenacadie Provincial Wildlife Park. Brought to Nova Scotia by a Boston merchant in 1760, they are found nowhere else in the world.

TIMELINE

1497 John Cabot, exploring for England, lands on Cape Breton Island.

1752 Canada's first newspaper, "The Halifax Gazette," is published.

1984 Tides in the Bay of Fundy are used to produce electricity.

1605 Port Royal, one of North America's oldest cities, is established. It is later called Annapolis Royal.

1820 Cape Breton Island becomes part of Nova Scotia.

1998 The fastest car ferry in North America makes its first trip between Maine and Nova Scotia. It reduces the trip by 3.5 hours.

Ontario

NAME From the Iroquoian word "kandario," meaning "sparkling water" and the Huron words "ontari" for "lake" and "io" for "beautiful."

CAPITAL Toronto

AREA 412,581 square miles (1,068,585 square kilometers)

POPULATION 11,410,046

PROVINCE July 1, 1867 (one of the original four provinces)

HIGHEST POINT Ishpatina Ridge (2,275 feet; 693 meters)

LOWEST POINT Sea level

INDUSTRIES Chemicals, computer equipment, electrical equipment, food products, mining, paper products, transportation equipment

AGRICULTURE Barley, cattle, chickens, corn, dairy products, eggs, hogs, wheat

MOTTO Loyal it began, loyal it remains.

FLAG The flag shows the British Union Jack and Ontario's shield with the cross of St. George on it, representing the province's ties with Great Britain. The three maple leaves stand for Canada. The flag was adopted in 1965.

BIRD The **common loon,** chosen in 1994, lives in northern lakes and is known for its haunting cry. It is a strong, underwater swimmer and takes flight from the surface of the water, not from land.

FLOWER The **white trillium** is also known as the "wake robin," because it blooms in the spring just as robins are returning from their winter homes. The flower was selected in 1937.

TREE Early settlers steeped the bark of the **Eastern white pine** with other ingredients to make a cough syrup. The inner bark was used to treat wounds. The tree was adopted in 1984.

AAA GEMS:
Selected Must-See Points of Interest

AFRICAN LION SAFARI AND GAME FARM (Cambridge) – A drive-through tour makes it seem as if you are in Africa. More than 1,000 animals – including cheetahs, lions, tigers, and giraffes – roam freely here.

HOCKEY HALL OF FAME (Toronto) – Explore a locker room, play virtual-reality hockey, announce a play-by-play of a game, see historic Stanley Cups and other hockey memorabilia, and more.

NATIONAL MUSEUM OF SCIENCE AND TECHNOLOGY (Ottawa) – Who, what, where, when, why, and how are explored here. Canada's largest refracting telescope is among the featured hands-on exhibits.

Inside Scoop

CAMP X, a secret place where World War II spies were trained, was located in Whitby. One of its students was author Ian Fleming, the creator of James Bond.

WHEN THE Rideau Canal in Ottawa freezes each winter, it becomes one of the world's longest skating rinks.

WAYNE GRETZKY, the National Hockey League's all-time top scorer, was born in Brantford in 1961 and was on the local All-Star team when he was 6 years old.

Toronto is Canada's largest city, with more than 4.6 million people. Towering over its skyline is CN Tower, which features arcades, restaurants, and the Sky Pod, the world's highest (1,465 feet; 44 meter) man-made observatory.

TIMELINE

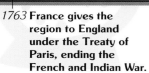

1610 French and English explorers visit the area.

1857 Queen Victoria names Ottawa the capital of Canada.

1959 The St. Lawrence Seaway opens.

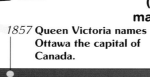

1763 France gives the region to England under the Treaty of Paris, ending the French and Indian War.

1829 The Welland Canal, providing a route for ships between Lake Ontario and Lake Erie, is completed.

1992–93 The Toronto Blue Jays win the World Series in two consecutive years.

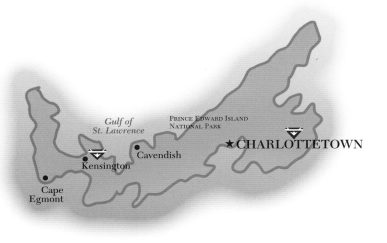

Gulf of St. Lawrence

PRINCE EDWARD ISLAND NATIONAL PARK

★CHARLOTTETOWN

Cavendish

Kensington

Cape Egmont

| 0 | | 50 Miles |
| 0 | 50 Kilometers | |

AAA GEMS:
Selected Must-See Points of Interest

CONFEDERATION CENTRE OF THE ARTS
(Charlottetown) – More than 15,000 works of Canadian art and history are displayed here. Watch original plays performed during the summer Charlottetown Festival.

WOODLEIGH REPLICA & GARDENS (Kensington) – Thirty large-scale models of British castles and cathedrals, some big enough to enter, are surrounded by English-style country gardens.

Inside Scoop

LUCY MAUD MONTGOMERY, born in Clifton and raised in Cavendish, wrote about her childhood on Prince Edward Island in "Anne of Green Gables." Her book, published in 1908, has been translated into 15 languages.

IRISH MOSS, collected from the Prince Edward Island coast, is Canada's most important seaweed. A substance in the moss, carrageen, is used to thicken cosmetics, ice cream, and cake mixes.

BOTTLE HOUSES, built in the early 1980s at Cape Egmont, were made from many kinds of bottles. The largest used 12,000 bottles and measured 18 feet by 24 feet (5.5 by 7.3 meters).

NAME In honor of Edward, Duke of Kent, the father of Queen Victoria.

CAPITAL Charlottetown

AREA 2,185 square miles (5,560 square kilometers)

POPULATION 135,294

PROVINCE July 1, 1873 (7th province)

HIGHEST POINT Queen's County (465 feet; 142 meters)

LOWEST POINT Sea level

INDUSTRIES Clothing, fertilizer, food products, medical instruments, tourism, wood products

AGRICULTURE Barley, cattle, hay, hogs, Irish moss, milk, potatoes, seafood, tobacco

MOTTO The small under the protection of the great.

FLAG The flag's design is based on the province's coat of arms, which uses the same symbols. The lion and the large oak represent England. The three young oak trees are for the province's three counties: King's, Queen's, and Prince. The flag was adopted in 1964.

BIRD The **blue jay** was chosen by a vote in the province in 1977. It lives in the province year-round.

FLOWER The **showy lady's slipper** (also called the pink-and-white lady's slipper) was chosen in 1947. Its name comes from the shape of the petals, which look like slippers.

TREE The **Northern red oak's** wood was used for barrels and furniture, and tannic acid from the tree was used in making leather. The tree was adopted in 1987.

Prince Edward Island is known for its great beaches, campgrounds, and outdoor activities like kayaking.

TIMELINE

1534 French navigator Jacques Cartier is the first European to visit the island.

1769 The island becomes a separate British colony.

1603 Samuel de Champlain claims the island for France and names it Isle St. Jean. The English call it St. John.

1799 The Isle of St. Jean is renamed Prince Edward Island.

1997 The Confederation Bridge, considered to be the longest bridge over ice-covered waters, opens. It connects the island to New Brunswick.

Québec

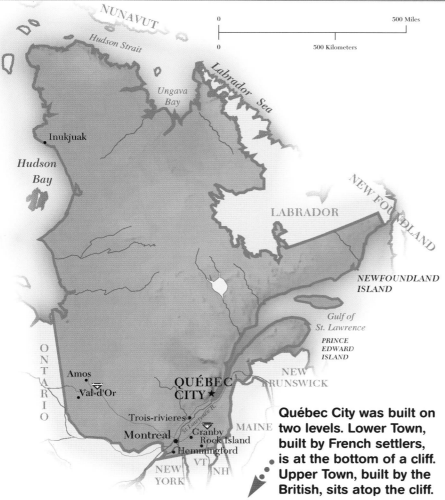

Québec City was built on two levels. Lower Town, built by French settlers, is at the bottom of a cliff. Upper Town, built by the British, sits atop the cliff.

Inside Scoop

THE HASKELL OPERA HOUSE in Rock Island was built before the border between Canada and the United States was set. As a result, audiences now sit in the United States while watching performances on a stage in Canada.

MONTRÉAL is the second largest French-speaking city after Paris.

ICE HOCKEY was first played in Québec in the early 1800s. British soldiers played the game with sticks and a ball.

TIMELINE

1534 French explorer Jacques Cartier claims the region for France.

1763 France surrenders the region to England after the French and Indian War.

1974 French is declared Québec's official language.

1608 Samuel de Champlain, of France, sets up the first European settlement in Canada near present-day Québec City.

1967 Fifty million visitors attend Expo '67, Montréal's international fair held in honor of Canada's 100th birthday.

2000 The 1,000-mile (1,609-kilometer) recreational Trans-Canada Trail, the longest of its kind, opens to hikers.

FRESH FACTS

NAME From an Algonquian Indian word meaning "where the river narrows," because the St. Lawrence becomes narrow near present-day Quebec City.

CAPITAL Québec City

AREA 594,860 square miles (1,540,687 square kilometers)

POPULATION 7,237,479

PROVINCE July 1, 1867 (one of the original four provinces)

HIGHEST POINT Mont d'Iberville (5,322 feet; 1,622 meters)

LOWEST POINT Sea level

INDUSTRIES Clothing, electric power, food products, mining, paper products, transportation equipment, tourism, wood products

AGRICULTURE Cattle, chickens, corn, dairy products, fruit, grains, hogs, maple syrup, sheep, turkeys, vegetables

MOTTO I remember.

FLAG The flag, adopted in 1948, displays the white fleur de lis, the flower of the French court, symbolizing the province's ties to France.

BIRD Unlike other owls, the **snowy owl** hunts in the day and at night. The bird was adopted in 1987.

FLOWER In 1999, the province voted for the **blue flag iris** to be its new official flower, replacing the Madonna lily.

TREE The inner bark of a **yellow birch** smells like wintergreen. The tree, whose wood is used for furniture, was adopted in 1993.

AAA GEMS:
Selected Must-See Points of Interest

GRANBY ZOO (Granby) — More than 1,000 wild and exotic animals from five continents live here. Of special interest are a serpentarium, the AFRIKA Pavilion, and a Meet the Keepers presentation.

THE CITY OF GOLD (Val d'Or) — Descend deep underground into a gold mine where guides tell you how gold is extracted. When you surface, visit the museum, laboratory, and a 1935 mining village.

Saskatchewan

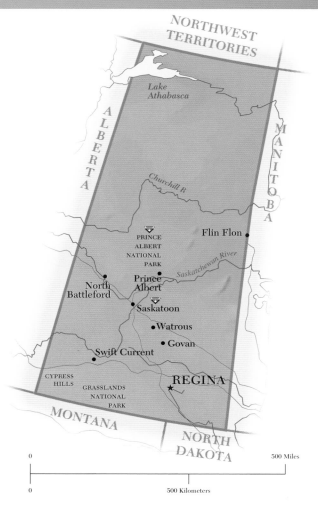

NORTHWEST TERRITORIES

Lake Athabasca

ALBERTA

MANITOBA

Churchill R.

PRINCE ALBERT NATIONAL PARK

Flin Flon

Saskatchewan River

Prince Albert

North Battleford

Saskatoon

Watrous

Govan

Swift Current

CYPRESS HILLS

GRASSLANDS NATIONAL PARK

REGINA

MONTANA

NORTH DAKOTA

0 — 500 Miles
0 — 500 Kilometers

AAA GEMS:
Selected Must-See Points of Interest

PRINCE ALBERT NATIONAL PARK – You can drive, hike, bike, ride in a boat, play golf, or admire the scenery and wildlife here. A herd of bison wander freely, and elk, deer, timber wolves, and bears are plentiful. The village of Waskesiu is within the park boundaries.

WANUSKEWIN HERITAGE PARK (Saskatoon) – You can build a tepee, tan a hide, bake a bannock (a thick, flat cake), and learn much more about the Northern Plains Indians at this museum and theater.

Sage, sharptail grouse, and Canada's only black-tailed prairie dogs can all be found in the rugged countryside of Grassland National Park.

FRESH FACTS

NAME From the Cree Indian word "kisiskatchewan," meaning "river that flows swiftly."

CAPITAL Regina

AREA 251,866 square miles (652,330 square kilometers)

POPULATION 978,933

PROVINCE Sept. 1, 1905 (9th province)

HIGHEST POINT Cypress Hills (4,567 feet; 1,392 meters)

LOWEST POINT Lake Athabasca (700 feet; 213 meters)

INDUSTRIES Chemicals, electrical equipment, food products, mining, printed materials

AGRICULTURE Barley, canola, cattle, oats, rye, wheat

MOTTO From many people's strength.

FLAG The green band represents the northern forests, and the gold band symbolizes the province's wheat fields. The shield and flower of the province are also displayed. The flag was adopted in 1969.

 **BIRD** The **sharp-tailed grouse,** chosen in 1945, is named for its pointy tail. The bird, which looks like a chicken, lives mostly on the ground, burrowing itself into snowdrifts at night to keep warm.

FLOWER The **Western red lily,** chosen in 1941, has several other names: wood lily, prairie lily, and wild tiger lily.

TREE The **white birch,** chosen in 1988, is sometimes called the canoe birch or paper birch. Its white bark peels off in thin layers. Native peoples used the bark as paper and to make canoes.

Inside Scoop

SWIMMERS don't have to worry about sinking at Little Manitou Lake, in Watrous, because its water is three times saltier than any ocean.

THE FIRST ambulance service by air in North America was started in Regina in 1946.

SASKATCHEWAN is called Canada's "Breadbasket" because it produces more wheat than any other place in the country.

ESTABLISHED IN 1887, the Last Mountain Bird Observatory near Govan is the world's oldest bird sanctuary. Pelicans, ducks, Canada geese, and other birds cannot be hunted here.

TIMELINE

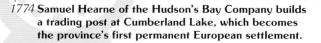

1690 English explorer Henry Kelsey of the Hudson's Bay Company enters the region.

1947 Saskatchewan becomes the first province to give its residents free hospital care.

1774 Samuel Hearne of the Hudson's Bay Company builds a trading post at Cumberland Lake, which becomes the province's first permanent European settlement.

1974 The first female Royal Canadian Mounted Police recruits begin training in Regina.

Yukon Territory

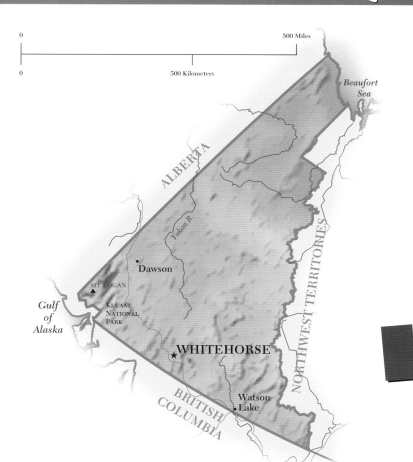

NAME From the Loucheux Indian word "yu-kun-ah," meaning "great river."

CAPITAL Whitehorse

AREA 186,661 square miles (483,450 square kilometers)

POPULATION 28,674

TERRITORY June 13, 1898 (2nd territory)

HIGHEST POINT Mount Logan (19,545 feet; 5,959 meters)

LOWEST POINT Sea level

INDUSTRIES Food products, fur, gold mining, lumber, metal products, mining, printed materials, tourism

AGRICULTURE Fish, grains, hay, livestock, vegetables

MOTTO None

FLAG The green stripe is for forests, the white for snow, and the blue for the sea. The coat of arms is framed by fireweed, the official flower. The flag was adopted in 1968.

BIRD Native people living in the northwest believe the **common raven** to be a sacred bird. It was adopted in 1985.

FLOWER The **fireweed,** adopted in 1957, is often the first plant to grow and blossom after a forest fire. Some people cook and eat its young greens.

TREE None.

Mount Logan, the highest mountain in Canada at 19,545 feet (5,959 meters), is located in Kluane National Park. The park also has some of the largest icefields south of the Arctic Circle.

Inside Scoop

TOP SLED-DOG TEAMS from all over North America compete in the annual Yukon Quest Sled-Dog Race, known as the toughest race of its kind. It covers 1,000 miles (1,609 kilometers) between Whitehorse and Fairbanks, Alaska.

THE WORLD'S LARGEST weather vane, at the Whitehorse airport, is made from an airplane and sits on a rotating pedestal.

A HOMESICK construction worker posted a signpost at Watson Lake in 1942 showing the mileage to Danville, Ill., his hometown. Since then, other people have added more than 20,000 signs to what is called "Signpost Forest."

GOLD PROSPECTORS headed to Dawson had to bring a year's supply of food along with their gear.

TIMELINE

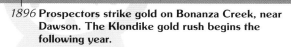

1842 Canadian fur trader Robert Campbell establishes a fur trading post for the Hudson's Bay Company.

1935 Gold rush pioneer Martha Munger Black, known as the "Mother of the Yukon," is elected to Canada's House of Commons at age 70.

1896 Prospectors strike gold on Bonanza Creek, near Dawson. The Klondike gold rush begins the following year.

1959 The world's longest fish ladder is built for chinook salmon at Whitehorse Rapids on the Yukon River.

The 100th anniversary of the *2002* land-claims process by Yukon's First Nations is celebrated; eight of Yukon's 14 First Nations are now self-governing.

The Statue of Liberty in New York Harbor.

FRESH FACTS

NAME Used for the first time in the Declaration of Independence in 1776.

CAPITAL Washington, D.C. (District of Columbia)

ABBREVIATION U.S.

NICKNAME United States, America or U.S.A.

AREA 3,537,440 square miles (9,162,000 square kilometers)

POPULATION 281,421,906

INDEPENDENCE July 4, 1776

HIGHEST POINT Mount McKinley (Denali), Alaska (20,320 feet, 6,194 meters)

LOWEST POINT Death Valley (282 feet; 86 meters below sea level)

OTHER POINTS Point Barrow, Alaska (northernmost); Ka Lee (South Cape), Hawaii (southernmost); West Quoddy, Maine (easternmost); Cape Wrangell, Alaska (westernmost).

INDUSTRIES Airplanes, chemicals, computing, entertainment, fabricated metal products, machinery, motor vehicles, plastics, petroleum products, pharmaceuticals, paper, printed material, processed food, telecommunications, tourism

AGRICULTURE Cattle, chickens, corn, cotton, hogs, milk, soybeans, wheat

MOTTO In God we trust.

FLAG Sometimes called "The Stars and Stripes" or "Old Glory," the U.S. flag has 13 stripes for the original 13 colonies and 50 five-point stars for the current 50 states. The flag was designed in 1777.

BIRD The **bald eagle** became the national bird in 1782. It symbolizes freedom and power. The bald eagle is not really bald—its head is covered with white feathers.

FLOWER The **rose** was selected in 1986 as the nation's flower. It symbolizes life, love, beauty, and eternity.

TREE None

SONG "The Star-Spangled Banner" was adopted as the national anthem in 1931.

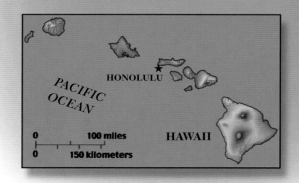

TIMELINE

1620 The Pilgrims arrive at Plymouth, Massachusetts.

1492 Christopher Columbus lands in the New World.

1776 The Declaration of Independence is adopted in Philadelphia.

1789 George Washington becomes the first president of the United States.

1863 President Abraham Lincoln issues the Emancipation Proclamation, freeing all slaves.

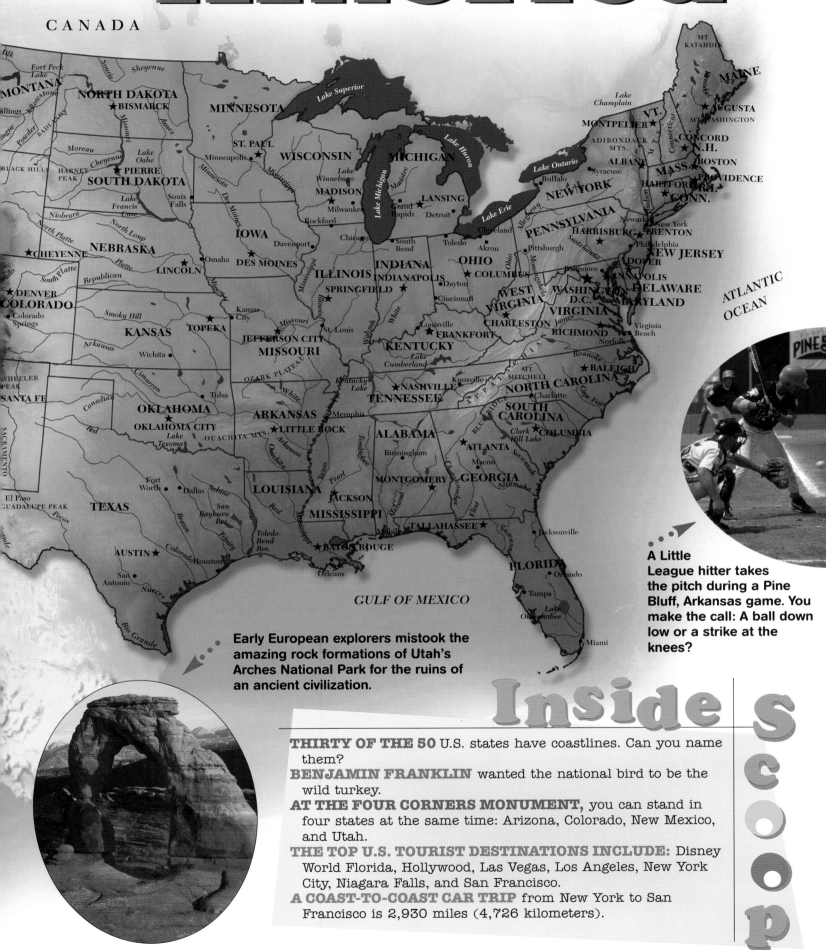

CANADA

MT. KATAHDIN

MONTANA
NORTH DAKOTA
★BISMARCK
MINNESOTA
Lake Superior
MAINE
VT.
MONTPELIER
Lake Champlain
ADIRONDACK MTS.
MT. WASHINGTON
AUGUSTA
★CONCORD
N.H.

BLACK HILLS
HARNEY PEAK
SOUTH DAKOTA
★PIERRE
Lake Oahe
ST. PAUL
Minneapolis ★
WISCONSIN
MADISON
Milwaukee
Lake Winnebago
MICHIGAN
Lake Huron
Grand Rapids
LANSING
Detroit
Lake Ontario
Buffalo
ALBANY
Syracuse
NEW YORK
MASS.
HARTFORD
CONN.
BOSTON
PROVIDENCE
R.I.

CHEYENNE
NEBRASKA
IOWA
Davenport
Rockford
Chicago
South Bend
Toledo
Cleveland
Akron
Pittsburgh
PENNSYLVANIA
HARRISBURG
TRENTON
Newark ★New York
Philadelphia
NEW JERSEY

DENVER
COLORADO
Colorado Springs
LINCOLN
Omaha
DES MOINES
ILLINOIS
INDIANA
INDIANAPOLIS
SPRINGFIELD
Dayton
Cincinnati
OHIO
COLUMBUS
WEST VIRGINIA
CHARLESTON
VIRGINIA
WASHINGTON D.C.
ANNAPOLIS
MARYLAND
DELAWARE
DOVER
ATLANTIC OCEAN

SANTA FE
WHEELER PEAK
KANSAS
TOPEKA
Wichita
Kansas City
JEFFERSON CITY
MISSOURI
St. Louis
FRANKFORT
KENTUCKY
Louisville
Lake Cumberland
RICHMOND
Norfolk
Virginia Beach
RALEIGH
MT. MITCHELL
NORTH CAROLINA

OKLAHOMA
OKLAHOMA CITY
Lake Texoma
OUACHITA MTS.
ARKANSAS
LITTLE ROCK
Tulsa
Memphis
NASHVILLE
Knoxville
TENNESSEE
Charlotte
SOUTH CAROLINA
COLUMBIA
Clark Hill Lake

TEXAS
El Paso
GUADALUPE PEAK
Fort Worth
Dallas
San Rayburn Res.
LOUISIANA
JACKSON
MISSISSIPPI
ALABAMA
Birmingham
MONTGOMERY
Macon
GEORGIA
ATLANTA
Cape Fear

AUSTIN
San Antonio
Houston
Toledo Bend Res.
BATON ROUGE
New Orleans
Mobile
TALLAHASSEE
Jacksonville
Orlando
FLORIDA

Rio Grande

GULF OF MEXICO

Tampa
Lake Okeechobee
Miami

A Little League hitter takes the pitch during a Pine Bluff, Arkansas game. You make the call: A ball down low or a strike at the knees?

Early European explorers mistook the amazing rock formations of Utah's Arches National Park for the ruins of an ancient civilization.

Inside Scoop

THIRTY OF THE 50 U.S. states have coastlines. Can you name them?

BENJAMIN FRANKLIN wanted the national bird to be the wild turkey.

AT THE FOUR CORNERS MONUMENT, you can stand in four states at the same time: Arizona, Colorado, New Mexico, and Utah.

THE TOP U.S. TOURIST DESTINATIONS INCLUDE: Disney World Florida, Hollywood, Las Vegas, Los Angeles, New York City, Niagara Falls, and San Francisco.

A COAST-TO-COAST CAR TRIP from New York to San Francisco is 2,930 miles (4,726 kilometers).

1941 **The United States enters World War II.**

1945 **The United States becomes a charter member of the United Nations.**

1969 **Two American astronauts, Neil Armstrong and Edwin Aldrin, are the first people to walk on the moon.**

The United States, with its allies, begins a war against terrorism. *2001*

AAA GEMS:
Selected Must-See Points of Interest

ANNISTON MUSEUM OF NATURAL HISTORY – This museum features more than 600 types of birds, 100 African animals, Egyptian mummies, dinosaurs, fossils, and gemstones.

OLD ALABAMA TOWN (Montgomery) – A restored village with more than 50 buildings shows how people lived during the 1800s and early 1900s.

USS ALABAMA BATTLESHIP MEMORIAL PARK (Mobile) – Tour the USS Alabama, a World War II–era battleship, and the USS Drum, a submarine.

U.S. SPACE AND ROCKET CENTER (Huntsville) – Hands-on exhibits, awesome rides, and the world's largest collection of rockets and space memorabilia offer far-out adventures about outer space.

VISIONLAND (Bessemer) – Thrill rides, a water park, and a carousel are fun for kids of all ages.

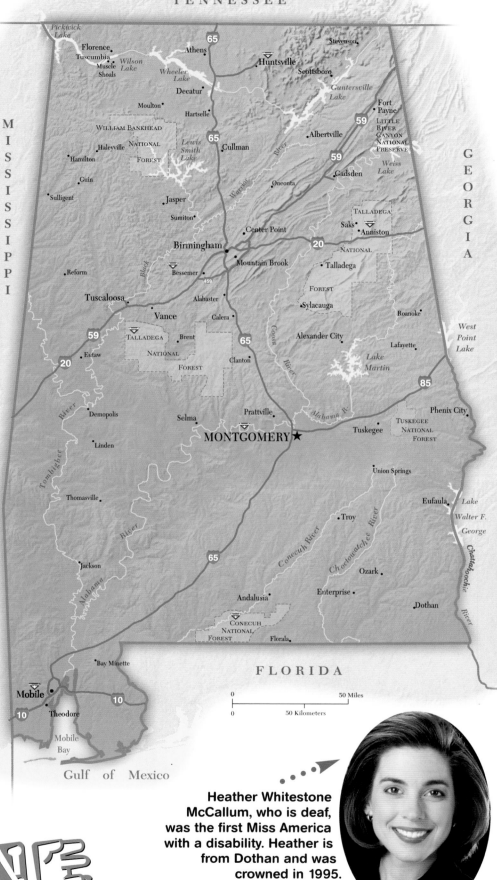

Thousands of children and adults have attended U.S. Space Camp in Huntsville to learn about space exploration. In this photo, a young trainee tries out an MMU (manned maneuvering unit) similar to those used by space shuttle astronauts.

Heather Whitestone McCallum, who is deaf, was the first Miss America with a disability. Heather is from Dothan and was crowned in 1995.

TIMELINE

1814 Gen. Andrew Jackson defeats the Creek Indians at the Battle of Horseshoe Bend. The Creeks surrender nearly half of present-day Alabama.

1886 America's first electric trolley streetcars start operating in Montgomery.

1919 The Boll Weevil Monument is dedicated in Enterprise, honoring the tiny beetle that prompted farmers to grow a variety of crops after the insect ruined the cotton crop.

1540 Hernando de Soto of Spain explores the region.

1861 Montgomery becomes the first capital of the Confederate States of America.

FRESH FACTS

NAME Based on the Creek Indian word "alibamu," meaning "thicket clearers," and the name of a Creek Indian town.

ABBREVIATION Ala.

CAPITAL Montgomery

NICKNAME The Heart of Dixie (also, Yellowhammer State)

AREA 52,419 square miles (135,765 square kilometers)

POPULATION 4,447,100

STATEHOOD Dec. 14, 1819 (22nd state)

HIGHEST POINT Cheaha Mountain (2,407 feet; 733 meters)

LOWEST POINT Sea level

INDUSTRIES Chemicals, clothing, food products, lumber, metals, mining, paper products, plastics, rubber, textiles

AGRICULTURE Cattle, chickens, cotton, peanuts, sweet potatoes, young plants

MOTTO We dare defend our rights.

FLAG Adopted in 1895, the flag is similar to the one flown by the Confederacy during the Civil War.

BIRD The **yellowhammer** was named for the yellow on the underside of its wings and the way this member of the woodpecker family hammers on tree trunks. The bird was adopted in 1927.

FLOWER In 1959, the **camellia** replaced the goldenrod. It blooms nine months of the year.

TREE The **Southern longleaf pine,** adopted in 1997, is found mostly in the lower two-thirds of the state. It can grow to be 150 feet (45 meters) tall and has cones as long as 10 inches (25 centimeters).

SONG "Alabama" (words by Julia S. Tutwiler; music by Edna G. Gussen)

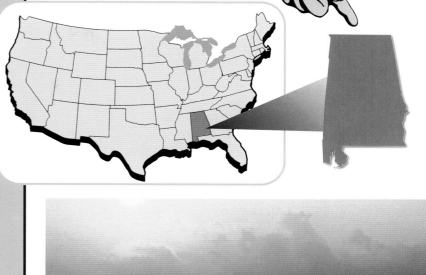

Alabama's Gulf Shores, on the Gulf of Mexico, feature 50 miles of beautiful beaches with sand so white that it has often been compared to sugar.

Inside Scoop

ALABAMA was the first state to use the emergency telephone number 911. Sen. Rankin Fite placed the first call from Halleyville on Feb. 16, 1968.

GEORGE WASHINGTON CARVER, who was born a slave and became a great scientist at the Tuskegee Institute, invented more than 300 uses for the peanut and more than 100 for the sweet potato.

LITTLE RIVER ON LOOKOUT MOUNTAIN is the nation's only river that runs entirely on top of a mountain. It forms the Little River Canyon, known as "The Grand Canyon of the South."

HUNTSVILLE is called "The Rocket Capital of the World."

A TEEN IN DECATUR started the very first Red Cross Club at her high school. Many of the club's projects helped other kids.

1955 Rosa Parks is arrested when she refuses to give up her bus seat to a white man. The Montgomery bus boycott begins.

1965 Dr. Martin Luther King, Jr. leads a march from Selma to Montgomery to support voter registration for African-Americans.

1955 The George C. Marshall Space Flight Center opens in Huntsville to develop spacecraft. Its successes include the Saturn V rocket that launched Apollo 11 to the moon, the space shuttles, and the Hubble Space Telescope.

1992 Mae Jemison, born in Decatur, blasts into space on the Space Shuttle Endeavour, becoming the first African-American woman astronaut.

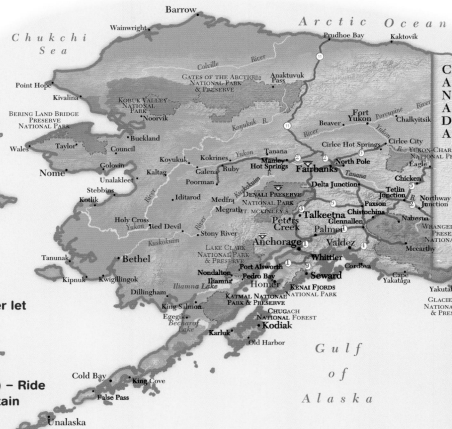

AAA GEMS:
Selected Must-See Points of Interest

ALASKA NATIVE HERITAGE CENTER
(Anchorage) – Learn why members of the Tlingit tribe carve totem poles and about other traditions of native Alaskans.

DENALI NATIONAL PARK AND PRESERVE – Denali, which means "The Great One" or "The High One," is the Athabascan Indian name for Mount McKinley, North America's highest peak. The park is home to grizzly bears, moose, caribou, Dall's sheep, and many other animals.

GASTINEAU SALMON HATCHERY
(Juneau) – More than 160 million salmon eggs hatch here annually.

MENDENHALL GLACIER (Juneau) – Trails on both sides of the 12-mile- (19-kilometer-) long glacier let you see this river of blue ice up close.

RIVERBOAT DISCOVERY (Fairbanks) – A trip aboard the Discovery III offers views of the Alaskan wilderness and an old Athabascan Indian village.

WHITE PASS AND YUKON ROUTE (Skagway) – Ride this narrow-gauge railroad as it chugs across mountain rivers and chasms.

The first woman ever to compete in the 1,150-mile (1,850-kilometer) Iditarod Trail Sled Dog Race, Susan Butcher, was also the first to win the race three years in a row (1986, 1987, 1988).

Inside Scoop

THE SUN DOESN'T SET for almost three months during the summer in northernmost Alaska.

ALASKA has more caribou than people.

THE IDITAROD is a dog sled race held every year. In 1925, 20 volunteer mushers (dog sledders) rushed medicine from Anchorage to Nome during a children's diphtheria epidemic.

ALASKA IS THE LARGEST STATE. If placed on top of the 48 lower states, Alaska would extend from coast to coast.

SEVENTEEN OF THE 20 highest peaks in the United States are in Alaska.

THERE ARE MORE ACTIVE VOLCANOES and ice fields in Alaska than in the rest of the inhabited world.

MALASPINA, one of Alaska's 5,000 glaciers, is larger than the state of Rhode Island.

AN EIGHTH GRADER in Anchorage started a weekly musical performance by kids called "Musical Smiles" at two assisted-living homes to entertain their elderly residents. He won Alaska's Prudential Spirit of Community Award in 2000 for his efforts.

TIMELINE

1784 Russian whalers and fur traders establish the first permanent settlement on Kodiak Island.

1867 U.S. Secretary of State William H. Seward purchases Alaska from Russia for $7.2 million or about two cents an acre (hectare).

1912 Alaska becomes a U.S. territory.

1741 Danish explorer Vitus Bering, working for the Russian czar, reaches Alaska.

1880 Gold is discovered near Juneau. Soon more discoveries set off gold rushes in other parts of Alaska.

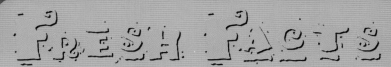

NAME Based on the Russian version of an Aleutian word "alakshak," meaning "peninsula" or "land that is not an island."

ABBREVIATION None

CAPITAL Juneau (only U.S. capital city accessible only by boat or plane)

NICKNAME The Last Frontier (also, Land of the Midnight Sun)

AREA 663,267 square miles (1,717,861 square kilometers)

POPULATION 626,932

STATEHOOD Jan. 3, 1959 (49th state)

HIGHEST POINT Mount McKinley (20,320 feet; 6,194 meters)

LOWEST POINT Sea level

INDUSTRIES Fishing, furs, lumber, mining, natural gas, petroleum, tourism, wood products

AGRICULTURE Barley, dairy products, hay, livestock, oats, seafood, young plants

MOTTO North to the future.

FLAG Adopted in 1959, the state's flag was first designed in 1927 by a 13-year-old from Cognac. The blue field symbolizes the sky, sea, mountain lakes, and wildflowers. The seven gold stars stand for the Big Dipper and the eighth is for the North Star, because Alaska is the northernmost state.

BIRD During the winter, **willow ptarmigans** grow hair-like feathers on their feet, which let them glide across the snow as though they were wearing snowshoes. The ptarmigan was adopted in 1955.

FLOWER Found throughout the Arctic region, the **blue forget-me-not** was chosen as the state flower in 1949.

TREE The **Sitka spruce,** adopted in 1962, is the largest type of spruce tree. It grows near streams where its thick roots protect the streams' banks from erosion.

SONG "Alaska's Flag" (words by Marie Drake; music by Elinor Dusenbury)

YUKON

BRITISH COLUMBIA

kwan
Skagway
JUNEAU
lican
Petersburg
NAL
Craig • Ketchican
FOREST • Metlakatla

At 20,320 feet (6,194 meters), Alaska's Mount McKinley is North America's highest mountain.

Alaska's vast wilderness is home to grizzly, black, and polar bears. Although bears usually try to avoid humans, when threatened they can be dangerous. The Alaska Public Lands Information Center publishes this sticker to teach hikers about bear safety.

• BE A NOISY HIKER...
Sing, talk, wear a bell.

• GIVE BEARS SPACE...
Watch & photograph from a distance.

• RESPECT A BEAR'S MEAL...
Stay away from dead animals.

• KEEP A CLEAN CAMP...
Cook & store food away from camp.

• LEAVE YOUR DOG AT HOME...
Bears and pets don't mix.

BEAR SAFETY IN ALASKA

ALASKA PUBLIC LANDS INFORMATION CENTERS

Wildlife deserve our respect and good manners! Alaska

1964 The strongest earthquake ever recorded in North America, 9.2 on the Richter scale, strikes Alaska.

1977 The Trans-Alaska Pipeline is completed. It transports 88,000 barrels of oil every day.

1943 The Alaska-Canada Highway (1,397 miles; 2,248 kilometers), originally built as a military supply road, is completed.

1968 Oil is discovered near Prudhoe Bay.

1989 The Exxon Valdez spills 11 million gallons (42 million liters) of oil into Prince William Sound, the biggest oil spill in U.S. history to date.

AAA GEMS:
Selected Must-See Points of Interest

CANYON DE CHELLY NATIONAL MONUMENT (Navajo Indian Reservation) – "The Ancient Ones," or Anasazi, built these amazing, multi-level, adobe houses into the steep red cliffs more than 700 years ago. The ruins provide insights into the cultures of the tribes who lived there.

GRAND CANYON NATIONAL PARK – One of the seven natural wonders of the world, the awesome Grand Canyon reveals more than 1 billion years of our Earth's history.

HOOVER DAM (Lake Mead National Recreation Area) – Straddling the Arizona-Nevada border, the Hoover Dam provides water and electrical power to California and the Southwest. The special hard-hat tour allows a close-up look at how the turbines operate.

PETRIFIED FOREST NATIONAL PARK – Petrified wood (buried trees that have turned to gem-like, multi-colored stone after millions of years) plus petroglyphs (rock carvings made by the Earth's earliest peoples) make this a magnificent and mysterious place.

TOMBSTONE – Ride a stagecoach through "The Town Too Tough to Die" and see a re-enactment of the 1881 gunfight at the O.K. Corral, the most famous gunfight of the Wild West.

The Ostrich Race is one of the more unusual events at the Chandler Ostrich Festival, held each year in March.

One of the most popular ways to explore the Grand Canyon is on the back of a mule. Mule rides into the canyon began in 1891.

TIMELINE

1539 Franciscan friar Marcos de Niza searches for the fabled Seven Cities of Cibola, cities thought to be filled with treasure.

1848 Mexico gives up most of present-day Arizona to the United States.

1853 The United States buys the remaining part of Arizona from Mexico in the Gadsden Purchase.

1877 The Southern Pacific Railroad pulls into Arizona.

1911 The Theodore Roosevelt Dam on the Salt River brings water to Arizona's south-central region.

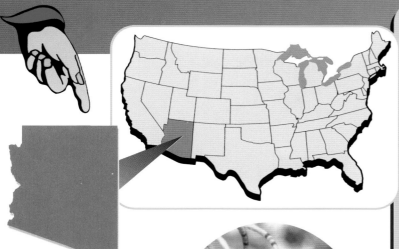

An American Indian dancer performs a Hoop Dance at the Heard Museum in Phoenix. The Hoop Dance requires great agility and coordination in moving large hoops over and around the body, legs, and arms in a dizzying number of shapes.

FRESH FACTS

NAME From the Pima Indian word "arizonac," meaning "little spring place," and the Aztec Indian word "arizuma," meaning "silver-bearing."

ABBREVIATION Ariz.

CAPITAL Phoenix

NICKNAME Grand Canyon State

AREA 113,998 square miles (295,254 square kilometers)

POPULATION 5,130,632

STATEHOOD Feb. 14, 1912 (48th state)

HIGHEST POINT Humphreys Peak (12,633 feet; 3,851 meters)

LOWEST POINT Colorado River (70 feet; 21 meters)

INDUSTRIES Construction, copper mining, electrical equipment, food products, metals, printing and publishing, tourism, transportation equipment

AGRICULTURE Barley, broccoli, cattle, cauliflower, cotton, lettuce, sorghum

MOTTO God enriches.

FLAG The red and yellow rays symbolize the original 13 colonies, the setting sun, and the colors flown by the Spanish conquistadors. The copper-colored star celebrates Arizona as the nation's biggest copper producer. The flag was adopted in 1917.

BIRD The **cactus wren,** adopted in 1973, is the largest wren in the United States, measuring 7–8 inches (18–20 centimeters) in length. It often builds its nest on a cactus arm.

FLOWER The **saguaro** cactus blossom was adopted in 1931. The saguaro cactus can grow to more than 50 feet (15 meters) high. The Papago and Pima Indians made a syrup from the saguaro's red fruit.

TREE Adopted in 1954, the **paloverde,** Spanish for "green stick," is a short tree with yellow to yellow-green bark that can survive with little water.

SONG "Arizona" (words by Margaret R. Clifford; music by Maurice Blumenthal)

Inside Scoop

A METEORITE SMASHED into Earth about 50,000 years ago, creating a huge hole in Coconino County named the Barringer Meteor Crater. It measures 4,180 feet (1,275 meters) wide by 570 feet (175 meters) deep.

THE COPPER on the dome of the state's Capitol building is equivalent to 4,800,000 copper pennies.

EACH JANUARY, the Hashknife Pony Express re-enacts the pony express, traveling 200 miles (322 kilometers)—one-tenth of the original route—by horseback to deliver 20,000 first-class letters.

TUCSON is called "The Astronomy Capital of the World." About 30 telescopes are mounted near the city.

A 12-YEAR-OLD FROM Glendale is one of America's fastest Go-Kart racers. He is a three-time Junior One first-place driving champion and the winner of more than 55 main event races.

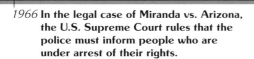

1948 Voting rights are granted to Arizona's American Indians.

1971 The original London Bridge, built in the 1800s, is taken apart and rebuilt over Lake Havasu.

The Arizona Diamondbacks **2001** win the World Series.

1966 In the legal case of Miranda vs. Arizona, the U.S. Supreme Court rules that the police must inform people who are under arrest of their rights.

1981 Arizona-born Sandra Day O'Connor becomes the first woman justice appointed to the U.S. Supreme Court.

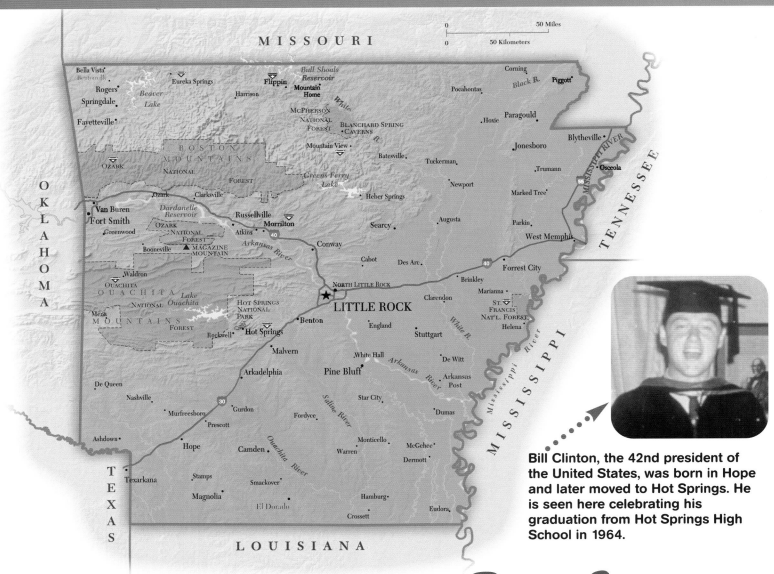

Bill Clinton, the 42nd president of the United States, was born in Hope and later moved to Hot Springs. He is seen here celebrating his graduation from Hot Springs High School in 1964.

Whitaker Point, which is also known as Hawksbill Crag, is one of the most famous landmarks in the Ozark Mountains. The point is a spectacular rock outcrop that juts from a high bluff located in the Upper Buffalo Wilderness Area.

Inside Scoop

THE TOWN OF TEXARKANA belongs to both Arkansas and Texas. The post office straddles the border and has a door in each state.

THE NATION'S ONLY diamond mine is near Murfreesboro and operated from 1908 to 1925 before becoming a tourist attraction. The largest diamond found there is 40.23 carats.

MANY VISITORS HAVE BATHED in Arkansas' hot springs, including President Franklin D. Roosevelt, gangster Al Capone, and baseball great Babe Ruth.

EVERY THANKSGIVING WEEK, more than 60,000 people attend the World Championship Duck Calling Contest, the state's oldest festival, held in Stuttgart.

AN 18-YEAR-OLD from Sulphur Rock who has Down Syndrome and heart problems served as a state 4-H ambassador and was selected to be an Arkansas delegate to a 4-H citizenship conference in Washington, D.C.

TIMELINE

1673 Jacques Marquette, a French missionary, and Louis Jolliet, a French-Canadian explorer, arrive at the mouth of the Arkansas River.

1803 The United States acquires Arkansas as part of the Louisiana Purchase.

1817 Fort Smith is erected to protect pioneers traveling west. During the 1849 gold rush, it becomes an important outfitting station.

1541 Spanish explorer Hernando de Soto is the first European to visit the region.

1686 The first European permanent settlement in the lower Mississippi Valley is established at Arkansas Post.

1921 Oil is discovered near El Dorado.

FRESH FACTS

NAME From the French version of the Sioux Indian word "acansa," meaning "downstream place."

ABBREVIATION Ark.

CAPITAL Little Rock

NICKNAME The Natural State (also, The Razorback State)

AREA 53,183 square miles (137,742 square kilometers)

POPULATION 2,673,400

STATEHOOD June 15, 1836 (25th state)

HIGHEST POINT Magazine Mountain (2,753 feet; 839 meters)

LOWEST POINT Ouachita River (55 feet; 17 meters)

INDUSTRIES Chemicals, electrical equipment, food products, machinery, metals, paper products, steel, tourism, wood products

AGRICULTURE Cattle, chickens, cotton, rice, sorghum, soybeans

MOTTO The people rule.

FLAG The large diamond symbolizes Arkansas' diamond mine; the 25 stars represent Arkansas as the 25th state; the star above the state name shows it was a Confederate state during the Civil War; and the three stars below are for the three powers that owned the land: France, Spain, and the United States. The flag was adopted in 1913.

BIRD The **mockingbird,** adopted in 1929, gets its name from the way it mimics the songs of other birds. It can change its song as often as 30 times in 10 minutes.

FLOWER The **apple blossom** was adopted in 1901 because Arkansas was once a major apple-producing state.

TREE The **pine** tree was adopted in 1939. Fifty-four percent of the state's forests are pine woods.

SONGS "Arkansas" (words and music by Wayland Holyfield). "Oh, Arkansas" (words by Gary Klaff; music by Terry Rose).

AAA GEMS: Selected Must-See Points of Interest

BLANCHARD SPRINGS CAVERNS (Mountain View) — Mineral deposits create fantastic columns, stalactites, and stalagmites.

HOT SPRINGS NATIONAL PARK — Hike through the Ouachita Mountains or sample one of the 47 hot springs. The water bubbling up from underground fell as rain about 4,000 years ago! Be careful, though. The water is hot — about 143° F (62° C).

MID-AMERICA SCIENCE MUSEUM (Hot Springs) — Explore perceptions, types of energy, matter, and life cycles with fun, interactive exhibits.

OZARK FOLK CENTER (Mountain View) — One hundred years (1820–1920) of life in the Ozark Mountains are captured through craft demonstrations, music, and food.

PETIT JEAN STATE PARK (Morrilton) — Arkansas' first state park is named after the legend of Petit Jean, a French girl who disguised herself as a boy so she could follow her true love to America.

WHITE RIVER SCENIC RAILROAD (Flippin) — See the Ozark Mountains and the spectacular scenery by train.

Blues music has a long history in Arkansas. Helena's annual King Biscuit Blues Festival, named after a radio program called "King Biscuit Time" that started in 1941, has helped keep the tradition alive.

1927 **Rising waters on the Mississippi River flood half the state.**

1932 **Hattie Caraway becomes the first woman to be elected to the U.S. Senate.**

1957 **President Dwight D. Eisenhower sends federal troops to Little Rock to escort black students to Central High School.**

1962 **Sam Walton opens the first Wal-Mart store in Rogers.**

Gov. William J. Clinton from Hope is elected the *1992* 42nd president of the United States, the first from Arkansas, and re-elected in 1996.

1974 **Jockey Bill Shoemaker wins his 100th stakes race and more than $100,000 at Oaklawn Park in Hot Springs.**

California

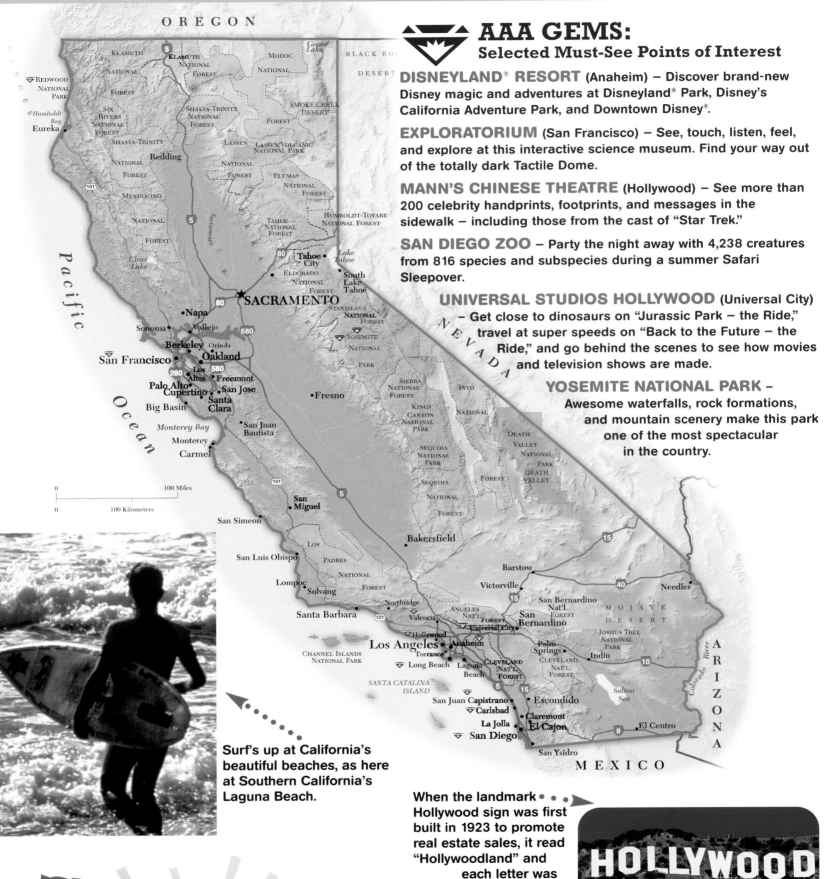

KLAMUTH NATIONAL FOREST
KLAMUTH NATIONAL FOREST
MODOC NATIONAL FOREST
BLACK ROC
DESERT
Goose Lake

REDWOOD NATIONAL PARK
SIX RIVERS NATIONAL FOREST
SHASTA-TRINITY NATIONAL FOREST
SHASTA-TRINITY NATIONAL FOREST
SMOKE CREEK DESERT

Humboldt Bay
Eureka

SHASTA-TRINITY NATIONAL FOREST
LASSEN
LASSEN VOLCANIC NATIONAL PARK

MENDOCINO NATIONAL FOREST
Redding
PLUMAS NATIONAL FOREST
HUMBOLDT-TOYABE NATIONAL FOREST

Clear Lake
TAHOE NATIONAL FOREST

Tahoe City
Lake Tahoe

ELDORADO NATIONAL FOREST
South Lake Tahoe

SACRAMENTO
STANISLAUS NATIONAL FOREST

Napa
Sonoma   Vallejo
Berkeley   Orinda
San Francisco   Oakland
Palo Alto   Freemont
Cupertino   San Jose
Big Basin   Santa Clara

YOSEMITE NATIONAL PARK

NEVADA

Fresno

SIERRA NATIONAL FOREST
KINGS CANYON NATIONAL PARK
INYO NATIONAL FOREST

Monterey Bay
Monterey
Carmel

San Juan Bautista

DEATH VALLEY NATIONAL PARK
DEATH VALLEY

SEQUOIA NATIONAL PARK
SEQUOIA NATIONAL FOREST

San Simeon

San Miguel

Bakersfield

San Luis Obispo
LOS PADRES NATIONAL FOREST

Lompoc
Solvang

Barstow
Victorville
Needles

Santa Barbara
Northridge
Valencia
ANGELES NAT'L FOREST
Universal City
Hollywood
Los Angeles   Anaheim
Torrance
Long Beach
Laguna Beach
San Juan Capistrano
Carlsbad
La Jolla   El Cajon
San Diego
San Ysidro

San Bernardino Nat'l. Forest
San Bernardino
CLEVELAND NAT'L FOREST
CLEVELAND NAT'L FOREST
MOJAVE DESERT
JOSHUA TREE NATIONAL PARK
Palm Springs
Indio
Salton Sea
Escondido
Claremont

ARIZONA
Colorado River
El Centro

MEXICO

CHANNEL ISLANDS NATIONAL PARK
SANTA CATALINA ISLAND

Pacific Ocean

0   100 Miles
0   100 Kilometers

AAA GEMS:
Selected Must-See Points of Interest

DISNEYLAND® RESORT (Anaheim) – Discover brand-new Disney magic and adventures at Disneyland® Park, Disney's California Adventure Park, and Downtown Disney®.

EXPLORATORIUM (San Francisco) – See, touch, listen, feel, and explore at this interactive science museum. Find your way out of the totally dark Tactile Dome.

MANN'S CHINESE THEATRE (Hollywood) – See more than 200 celebrity handprints, footprints, and messages in the sidewalk – including those from the cast of "Star Trek."

SAN DIEGO ZOO – Party the night away with 4,238 creatures from 816 species and subspecies during a summer Safari Sleepover.

UNIVERSAL STUDIOS HOLLYWOOD (Universal City) – Get close to dinosaurs on "Jurassic Park – the Ride," travel at super speeds on "Back to the Future – the Ride," and go behind the scenes to see how movies and television shows are made.

YOSEMITE NATIONAL PARK – Awesome waterfalls, rock formations, and mountain scenery make this park one of the most spectacular in the country.

Surf's up at California's beautiful beaches, as here at Southern California's Laguna Beach.

When the landmark Hollywood sign was first built in 1923 to promote real estate sales, it read "Hollywoodland" and each letter was covered with thousands of lightbulbs.

TIMELINE

1579 Sir Francis Drake claims California for England.

1769 Franciscan friar Junipero Serra establishes the San Diego de Alcala Mission, the first of many.

1841 The first wagon train arrives in California.

1853 In San Francisco, Levi Strauss makes brown canvas pants for gold miners, then switches to blue denim—the first blue jeans.

1542 Juan Rodriquez Cabrillo, sailing from Mexico, is the first European to discover the California coast.

1822 California becomes part of Mexico.

1848 Mexico surrenders California in the Treaty of Guadaloupe Hidalgo. Gold is found at Sutter's Mill.

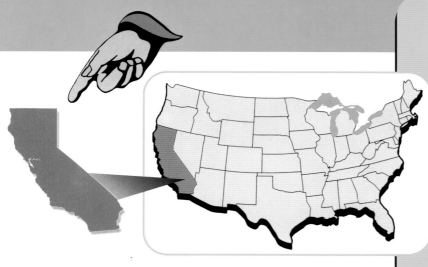

NAME From "Califia," a legendary island filled with gold that was described in a popular novel by Garci Ordonez de Montalvo and published in Spain in 1510.

ABBREVIATION Calif.

CAPITAL Sacramento

NICKNAME Golden State

AREA 163,696 square miles (423,972 square kilometers)

POPULATION 33,871,648

STATEHOOD Sept. 9, 1850 (31st state)

HIGHEST POINT Mount Whitney (14,495 feet; 4,418 meters)

LOWEST POINT Death Valley (282 feet; 86 meters below sea level)

INDUSTRIES Clothes, electrical and electronic equipment, entertainment, food products, machinery, telecommunications, tourism, wine

AGRICULTURE Cattle, dairy products, grapes, lettuce, strawberries, tomatoes, young plants

MOTTO I have found it. (Eureka!)

FLAG Adopted in 1911, the flag is similar to the one flown at Sonoma during the 1846 California revolt against Mexican rule. The grizzly bear symbolizes strength, and the star refers to the Lone Star of Texas, the state that won its independence from Mexico in 1836.

CALIFORNIA REPUBLIC

BIRD The **California valley quail,** adopted in 1931, is a lively, hardy, and adaptable bird. The curved, black plume atop its head makes the bird easy to identify.

FLOWER The **golden poppy,** adopted in 1903, was used by American Indians as a source of food and for oil they applied to their hair.

TREE The **California redwood,** adopted in 1937 as the state tree, is found only on the Pacific Coast. It is the world's tallest tree.

SONG "I Love You, California" (words by F.B. Silverwood; music by Alfred F. Frankenstein)

First opened in 1937, San Francisco's Golden Gate Bridge is one of the longest suspension bridges in the world. Each of the two cables that support the bridge's floor is 7,659 feet (2,334 meters) long and contains 27,572 parallel wires, enough to circle the Earth's equator more than three times.

Inside Scoop

THE CHINESE NEW YEAR'S festival in San Francisco is the biggest in the country.

THE GENERAL SHERMAN TREE, a giant sequoia redwood in Sequoia National Park, is considered to be the world's largest tree overall.

YOSEMITE FALLS is 14 times higher than Niagara Falls.

FROM 1996 until the beginning of 2002, Michelle Kwan from Torrance won the gold medal at six U.S. Figure Skating Championships, four world championships, and a bronze medal at the 2002 Winter Olympics.

MORE THAN 100 different languages are spoken in Los Angeles.

CALIFORNIA grows more food than any other state in the nation.

AT 17-YEARS-OLD, a dancer from Long Beach became the youngest member of the Alvin Ailey American Dance Theater.

1906 A powerful earthquake registering 8.3 on the Richter scale strikes San Francisco.

1910 The first film made in Hollywood, D.W. Griffith's "In Old California," is shown.

1913 The nation's highest temperature (134° F; 57° C) is recorded in Death Valley.

1928 Mickey Mouse debuts in "Steamboat Willie," the first animated cartoon combining sound and action.

1937 San Francisco's Golden Gate Bridge opens.

1945 The charter establishing the United Nations is adopted in San Francisco.

1963 California becomes the most populous state.

1976 Steven Jobs and Steve Wozniak, both in their 20s, start Apple Computer, Inc. in Los Altos.

The Kodak Theatre, the *2002* new home of the Academy Awards, opens in Los Angeles.

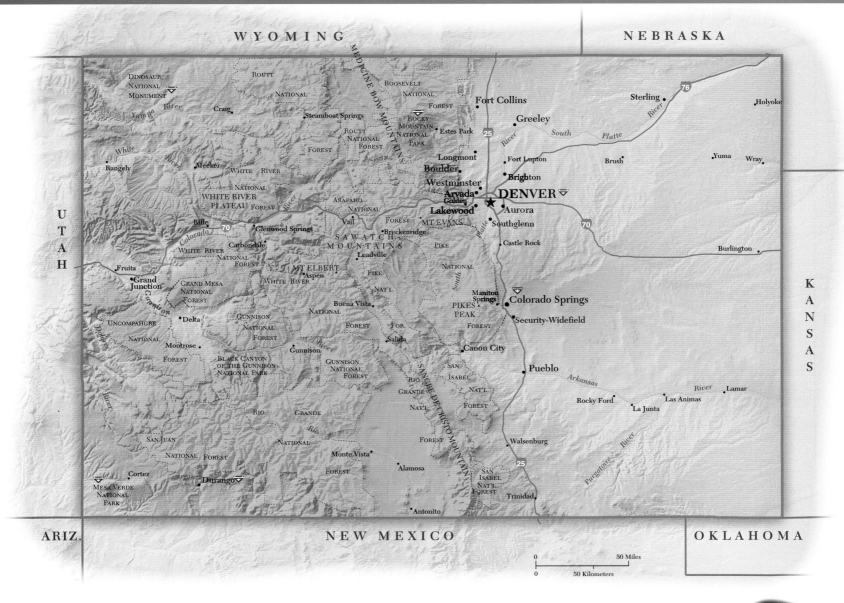

WYOMING
NEBRASKA

DINOSAUR NATIONAL MONUMENT

ROUTT

NATIONAL

Craig

Steamboat Springs

ROUTT NATIONAL FOREST

Rangely

Meeker

WHITE RIVER

NATIONAL

WHITE RIVER PLATEAU

FOREST

Rifle

Glenwood Springs

Carbondale

Fruita

Grand Junction

GRAND MESA NATIONAL FOREST

WHITE RIVER NATIONAL FOREST

Aspen

MT ELBERT

WHITE RIVER

Leadville

SAWATCH MOUNTAINS

Vail

Breckenridge

MT EVANS

PIKE

NATIONAL

FOREST

ROOSEVELT

NATIONAL

FOREST

ROCKY MOUNTAIN NATIONAL PARK

Fort Collins

Greeley

Estes Park

Longmont

Boulder

Westminster

Arvada

Golden

Lakewood

DENVER

Aurora

Southglenn

Castle Rock

Fort Lupton

Brighton

Sterling

Holyoke

South Platte River

Brush

Yuma

Wray

MEDICINE BOW MOUNTAINS

ARAPAHO NATIONAL FOREST

UTAH

White River

Yampa River

Colorado River

Uncompahgre

Delta

Montrose

GUNNISON NATIONAL FOREST

BLACK CANYON OF THE GUNNISON NATIONAL PARK

Gunnison

GUNNISON NATIONAL FOREST

Buena Vista

NATIONAL FOREST

Salida

For.

SAN ISABEL NAT'L FOREST

Manitou Springs

PIKES PEAK

Colorado Springs

Security-Widefield

PIKE NATIONAL FOREST

Canon City

Pueblo

Burlington

KANSAS

SAN JUAN NATIONAL FOREST

RIO GRANDE

RIO GRANDE NATIONAL FOREST

Monte Vista

FOREST

Alamosa

SANGRE DE CRISTO MOUNTAINS

Walsenburg

SAN ISABEL NAT'L FOREST

Trinidad

Arkansas River

Rocky Ford

La Junta

Las Animas

Lamar

Purgatoire River

Cortez

MESA VERDE NATIONAL PARK

Durango

Antonito

ARIZ.
NEW MEXICO
OKLAHOMA

0 50 Miles
0 50 Kilometers

AAA GEMS:
Selected Must-See Points of Interest

DENVER ZOO – Visit Sheep Mountain, Primate Panorama, a tropical rain forest, and more.
DINOSAUR NATIONAL MONUMENT – One of the walls of the visitor center is made of fossilized Jurassic dinosaur bones.
DURANGO AND SILVERTON NARROW GAUGE RAILROAD & MUSEUM – Take a 45-mile (72-kilometer) train ride between these two old mining towns.
MESA VERDE NATIONAL PARK – About 1,000 years ago, American Indians built their homes into cliffs, away from wild animals and other enemies. The park's 400 cliff dwellings are the best preserved in the nation.
PIKES PEAK (Colorado Springs) – Katherine Lee Bates was so inspired by the beautiful view from Pikes Peak that she sat down and wrote the words for "America the Beautiful" in 1893. If you don't want to hike to the top, you can get there by car, bus, or cog railway.
ROCKY MOUNTAIN NATIONAL PARK (Estes Park) – Elk and bighorn sheep roam these majestic mountains. Take a drive along Ridge Road, the highest through-road in the country.

More than 10 million skiers hit the slopes in Colorado each year.

TIMELINE

1682 Explorer René-Robert Cavelier, Sieur de la Salle, claims eastern Colorado for France.

1706 Juan de Ulibarri, a Spanish official, claims western Colorado for Spain.

1803 The United States buys eastern Colorado as part of the Louisiana Purchase.

1806 Explorer Zebulon Pike discovers the Rocky Mountains and tries to reach the top of one of them, later named Pikes Peak in his honor.

1848 The United States takes over western Colorado at the end of the Mexican War.

1859 Gold is discovered at North Clear Creek, attracting thousand of prospectors.

1894 The world's largest silver nugget, weighing 1,840 pounds (835 kilograms), is found near Aspen.

Fresh Facts

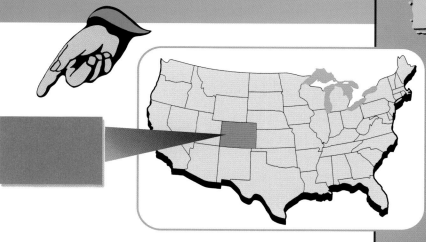

NAME From two Spanish words, "color" and "rojo," meaning "color red," describing the color of the Colorado River and much of the state's earth.

ABBREVIATION Colo.

CAPITAL Denver

NICKNAME Centennial State

AREA 104,094 square miles (269,603 square kilometers)

POPULATION 4,301,261

STATEHOOD Aug. 1, 1876 (38th state)

HIGHEST POINT Mount Elbert (14,433 feet; 4,399 meters)

LOWEST POINT Arkansas River (3,350 feet; 1,021 meters)

INDUSTRIES Beer, chemicals, construction, electronic equipment, food products, gold, machinery, metals, scientific instruments, tourism, transportation equipment

AGRICULTURE Cattle, corn, dairy products, hay, potatoes, wheat

MOTTO Nothing without Providence.

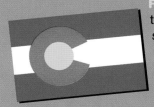

FLAG The blue stripes symbolize the sky, the white stripe stands for the state's snow-capped mountains, the C is for Colorado, and the golden ball within it represents Colorado's sunshine and gold deposits. The flag was adopted in 1911.

BIRD Male **lark buntings** sometimes perform an aerial show: They zoom almost straight up, then float down on air drafts, singing all the while. The bird was selected in 1931.

FLOWER The white and lavender **Rocky Mountain columbine** was chosen in 1899. In 1925, the General Assembly decreed that all citizens must protect this rare flower.

TREE The **Colorado blue spruce** was not officially adopted until 1939, although school children had voted on Arbor Day in 1892 for it to be the state tree.

SONG "Where the Columbines Grow" (words and music by A.J. Flynn)

The "Mile High City" of Denver, seen here at sunset, has grown from a small 19th-century mining camp into the economic and cultural capital of the Rockies.

Inside Scoop

BOULDER is the nation's only city that gets its water from a melting glacier.

SHIFTING SANDS in the Grand Sand Dunes National Monument create dunes 700 feet (213 meters) high. That's about the height of a 70-story building.

THE U.S. MINT in Denver makes 40 million coins a day — a total of 8 billion a year.

COLORADO has more mountains over 14,000 feet (4,267 meters) than any other state.

DURING THE 1859 GOLD RUSH, miners paid $15 for a bag of potatoes and $1 for each egg. They sold a pinch of gold dust for a mere 25 cents.

A 16-YEAR-OLD from Golden was a member of the swim team that went to Rome, Italy, in 2001 to participate in the World Deaf Games.

Many of the tallest mountains in North America are in Colorado, making the state "the place where miles stand on end."

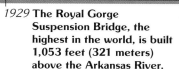

1906 The U.S. Mint at Denver issues its first coins.

1947 The state's first commercial ski resort opens for business in Aspen.

1929 The Royal Gorge Suspension Bridge, the highest in the world, is built 1,053 feet (321 meters) above the Arkansas River.

1958 Colorado Springs becomes the permanent home of the U.S. Air Force Academy.

1977 The Olympic Training Center opens in Colorado Springs.

1993 Denver welcomes the state's first major league baseball team, the Colorado Rockies.

Connecticut

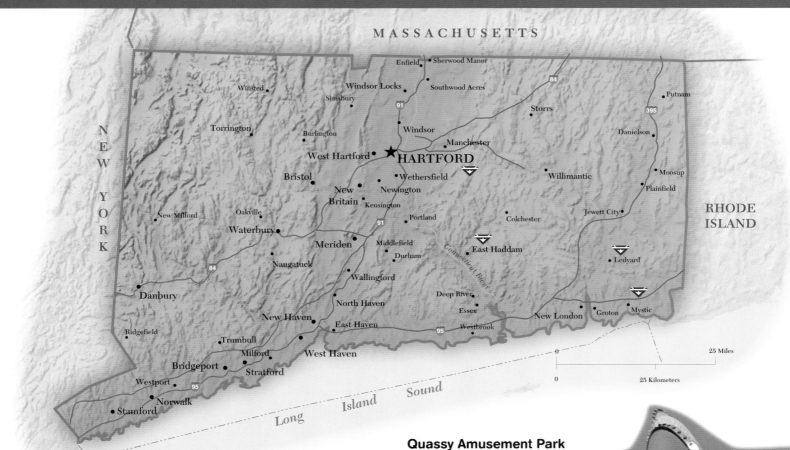

MASSACHUSETTS

Enfield • Sherwood Manor
Winsted • Windsor Locks • Southwood Acres
Simsbury • Storrs • Putnam
84
91
Torrington • Burlington • Windsor
West Hartford • ★ HARTFORD • Manchester • Danielson
Bristol • Wethersfield • Willimantic • Moosup
New Britain • Newington • Plainfield
New Milford • Oakville • Kensington • Portland • Colchester • Jewett City
Waterbury • 91 • East Haddam • Ledyard • RHODE ISLAND
84 • Meriden • Middlefield • Durham
Naugatuck • Wallingford • Deep River
Danbury • North Haven • Essex • New London • Groton • Mystic
Ridgefield • New Haven • East Haven • Westbrook • 95
Trumbull • West Haven
Milford • 95
Bridgeport • Stratford
Westport • 95
Norwalk
Stamford

N E W   Y O R K

Long Island Sound

0 ___ 25 Miles
0 ___ 25 Kilometers

Quassy Amusement Park in Middlebury features 24 rides, including the Tilt-A-Whirl and the Monster Rollercoaster, as well as a sandy lakeside beach, picnic areas, an arcade, and more.

◈ AAA GEMS:
Selected Must-See Points of Interest

GILLETTE CASTLE STATE PARK (East Haddam) — William Gillette, an actor who played the role of Sherlock Holmes, lived with 15 cats in this 24-room stone castle. The mansion is filled with cat pictures and statues as well as theatrical souvenirs.

MARK TWAIN HOUSE (Hartford) — Mark Twain, whose real name was Samuel Langhorne Clemens, lived in this 19-room house from 1874 to 1891 with his family while writing "The Adventures of Tom Sawyer," "The Adventures of Huckleberry Finn," and "A Connecticut Yankee in King Arthur's Court."

MASHANTUCKET PEQUOT MUSEUM & RESEARCH CENTER (Ledyard) — Realistic outdoor and indoor exhibits trace the history and culture of the Pequot Indians and other regional tribes.

MYSTIC SEAPORT — Visit this re-created seaport and learn about sailing, whaling, shipbuilding, and everyday life in the mid-1800s.

OLD STATE HOUSE (Hartford) — Built in 1797, the nation's oldest state house stages a re-enactment of the 1839-1841 freedom trial of enslaved Africans from the ship, the Amistad. In the upstairs museum are such curiosities as a two-headed calf and an 8.5-foot (2.6-meter) alligator.

Litchfield County in northwest Connecticut has some of the best biking trails in the northeastern United States.

TIMELINE

1636 Thomas Hooker leads a group of settlers from Massachusetts to Hartford.

1764 The first edition of the "Hartford Courant" is printed. It is the oldest U.S. newspaper in circulation today.

1639 Connecticut adopts the Fundamental Orders, the first written constitution establishing a democratic government.

1662 King Charles II grants the charter for Connecticut.

1800 Eli Whitney, of New Haven, uses standardized parts to manufacture rifles, foreshadowing modern mass-production methods.

FRESH FACTS

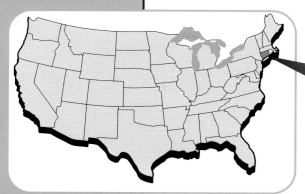

NAME From an Algonquian Indian word "quinnihtukqut," meaning "beside the long tidal river."

ABBREVIATION Conn.

CAPITAL Hartford

NICKNAME Constitution State (also, Nutmeg State)

AREA 5,543 square miles (14,356 square kilometers)

POPULATION 3,405,565

STATEHOOD Jan. 9, 1788 (5th state)

HIGHEST POINT Mount Frissell (2,380 feet; 725 meters)

LOWEST POINT Sea level

INDUSTRIES Aircraft parts, chemical products, electrical equipment, electronics, fabricated metal products, finance, insurance, machinery, real estate, scientific instruments, submarines

AGRICULTURE Christmas trees, dairy products, eggs, mushrooms, vegetables, young plants

MOTTO He who transplanted still sustains.

FLAG Adopted in 1897, the flag displays the state's coat of arms with its three grapevines, each with three bunches of purple grapes. Some historians think the vines represent the state's first English colonies: Hartford, Wethersfield, and Windsor. The state's motto is written on the ribbon below.

BIRD The **American robin,** with its cheery song, heralds the arrival of spring each year. It became the official state bird in 1943.

FLOWER American Indians called **mountain laurel** "spoon wood," because they fashioned spoons and other utensils from the plant. The flower was adopted in 1907.

TREE The **white oak** is a symbol of freedom in Connecticut. In 1687, the state's charter was hidden in a white oak when King James II of England sent armed troops to reclaim the charter — and all of Connecticut.

SONG "Yankee Doodle" (traditional)

Mystic Seaport, the leading maritime museum in the United States, entertains more than 1 million visitors a year.

Inside Scoop

SINCE 1966, jazz concerts are held in Hartford's Bushnell Park in the summer on Monday evenings. Famous musicians and local kids perform.

YALE STUDENTS used empty pie tins from Mrs. Frisbie Pies as flying discs across the school lawn in 1920. They called the tins "Frisbies."

THE NEW HAVEN DISTRICT TELEPHONE COMPANY published the world's first telephone book in February 1878. It contained 50 names.

THE FOOTBALL TACKLING DUMMY was invented at Yale University in New Haven in 1889 by Amos Alonzo Stagg, a Yale divinity student and football player. He later became one of the most successful coaches in the history of college football.

AN 18-YEAR-OLD from Burlington became an apprentice firefighter and certified EMT for the Burlington Volunteer Fire Department. For all her volunteer work, she was awarded Prudential's Connecticut Spirit of Community Award in 2000.

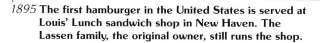

1806 Noah Webster publishes his first dictionary. It helps to standardize American spellings and meanings.

1895 The first hamburger in the United States is served at Louis' Lunch sandwich shop in New Haven. The Lassen family, the original owner, still runs the shop.

1954 The USS Nautilus, the world's first atomic-powered submarine, is launched at Groton. In 1958, it is the first submarine to sail under the ice at the North Pole.

1974 Ella Grasso is elected the state's first female governor, the first woman in America to become a governor without taking over the position from her husband.

Delaware

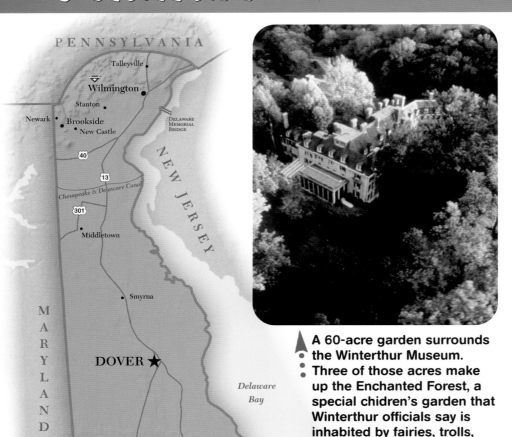

AAA GEMS:
Selected Must-See Points of Interest

BRANDYWINE RIVER MUSEUM
(Wilmington) – A converted gristmill from the 1800s displays American art.

HAGLEY MUSEUM (Wilmington) – The museum and restored mills trace the development of water power on the Brandywine River.

LONGWOOD GARDENS (Wilmington) – Formal gardens, elaborate fountains, and exotic tropical plants add colorful beauty to the area.

NEMOURS MANSION AND GARDENS (Wilmington) – Built in 1909, this French-style chateau has 102 rooms. It is decorated with many antiques and old paintings.

WINTERTHUR MUSEUM AND GARDEN (Wilmington) – Galleries explore the history of American decorative arts.

A 60-acre garden surrounds the Winterthur Museum. Three of those acres make up the Enchanted Forest, a special chidren's garden that Winterthur officials say is inhabited by fairies, trolls, and other fanciful folk!

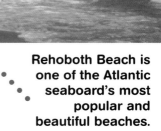

Rehoboth Beach is one of the Atlantic seaboard's most popular and beautiful beaches.

The annual Delaware State Fair features monster truck rallies, rodeo events, and much, much more!

TIMELINE

1609 Henry Hudson, working for the Dutch, explores Delaware Bay.

1631 The Dutch become the first Europeans to live in the area.

1638 Swedish colonists build Fort Christina, the first permanent settlement in Delaware. It is later seized by the Dutch.

1664 England captures Dutch territory on the Delaware River.

1682 William Penn takes over the region, allowing Delaware to have its own legislature 22 years later.

1802 Eleuthere Irenee du Pont sets up a gunpowder mill at Brandywine Creek that later grows into the DuPont Company, a leading manufacturer of chemicals and chemical products.

FRESH FACTS

NAME From the Delaware River, which was named for Lord De La Warr (Sir Thomas West), first governor of the Virginia Company.

ABBREVIATION Del.

CAPITAL Dover

NICKNAME First State (also, Diamond State)

AREA 2,489 square miles (6,646 square kilometers)

POPULATION 783,600

STATEHOOD Dec. 7, 1787 (1st state)

HIGHEST POINT Ebright Road, New Castle County (442 feet; 135 meters)

LOWEST POINT Sea level

INDUSTRIES Chemicals, finance, food products, nylon, paper products, plastic products, rubber products, scientific instruments, tourism, transportation equipment

AGRICULTURE Chickens, corn, dairy products, seafood, soybeans, young plants

MOTTO Liberty and Independence.

FLAG The wheat, corn, ox, and farmer symbolize agriculture. The ship symbolizes commerce. The colors symbolize Gen. George Washington's uniform. The flag was adopted in 1913.

DECEMBER 7, 1787

BIRD Adopted in 1939, the **blue hen chicken,** known for its fighting ability, accompanied Delaware soldiers during the Revolutionary War.

FLOWER The **peach blossom,** adopted in 1955, represents the many peach trees that grew in Delaware in the 1800s.

TREE The dark-green leaves and red berries of the **American holly** were once used to make Christmas wreaths by residents of Sussex County. The tree was adopted in 1939.

SONG "Our Delaware" (words by George B. Hynson; music by Will M.S. Brown)

A model of a Swedish ship called Kalmar Nyckel sails under Delaware Memorial Bridge in Chesapeake Bay. The ship brought Swedish and Finnish settlers to the 17th century Delaware Valley colony known as New Sweden.

Inside Scoop

THE FIRST LOG CABINS in the United States were built in Delaware in 1638 by Swedish colonists.

ALTHOUGH VERY SICK, Caesar Rodney rode 80 miles (129 kilometers) on horseback at night from Wilmington to Philadelphia, Pa., to cast the tie-breaking vote for independence in 1776.

THE WORLD'S LARGEST CARGO PLANES are stationed at Dover Air Force Base. Each plane can transport 48 Cadillac automobiles or 25,844,746 Ping-Pong balls.

AFTER A SHIP became stuck on a Delaware River sandbar, the ship's pea cargo started collecting sand. Eventually an island formed, which was named Pea Patch Island.

A TEEN FROM Wilmington organized a group of friends and other students to make meals for the families of children who were staying at a Ronald McDonald House while they received medical treatment. The teen's efforts won her a Prudential Community Spirit award.

1935 Nylon, the first synthetic fabric, is developed by a DuPont chemist, Dr. W.H. Carothers.

1951 The Delaware Memorial Bridge is built, linking Delaware and New Jersey.

1829 The Chesapeake & Delaware Canal is completed, providing a nearly 300-mile (482-kilometer) shortcut for ships traveling between Baltimore, Md. and Philadelphia, Pa.

1971 Delaware passes the Coastal Zone Act to protect wetlands.

FRESH FACTS

NAME The name honors Christopher Columbus. The district is also called Washington, D.C., in honor of George Washington, the country's first president.

ABBREVIATION D.C.

NICKNAME The Nation's Capital (also, D.C.)

AREA 68 square miles (176 square kilometers)

POPULATION 572,059

HIGHEST POINT Tenleytown (410 feet; 125 meters)

LOWEST POINT Potomac River (1 foot; 30 centimeters)

INDUSTRIES Government, tourism

MOTTO Justice for all.

FLAG Adopted in 1938, the flag was based on the design of George Washington's coat of arms.

BIRD The flute-like song of the **wood thrush** is one of the most beautiful of all songbirds.

FLOWER The **American beauty rose** symbolizes life, love, beauty, and eternity.

TREE Adopted in 1960, the **scarlet oak** is named for the brilliant color its leaves turn in autumn.

SONG None

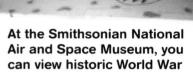

At the Smithsonian National Air and Space Museum, you can view historic World War II fighter planes.

One of Washington's most frequently visited monuments, the Lincoln Memorial honors the 16th president of the United States, Abraham Lincoln.

Inside Scoop

GEORGE WASHINGTON was 6'2" (1.9 meters) tall and wore size 13 shoes.

NEW YORK and Philadelphia each served as the nation's capital before the U.S. Congress chose the District of Columbia.

EACH SPRING, Washington, D.C. is made more beautiful by pink and white cherry tree blossoms. The cherry trees were a gift from the city of Tokyo, Japan, in 1912.

PRESIDENTS JOHN ADAMS, Thomas Jefferson, and James Monroe all died on July 4. Adams and Jefferson both died in 1826, exactly 50 years after signing the Declaration of Independence.

BEAN SOUP has been served at the U.S. Capitol every day since House Speaker Joe Cannon decreed it in 1907.

THE DISTRICT'S north-south streets are named with numbers. The east-west streets are named with letters of the alphabet.

A 14-YEAR-OLD volunteered on a pilot project sponsored by U.S. Aid for International Development that encouraged middle schoolers to learn more about foreign countries through research and volunteer activities.

TIMELINE

1793 President George Washington lays the cornerstone of the U.S. Capitol building.

1814 British troops set fire to the White House, the Capitol, and other buildings during the War of 1812. Dolley Madison, wife of the fourth president, carries a painting of George Washington to safety.

1867 Howard University is established to provide education for freed African-American slaves and their descendants.

1912 President Howard Taft is the first U.S. president to throw the first pitch in the opening game of the baseball season. The game was between the Washington Senators and the Philadelphia Athletics.

AAA GEMS:
Selected Must-See Points of Interest

LINCOLN MEMORIAL – The majestic marble structure has 36 columns, one for each state in the Union at the time President Lincoln was killed.

SMITHSONIAN NATIONAL AIR AND SPACE MUSEUM – Trace our advances in air and space technology – from early airplanes to high-tech spacecraft.

SMITHSONIAN NATIONAL ZOOLOGICAL PARK – The panda bears are the zoo's most famous inhabitants, but there are many other fascinating animals to see.

THE SMITHSONIAN INSTITUTION – Sixteen museums and galleries are part of the Smithsonian. Highlights include the Hope Diamond (the world's largest blue diamond) and Dorothy's red slippers (from the "Wizard of Oz" film).

THOMAS JEFFERSON MEMORIAL – A bronze statue of the nation's third president stands in the center of this circular building. Jefferson's most important writings are inscribed on the wall panels.

UNITED STATES CAPITOL – One of the nation's most familiar landmarks, the Capitol is where the members of the U.S. Senate and House of Representatives make the nation's laws. The statue at the top of the dome is named Freedom.

VIETNAM VETERANS MEMORIAL – This memorial honors the Americans who served in the U.S. armed forces during the Vietnam War.

WASHINGTON MONUMENT – Honoring our first president, the marble obelisk soars 555 feet (169 meters) high. Take the 897 steps or the elevator to the viewing platform.

WHITE HOUSE – The White House has been the home and workplace of every U.S. president except George Washington. It now has 132 rooms, 147 windows, and 35 bathrooms.

MARYLAND

Chevy Chase

Potomac River

WASHINGTON D.C.

Arlington

VIRGINIA

Capitol Heights

MARYLAND

Alexandria

0   5 Miles
0   5 Kilometers

In 2001, basketball legend Michael Jordan came out of retirement to join the Washington Wizards basketball team.

The Lincoln Memorial

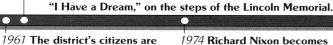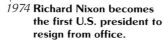

1963 Dr. Martin Luther King, Jr. delivers his famous speech, "I Have a Dream," on the steps of the Lincoln Memorial.

1995 The "Million Man March" supports self-reliance and responsibility among African-Americans. It inspires the 1997 "Million Woman March" in Philadelphia.

1961 The district's citizens are granted the right to vote in presidential elections.

1974 Richard Nixon becomes the first U.S. president to resign from office.

George W. Bush is elected the 43rd president of the **2000** United States. Presidents Bush and John Quincy Adams, the nation's sixth president, are the only sons of former presidents to be elected to the position.

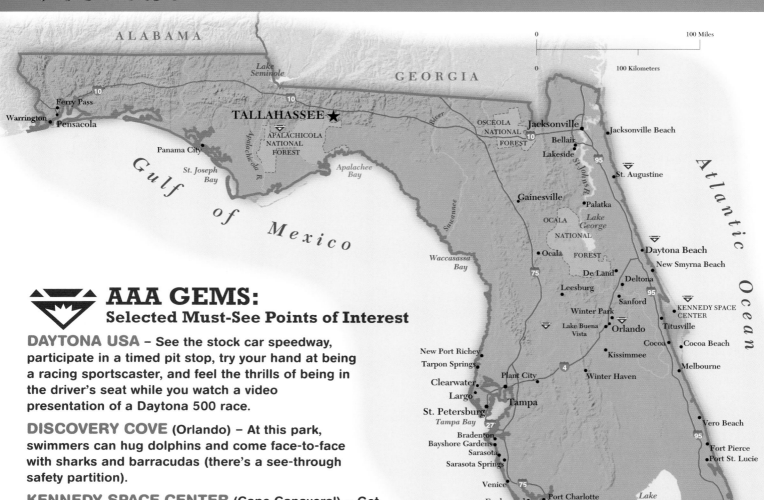

ALABAMA

GEORGIA

ATLANTIC OCEAN

Gulf of Mexico

0   100 Miles
0   100 Kilometers

Warrington
Ferry Pass
Pensacola
Panama City
St. Joseph Bay
Lake Seminole
TALLAHASSEE ★
APALACHICOLA NATIONAL FOREST
Apalachicola R.
Apalachee Bay
OSCEOLA NATIONAL FOREST
Jacksonville
Jacksonville Beach
Bellair
Lakeside
St. Augustine
St. Johns R.
Gainesville
Palatka
Lake George
OCALA NATIONAL FOREST
Ocala
Daytona Beach
New Smyrna Beach
De Land
Deltona
Leesburg
Sanford
KENNEDY SPACE CENTER
Winter Park
Lake Buena Vista
Orlando
Titusville
Cocoa
Cocoa Beach
Waccasassa Bay
Suwannee
New Port Richey
Tarpon Springs
Kissimmee
Clearwater
Plant City
Winter Haven
Melbourne
Largo
St. Petersburg
Tampa
Tampa Bay
Bradenton
Bayshore Gardens
Sarasota
Sarasota Springs
Vero Beach
Venice
Englewood
Port Charlotte
Lake Okeechobee
Fort Pierce
Port St. Lucie
Charlotte Harbor
Fort Myers
Cape Coral
Belle Glade
North Palm Beach
West Palm Beach
Lake Worth
Boynton Beach
Delray Beach
Immokalee
Margate
Boca Raton
Fort Lauderdale
Naples
Dania Beach
Hialeah
Miami Beach
Tamiami
Miami
Kendall
EVERGLADES NATIONAL PARK
Homestead
BISCAYNE NATIONAL PARK
Whitewater Bay
Florida Bay
Key West

◆ AAA GEMS:
Selected Must-See Points of Interest

DAYTONA USA – See the stock car speedway, participate in a timed pit stop, try your hand at being a racing sportscaster, and feel the thrills of being in the driver's seat while you watch a video presentation of a Daytona 500 race.

DISCOVERY COVE (Orlando) – At this park, swimmers can hug dolphins and come face-to-face with sharks and barracudas (there's a see-through safety partition).

KENNEDY SPACE CENTER (Cape Canaveral) – Get a close-up view of a launch pad, tour a space station, take rides in a space simulator and a mock space shuttle, watch IMAX movies and multimedia displays, and see spacecraft up close. Visit the Astronaut Memorial, dedicated to astronauts who have died in the line of duty.

SEAWORLD ORLANDO – Specialties here are the killer-whale show with Shamu and host Jack Hanna, a Cirque de la Mer show featuring acrobatics, a water-skiing show, and both dry and wet coaster rides.

ST. AUGUSTINE ALLIGATOR FARM – Twenty-two crocodilian species are represented here, as well as tropical birds, monkeys, and other exotic creatures.

UNIVERSAL ORLANDO – Exciting movie-themed and character-themed rides and shows are the highlights at Universal Studios and the Islands of Adventure.

WALT DISNEY WORLD® RESORT (Lake Buena Vista) – The awesome complex includes the Magic Kingdom® Park, Epcot®, Disney-MGM Studios, Disney's Animal Kingdom® Theme Park, and three water parks.

TIMELINE

These teen Cuban-American girls are celebrating the Calle Ocho festival in Miami's Little Havana neighborhood.

1513 Juan Ponce de León claims the area for Spain.

1565 St. Augustine is founded by Spain. It is the oldest permanent city settled by Europeans in the United States.

1539 Hernando de Soto guides an expedition through the region.

1819 Spain sells Florida to the United States for $5 million.

1919 Miami Beach is founded. A land boom begins, and the population of Florida increases rapidly.

Fresh Facts

NAME Explorer Ponce de León names the state "La Florida" in 1513 for the Feast of Flowers celebration held in Spain on Easter Sunday, the day he lands on Florida's coast.

ABREVIATION Fla.

CAPITAL Tallahassee

NICKNAME Sunshine State

AREA 65,755 square miles (170,305 square kilometers)

POPULATION 15,982,378

STATEHOOD March 3, 1845 (27th state)

HIGHEST POINT Walton County (345 feet;105 meters)

LOWEST POINT Sea level

INDUSTRIES Construction, electrical and electronic equipment, food products, printing and publishing, tourism, trade, transportation equipment

AGRICULTURE Grapefruit, lemons, melons, oranges, strawberries, sugar cane, vegetables, young plants

MOTTO In God we trust.

FLAG The state seal in the middle shows a Seminole Indian woman, representing the state's American Indian heritage. The steamboat stands for Florida's waterways, and the sun's rays are for the state's abundant sunshine. The flag was adopted in 1899.

BIRD Mockingbirds learn new songs throughout their lives. They imitate the songs of other birds as well as sounds made by other animals. Florida adopted the bird in 1929.

FLOWER Adopted in 1909, the sweet-smelling **orange blossom** represents the state's most important crop.

TREE The Seminole Indians used the **Sabal palmetto's** long, thick leaves to thatch their homes. Early settlers used the palmetto for food and for wood to build forts. The tree was adopted in 1953.

SONG "Old Folks at Home" (also known as "Swanee River"; words and music by Stephen C. Foster)

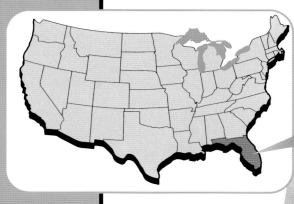

A space shuttle takes flight from Cape Canaveral on Florida's Atlantic coast. The first space shuttle was launched in 1981.

Inside Scoop

THERE ARE 882 islands in the Florida Keys.

GATORADE is named for the University of Florida's football team, the Gators, which helped test the new sports drink in 1965.

FIFTY-EIGHT HURRICANES have hit Florida since 1900 — more than anywhere else in the world.

EVERY MARCH Miami hosts the Calle Ocho (Spanish for "8th Street") festival, the largest Hispanic celebration in the United States.

THE SAND at Daytona Beach is so smooth from being pounded by ocean waves that the first organized stock car races were held there in 1936.

A 14-YEAR-OLD from Orlando rescued another teen who had been attacked by an 11-foot (3-meter) alligator in Little Lake Conway in 2001. She pulled her friend onto her boogie board and brought her safely to shore.

Alligators, which can reach 15 feet (4.6 meters) in length, are the largest reptiles in North America. They can be found in Florida's Everglades National Park, as well as in other swamps, rivers, and marshes.

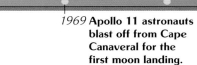

1947 Everglades National Park is created to protect the world's largest marsh.

1971 Walt Disney World® opens near Orlando. It becomes one of the world's greatest tourist attractions.

1969 Apollo 11 astronauts blast off from Cape Canaveral for the first moon landing.

1989 Ileana Ros-Lehtinen is elected to the U.S. House of Representatives, the first Hispanic-American woman to serve in the U.S. Congress.

Florida's electoral vote decides *2000* the outcome of the presidential election. George W. Bush wins by a narrow margin.

Georgia

AAA GEMS:

Selected Must-See Points of Interest

ANTEBELLUM PLANTATION (Atlanta) – Tour the 19 buildings and learn what plantation life was like in the Old South during the 1800s.

CALLAWAY GARDENS (Pine Mountain) – Special exhibits include azaleas and more than 1,000 butterflies in a glass conservatory. You can also bike, swim, fish, paddleboat, play miniature golf, and take scenic woodland drives.

CHICAMAUGA-CHATTANOOGA NATIONAL MILITARY PARK – The Confederacy won the 1863 battle of Chicamauga (Cherokee for "river of death"), but at a tragic price. More than 34,000 men were killed.

OKEFENOKEE SWAMP PARK (Waycross) – Huge alligators live in this swamp the Seminoles named "Land of the Trembling Earth." Take a boat ride to see the gators or walk through the wildlife refuge.

STONE MOUNTAIN (north of Atlanta) – Carved into the granite mountain is the world's largest sculpture, showing Confederate President Jefferson Davis, Gen. Thomas "Stonewall" Jackson, and Gen. Robert E. Lee. Gen. Lee is about the height of a nine-story building.

WORLD OF COCA-COLA ATLANTA – Quench your thirst for information about the development of this popular soft drink and enjoy free samples at a soda fountain of the future.

Chipper Jones, the hot-hitting star of the Atlanta Braves, has helped his baseball team win more division championships than any other team in baseball during the 1990s.

(Map of Georgia with surrounding states Tennessee, North Carolina, South Carolina, Florida, Alabama, and the Atlantic Ocean. Cities shown include Atlanta, Savannah, Augusta, Columbus, Macon, Albany, Valdosta, and many others.)

0   100 Miles
0   100 Kilometers

Black Rock Mountain State Park in north Georgia contains some of the oldest mountains on Earth. Scientists believe the base of Black Rock Mountain itself is about 1 billion years old.

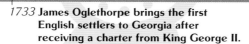
TIMELINE

1540 Hernando de Soto of Spain travels through Georgia.

1793 Eli Whitney invents the cotton gin near Savannah. It cleans cotton 50 times faster than a person can.

1733 James Oglethorpe brings the first English settlers to Georgia after receiving a charter from King George II.

1838 The Cherokee Indians are forced to relocate to Oklahoma Territory. Their march is known as the "Trail of Tears."

1864 To persuade the South to surrender during the Civil War, Union Gen. William T. Sherman sets fire to Atlanta and destroys much property on his "March to the Sea."

FRESH FACTS

NAME Named in honor of King George II of England, who ruled from 1727 to 1760.

ABBREVIATION Ga.

CAPITAL Atlanta

NICKNAME Peach State (also, Empire State of the South, Goober State)

AREA 59,425 square miles (153,911 square kilometers)

POPULATION 8,186,453

STATEHOOD Jan. 2, 1788 (4th state)

HIGHEST POINT Brasstown Bald Mountain (4,784 feet; 1,458 meters)

LOWEST POINT Sea level

INDUSTRIES Carpets, chemicals, clothing, cotton cloth, food products, lumber, paper products, retail trade, transportation equipment

AGRICULTURE Cattle, chickens, cotton, hogs, milk, peaches, peanuts, pecans, soybeans, tobacco

MOTTO Wisdom, justice, moderation.

FLAG Adopted in 2001, the flag shows the state seal surrounded by 13 white stars, symbolizing that Georgia was one of the original 13 colonies. Below is a ribbon showing the state's three previous flags, with the past and current American flag at each end.

BIRD The **brown thrasher** may have been named for its habit of tossing aside leaves with its beak when searching for food. This songbird winters in the South and was adopted in 1970.

FLOWER Legend says that the **Cherokee rose** was brought to Georgia by the Cherokee wife of a Seminole Indian. The flower was adopted in 1916.

TREE The **live oak** tree, adopted in 1937, keeps its leaves year-round. Spanish moss often hangs from its spreading branches. .

SONG "Georgia on My Mind" (words by Stuart Gorrell; music by Hoagy Carmichael)

The boyhood home of Dr. Martin Luther King, Jr. is in Atlanta.

Inside Scoop

GEORGIA GROWS about 800 billion peanuts every year, which, if laid end to end, would measure about 6 million miles (9,655,800 kilometers) — 25 times the distance between Earth and the moon.

THE MASTERS GOLF TOURNAMENT, begun in 1934, is played in Augusta every April.

THE SWEETEST ONION in the world, the Vidalia onion, is grown only in Vidalia and Glennville.

IN 1970, circus artist Karl Wallenda walked 1,000 feet (305 meters) on a tightrope 750 feet (229 meters) above the Tallulah Gorge in northeast Georgia. He was 75 years old.

THE SS SAVANNAH, the first steamship to cross the Atlantic, sailed from Georgia in 1819.

A 16-YEAR-OLD Marietta native and member of CNN's Student Bureau had photographs she had taken broadcast over the TV network.

1886 Atlanta pharmacist John S. Pemberton invents the syrup for Coca-Cola®, used at first as a medicine for settling upset stomachs.

1943 Georgia becomes the first state to allow 18-year-olds to vote.

1947 Jackie Robinson, from Cairo, is the first African-American to play major league baseball.

1964 Atlanta native Martin Luther King, Jr. is awarded the Nobel Peace Prize. At 35, he is the youngest to win the award.

1980 In Atlanta, CNN, the first 24-hour, all-news TV network, begins to broadcast.

Atlanta hosts the Summer Olympics. *1996*

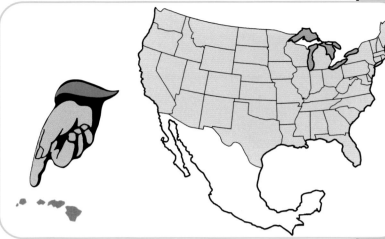

FRESH FACTS

NAME From Hawaiki, the former homeland of the Polynesian people, or Hawaii Loa, the Polynesian chief who may have discovered the Hawaiian Islands.

ABBREVIATION None

CAPITAL Honolulu

NICKNAME Aloha State (Aloha is the Hawaiian word for "love," "hello," and "good-bye.")

AREA 10,932 square miles (28,314 square kilometers)

POPULATION 1,211,537

STATEHOOD Aug. 21, 1959 (50th state)

HIGHEST POINT Mauna Kea, Island of Hawaii (13,796 feet; 4,205 meters)

LOWEST POINT Sea level

INDUSTRIES Clothing, food products (especially canned pineapple), petroleum, printing and publishing, refined sugar, tourism

AGRICULTURE Cattle, coffee, dairy products, flowers, macadamia nuts, pineapple, sugar cane

MOTTO The life of the land is perpetuated in righteousness.

FLAG Adopted in 1959, the flag has eight stripes, one for each of Hawaii's main islands. The Union Jack, the flag in the upper left corner, symbolizes the friendship of King Kamehameha I with England.

BIRD The **nene**, or Hawaiian goose, is better adapted to land than other geese. The nene's feet have long toes and are only partially webbed, allowing the bird to walk easily on rocks and hardened lava. The nene has been protected by law since the1940s and was adopted by the state in 1988.

FLOWER The flowers of the **yellow hibiscus** are sometimes strung, sewn, or braided to make flower necklaces, called leis, which are given to visitors upon arrival or departure from the islands. The tropical plant was adopted in 1988.

TREE The acorns of the **kukui**, or candlenut, tree have been used by natives for oil, relishes, and medicine. The tree was adopted in 1959.

SONG "Our Hawaii" (words by Henry Berger; music by King Kalakaua)

Inside Scoop

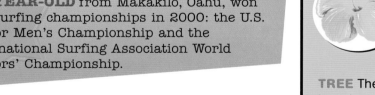

HAWAII IS the only state made up completely of islands – 132 of them.

MOUNT WAIALEALE, on Kauai, the wettest place on Earth, gets about 460 inches (1,168 centimeters) of rain a year.

POLYNESIANS, Hawaii's first settlers, invented surfing. They rode the waves with wooden boards curved at both ends.

THE WORLD'S LARGEST sea turtles, weighing up to 1,500 pounds (680 kilograms), are found in the waters off Hawaii.

THE HAWAIIAN LANGUAGE has only 12 letters – five vowels (a, e, i, o, u) and seven consonants (h, k, l, m, n, p, and w).

THE UKULELE, a four-stringed instrument similar to the guitar, was brought to Hawaii from Portugal.

A 17-YEAR-OLD from Makakilo, Oahu, won two surfing championships in 2000: the U.S. Junior Men's Championship and the International Surfing Association World Juniors' Championship.

TIMELINE

A.D. 300 Polynesians, probably from the Marquesas Islands in the South Pacific, begin to migrate to Hawaii.

1795 King Kamehameha I, a warrior from the Big Island, unifies Hawaii.

1840 King Kamehameha III gives Hawaii a constitution. A public school system is set up.

1778 Capt. James Cook lands on the islands and christens them Sandwich Islands, after a British earl for whom the sandwich is named.

1835 The first permanent sugar cane plantation is established on Kauai Island.

1885 Pineapple plants imported from Jamaica begin Hawaii's pineapple industry.

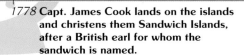
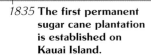

Hawaii's Mount Kilauea volcano has spewed over 250,000 cubic yards (191,000 cubic meters) of lava since its most recent eruption began in 1983.

AAA GEMS:
Selected Must-See Points of Interest

HALEAKALA NATIONAL PARK (Maui) – A huge volcanic valley sits atop Mount Haleakala. Hiking trails wind through a tropical forest, past waterfalls, streams, and turquoise pools where you can swim and snorkel.

HAWAII VOLCANOES NATIONAL PARK – There are two active volcanoes in this park: Mauna Loa, the world's largest, and Kilauea, the world's most active. You can drive past them, fly over them in a helicopter, or walk trails through thick forests to view the awesome lava areas.

MAUI MYTH & MAGIC THEATRE – Traditional Hawaiian music, dance, and acrobatic feats tell the history of Maui.

POLYNESIAN CULTURAL CENTER (Oahu) – Islanders demonstrate their arts and crafts and perform songs and dances at night. An IMAX film recounts the sea voyages of the islanders' ancestors.

SEA LIFE PARK (Oahu) – At this marine park right at the ocean, you can visit an aquarium with 2,000 kinds of fish, a sea lion feeding pool, a turtle lagoon, and a pirate's cove. "Splash U" lets you touch and interact with bottlenose dolphins.

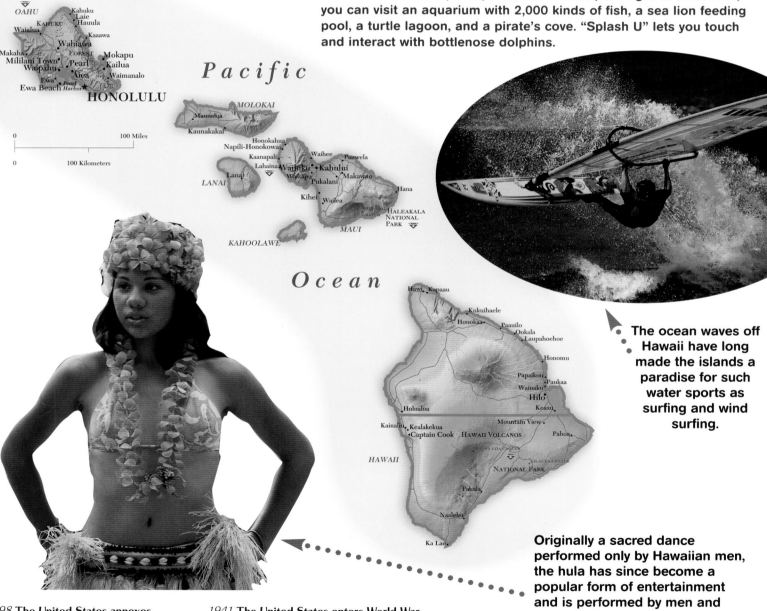

The ocean waves off Hawaii have long made the islands a paradise for such water sports as surfing and wind surfing.

Originally a sacred dance performed only by Hawaiian men, the hula has since become a popular form of entertainment and is performed by men and women alike.

1898 The United States annexes Hawaii. It becomes a U.S. territory two years later.

1941 The United States enters World War II as a result of the Japanese attack on Pearl Harbor on Oahu Island.

1936 The Hawaii Clipper becomes the first plane to bring tourists to Honolulu from the U.S. mainland.

1962 Daniel K. Inouye, representing Hawaii, is the first Japanese-American to be elected to the U.S. Senate.

1983 Mount Kilauea erupts, beginning the longest continuous flow of lava. As of 2002, the lava continues to flow.

CANADA

WASHINGTON

IDAHO PANHANDLE NATIONAL FOREST

Sandpoint

IDAHO PANHANDLE NATIONAL FOREST

Pond Oreille Lake

Hayden
Coeur d' Alene
Kellogg · Osburn 90
St. Maries
St. Joe River
NATIONAL FOREST

Moscow
CLEARWATER
Clearwater R. Orofino
Spalding
NATIONAL FOREST

Selway River

Grangeville
NEZ PERCE NATIONAL FOREST
BITTERROOT NATIONAL FOREST
Bitterroot River

Salmon River
PAYETTE NATIONAL FOREST

HELLS CANYON NATIONAL RECREATION AREA
Snake River

SALMON
Salmon
SALMON NATIONAL FOREST
River

BOISE
McCall
NATIONAL FOREST
Weiser
Fruitland
Emmett
Caldwell
Nampa
★ BOISE
Kuna
84
Mountain Home
SAWTOOTH NATIONAL FOREST
Sun Valley
HYNDMAN PEAK
NATIONAL FOREST
Arco
CHALLIS
NATIONAL
Salmon

MONTANA

BITTERROOT RANGE

TARGHEE NATIONAL FOREST
15
St. Anthony
TARGHEE NATIONAL FOREST
Rexburg
Rigby
Idaho Falls
Shelley
Blackfoot
CARIBOU NATIONAL FOREST
15
Pocatello
BONNEVILLE PEAK
Soda Springs
86
SAWTOOTH NATIONAL FOREST
CARIBOU NATIONAL FOREST
15
Franklin

YELLOWSTONE NATIONAL PARK

WYOMING

OREGON

Gooding
Jerome
Buhl
Twin Falls
Rupert
84
Burley
American Falls
CACHE PEAK
BLACK PINE PEAK
SAWTOOTH NATIONAL FOREST
MONUMENT PEAK
84

NEVADA   **UTAH**

0 —— 100 Miles
0 —— 100 Kilometers

◆ AAA GEMS:
Selected Must-See Points of Interest

CRATERS OF THE MOON NATIONAL MONUMENT (Arco) – The eerie, lunar-like volcanic landscape was formed by blazing hot lava that erupted from deep underground, and then cooled and hardened into unusual shapes. One cone is 700 feet (213 meters) high, about the height of a 70-story building. Some U.S. astronauts trained here.

DISCOVERY CENTER OF IDAHO (Boise) – This family-oriented museum invites people of all ages to explore and discover science with hands-on exhibits.

HELLS CANYON NATIONAL RECREATION AREA – Straddling the Idaho-Oregon border, this wilderness area includes the Snake River and Hells Canyon, the deepest gorge in North America. Trails, boat rides (in calm or white water), and scenic roads let you explore in different ways.

NEZ PERCE NATIONAL HISTORICAL PARK (Spalding) – Visit a fort, battlefields, and a museum honoring the culture and history of the Nez Perce Indians who once lived in this rugged area.

SUN VALLEY – Ski, ice skate, or ride snowmobiles in the winter at this scenic mountain spot. Swim, go white-water rafting, hike, camp out, and more in the summer.

The Stanley Lake area in the Sawtooth National Recreation Area is the whitewater headquarters of central Idaho, and a great spot for boating and fishing.

Mushroom-shaped Balanced Rock near Buhl is 40 feet (12 meters) high, yet stands on a base that is only a few feet thick.

TIMELINE

1805 Meriwether Lewis and William Clark explore Idaho on their way to the Pacific Ocean. They are helped by Shoshone and Nez Perce Indians living in the area.

1834 Fort Boise and Fort Hall, two trading posts, are set up.

1860 Mormons establish Franklin, the state's oldest town. Gold is discovered at Orofino Creek.

1877 The U.S. Army defeats the Nez Perce Indians.

1936 Sun Valley opens in the Sawtooth Mountains. It becomes a major ski resort.

NAME From the state's first gold mines and a steamship with the same name. Idaho is not from a Shoshone Indian word meaning "gem of the mountains."

ABBREVIATION None

CAPITAL Boise

NICKNAME Gem State

AREA 83,574 square miles (216,456 square kilometers)

POPULATION 1,293,953

STATEHOOD July 3, 1890 (43rd state)

HIGHEST POINT Borah Peak (12,662 feet; 3,859 meters)

LOWEST POINT Snake River at Lewiston (710 feet; 216 meters)

INDUSTRIES Chemicals, electronic parts, food products, lumber, machinery, paper, silver and other mining, tourism, wood products.

AGRICULTURE Barley, cattle, potatoes, sheep, sugar beets, wheat

MOTTO It is perpetual.

FLAG On the state seal is a woman who symbolizes liberty, justice, and equality. A miner represents the state's mineral resources. Other pictures stand for forestry, farming, and wildlife. The flag was first adopted in 1907 and re-adopted in 1957.

BIRD The **mountain bluebird** is truly an "early bird." It begins its morning song before dawn and sings until sunrise. It became the state bird in 1931.

FLOWER The **syringa,** adopted in 1931, is a shrub with fragrant flowers. American Indians used its stems for bows and arrows and its wood to make cradles.

TREE The nation's largest groves of **Western white pine** grow in northern Idaho. The tree, adopted by the state in 1935, is prized for its long, straight trunk. It is used to make furniture.

SONG "Here We Have Idaho" (chorus by McKinley Helm; verses by Albert J. Tompkins; music by Sallie Hume Douglas)

Inside Scoop

THE WORLD'S LARGEST potato chip is on display at the Potato Museum in Blackfoot. It is 14 feet (4 meters) by 25 feet (7 meters).

IDAHO LIES halfway between the North Pole and the Equator.

ONE OF THE WORLD'S LARGEST diamonds, weighing nearly 20 carats, was found near McCall.

PIONEERS boiled their eggs in some of Idaho's hot springs.

IDAHO GROWS more potatoes than any other state.

FEMALE BIKERS start pedaling in Boise in the Hewlett-Packard International Women's Challenge, the world's biggest bicycle race for women.

A 17-YEAR-OLD from Kuna worked with 12 other students from around the country to create a Web site for the National 4-H Club.

The Stanley Lake region in the Sawtooth National Recreation Area is the whitewater headquarters of central Idaho, and a great spot for boating and fishing.

1955 Arco is the first town to be totally powered by nuclear energy.

1959 An earthquake, registering 7.3 on the Richter scale, shakes up the Borah Peak region.

1968 Engineers complete the last of three dams to produce electric power from the Snake River.

1991 Larry Echo Hawk is the nation's first American Indian to be elected to state office.

After recovering from a broken leg and a knee injury, *1998* skier Picabo Street, an Idaho native, wins an Olympic gold in the women's super giant slalom.

AAA GEMS:
Selected Must-See Points of Interest

ADLER PLANETARIUM & ASTRONOMY MUSEUM
(Chicago) – Stargaze, take a virtual space trip, watch a multimedia space show, and see the outstanding collection of astronomical instruments and timepieces.

CAHOKIA MOUNDS STATE HISTORIC SITE
(Collinsville) – Monk's Mound, one of the site's 65 prehistoric American Indian mounds, is about 10 stories high and is the largest in the world. An empire of some 20,000 American Indians flourished here from A.D. 900 to 1500.

FIELD MUSEUM (Chicago) – One of the world's biggest natural history museums has special exhibits about T-Rex, Africa, ancient Egypt, gemstones, American Indian culture, and the history of chocolate.

JOHN G. SHEDD AQUARIUM
(Chicago) – See beluga whales, dolphins, penguins, and other aquatic animals in this huge indoor aquarium. Walk through a re-created Amazon rain forest and along a Pacific rocky coast. Check out feeding time at the coral reef and showtimes at the Oceanarium.

LINCOLN HOME NATIONAL HISTORIC SITE (Springfield) – Abraham Lincoln lived in this white frame house with his wife and children. It is the only home he ever owned.

MUSEUM OF SCIENCE AND INDUSTRY
(Chicago) – This museum is enormous. It contains a castle, a replica of a coal mine, an incubator that hatches baby chicks, a giant heart visitors can walk through, a virtual reality exhibit, and much more about science and technology.

The Spirit of Peoria offers old-time paddle boat cruises on the Illinois River.

In 1972, the Illinois House of Representatives officially declared the small town of Metropolis to be the "Hometown of Superman." Today, a large statue of the Man of Steel stands in downtown Metropolis.

TIMELINE

1673 Father Jacques Marquette, a French missionary, and Louis Jolliet, a French-Canadian explorer, are the first Europeans to explore Illinois.

1779 Jean Baptiste Pointe du Sable, from Haiti, builds a trading post at Checagou, the first structure in the city now called Chicago.

1860 Abraham Lincoln, from Springfield, is elected the 16th president of the United States and re-elected in 1864.

1763 France surrenders the territory to England under the Treaty of Paris, ending the French and Indian War.

1783 England surrenders Illinois to the United States after the Revolutionary War.

1868 Ulysses S. Grant, a Galena resident, is elected the 17th president of the United States and re-elected in 1872.

FRESH FACTS

NAME Based on the French version of "Illiniwek," the name of the American Indians who lived by the Illinois River.

ABBREVIATION Ill.

CAPITAL Springfield

NICKNAME Prairie State

AREA 57,914 square miles (149,997 square kilometers)

POPULATION 12,419,293

STATEHOOD Dec. 3, 1818 (21st state)

HIGHEST POINT Charles Mound (1,235 feet; 376 meters)

LOWEST POINT Mississippi River in Alexander County (279 feet; 85 meters)

INDUSTRIES Chemicals, electrical and electronic equipment, finance, food products, health care, insurance, machinery, metal products, printing and publishing, real estate, tourism, trade

AGRICULTURE Cattle, chickens, corn, hay, hogs, milk, sorghum, soybeans, wheat

MOTTO State sovereignty, national union.

FLAG The flag was the winner of a design contest sponsored by the Daughters of the American Revolution in 1912. It was created by Lucy Derwent of the Rockford Chapter and adopted by the state in 1915. The state name was added to the flag in 1969.

ILLINOIS

BIRD The **cardinal** was adopted in 1929 after school children voted for it over the bluebird by nearly 9,000 votes.

FLOWER School children chose the native **violet** to be the state flower. It was adopted in 1908.

TREE In 1973, 900,000 students voted for the **white oak** to become the state tree. It was adopted the same year.

SONG "Illinois" (words by C.H. Chamberlain; music by Archibald Johnston)

Inside Scoop

THE FIRST BIG FERRIS WHEEL, designed by George W. Ferris, started turning at Chicago's 1893 World's Columbian Exposition.

THE CHICAGO RIVER once flowed backward into Lake Michigan. In 1900 the Chicago Sanitary and Ship Canal opened and reversed the river's direction.

ABRAHAM LINCOLN was born in Kentucky and lived in Indiana before his family moved to Illinois.

IN 1992 Carol Mosely-Braun from Chicago became the first African-American woman elected to the U.S. Senate.

KASKASKIA ISLAND is the only part of the state that lies west of the Mississippi River.

MORE THAN HALF of the state's population lives in the Chicago metropolitan area.

TWO 14-YEAR-OLDS from St. Charles were members of a group of puppeteers who performed shows at children's hospitals.

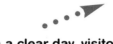

On a clear day, visitors to the top of Chicago's Sears Tower can see four states—Illinois, Michigan, Indiana, and Wisconsin.

1871 A raging fire destroys much of Chicago's wood buildings. The city is rebuilt, using bricks. It is now the third largest city in the country.

1885 The world's first metal-frame skyscraper, the 10-story Home Insurance Building, is constructed in Chicago.

1955 Ray Kroc opens the first McDonald's in Des Plaines.

1968 The first International Special Olympics Summer Games is held at Chicago's Soldier Field.

1973 Chicago's 1,450-foot (442-meter) Sears Tower opens which, at 110 stories, has the highest occupied floor of any building in North America.

1998 The Chicago Bulls claim their sixth National Basketball Association championship of the 1990s.

Indiana

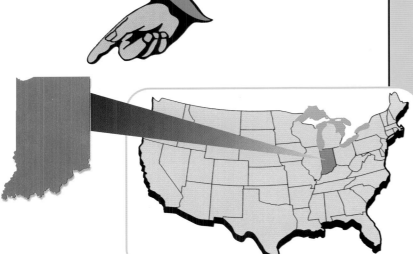

NAME Means "land of the Indians" and was named by the U.S. Congress.

ABBREVIATION Ind.

CAPITAL Indianapolis

NICKNAME Hoosier State

AREA 36,418 square miles (94,322 square kilometers)

POPULATION 6,080,485

STATEHOOD Dec. 11, 1816 (19th state)

HIGHEST POINT Wayne County (1,257 feet; 383 meters)

LOWEST POINT Posey County (320 feet; 98 meters)

INDUSTRIES Chemicals, electrical and electronic equipment, machinery, metals, motor vehicles, trade, transportation equipment

AGRICULTURE Cattle, chickens, corn, dairy products, hogs, popcorn, soybeans, wheat, young plants

MOTTO The crossroads of America.

FLAG The torch symbolizes liberty, and the stars surrounding it stand for the first 18 states to join the Union. The larger star at the top of the torch represents Indiana, the 19th state. The flag was adopted in 1917.

BIRD The **cardinal,** adopted in 1933, sings in a loud voice, repeating its musical notes several times. Often the male and female take turns singing, as if in response to each other.

FLOWER The **peony,** adopted in 1957, is Indiana's fourth state flower. The previous three were the carnation, the tulip tree flower, and the zinnia.

TREE The **tulip tree,** also called yellow poplar, is named for its bell-shaped flowers. It became official in 1931.

SONG "On the Banks of the Wabash, Far Away" (words and music by Paul Dresser)

Inside Scoop

MORE THAN 400,000 people attend the Indy 500, making it the world's biggest single-day sports event .

THE STATE'S NICKNAME, Hoosier, may have come from a common reply to a knock at the door: "Who's here?" or "Who's yer?" Or the name may refer to Samuel Hoosier, an employer in Kentucky in the 1820s who liked to hire workers from Indiana. No one is certain how the name came to be.

KNUTE ROCKNE won 105 of the 122 football games he coached at the University of Notre Dame during his 13 years as head coach from 1918–31. He had five undefeated seasons.

ROCK STAR MICHAEL JACKSON, from Gary, was the lead singer of the Jackson Five when he was just 5 years old. The other four group members were his brothers.

AN 18-YEAR-OLD from Valparaiso hosted a late-night talk show that he taped at his home. The show was broadcast on three public-access cable stations.

Timeline

1679 René-Robert Cavelier, Sieur de la Salle, explores Indiana on behalf of France.

1732 The French build a fort at Vincennes, Indiana's first permanent European settlement.

1763 The French surrender Indiana to England as part of the Treaty of Paris ending the French and Indian War.

1783 England surrenders Indiana to the United States after the Revolutionary War.

1800 The U.S. Congress creates the Indiana Territory.

1816 The right to a free public school education is made part of Indiana's constitution, the first state to guarantee this right in its constitution.

1842 The University of Notre Dame is founded near South Bend.

When the Ice Age ended more than 15,000 years ago, retreating glaciers created Lake Michigan and left the huge sand dunes that make up Indiana Dunes National Lakeshore.

AAA GEMS:
Selected Must-See Points of Interest

CHILDREN'S MUSEUM OF INDIANAPOLIS AND CINEDOME THEATER – The largest children's museum in the world has five floors of fun. Bucky, the first teenage T-Rex to be displayed anywhere, will debut in 2004.

COLLEGE FOOTBALL HALL OF FAME (South Bend) – Test your football skills, check out the Locker Room and the Hall of Honor, and watch an exciting game on a 360-degree screen.

EITELJORG MUSEUM OF AMERICAN INDIANS AND WESTERN ART (Indianapolis) – Famous paintings of the American West share the spotlight with objects used in daily life from Indian cultures throughout North America.

INDIANA DUNES NATIONAL LAKESHORE – Scenic trails crisscross a unique ecological area on the southern shore of Lake Michigan. The largest dune is 123 feet (37 meters) high and moves 4 to 5 feet (1.2 to 1.5 meters) southward each year.

INDIANAPOLIS MOTOR SPEEDWAY – See racing action past and present at the speedway's museum and the oval racecourse.

LINCOLN MUSEUM (Fort Wayne) – Abraham Lincoln spent 14 years of his youth in Indiana. This museum is the largest one devoted to his life. The last portrait of the 16th president to be painted is one of the highlights.

WYANDOTTE CAVES – An amazing network of tunnels, an underground mountain, and some of the world's largest helictites (unusual, curling formations) are the natural marvels that await cave explorers.

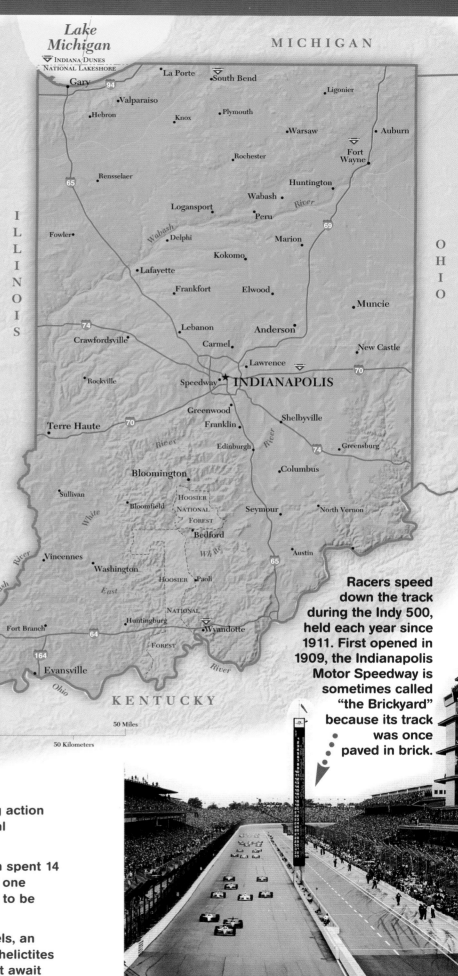

Racers speed down the track during the Indy 500, held each year since 1911. First opened in 1909, the Indianapolis Motor Speedway is sometimes called "the Brickyard" because its track was once paved in brick.

1911 The nation's first 500-mile (805-kilometer) automobile race speeds around the track at the Indianapolis Motor Speedway. The annual race is called the Indy 500.

1970 The Port of Indiana Harbor opens near Gary and greatly increases trade.

The NCAA Hall of Champions is built in 2000 White River State Park, honoring student-athletes in 22 different sports.

Iowa

NAME Based on the name of an Indian tribe called Ayuxwa, meaning "beautiful land" or "one who puts to sleep."

ABBREVIATION None

CAPITAL Des Moines

NICKNAME Hawkeye State

AREA 56,272 square miles (145,744 square kilometers)

POPULATION 2,926,324

STATEHOOD Dec. 28, 1846 (29th state)

HIGHEST POINT Osceola County (1,670 feet; 509 meters)

LOWEST POINT Lee County (480 feet; 146 meters)

INDUSTRIES Chemicals, communications, construction, electrical and electronic products, finance, food products, insurance, machinery, printing and publishing, trade

AGRICULTURE Cattle, chickens, corn, dairy products, hay, hogs, soybeans

MOTTO Our liberties we prize and our rights we will maintain.

FLAG Mrs. Dixie Cornell Gebhardt, who designed the flag in 1917, explained that the blue stripe stands for loyalty, justice, and truth; the white for purity; and the red for courage. The bald eagle carries a ribbon with the state's motto on it. The flag was adopted in 1921.

BIRD The **Eastern (American) goldfinch** is sometimes called the wild canary because of its color and canary-like song. It was adopted in 1933.

FLOWER The state of Iowa used the **wild rose** in 1897 to decorate a gift to the new battleship USS Iowa. The flower was adopted the same year.

TREE **Oak** trees grow throughout Iowa. They provide shade, food, and homes for many types of wildlife. The oak was adopted in 1961.

SONG "The Song of Iowa" (words by S.H.M. Byers; sung to the music of "O Tannenbaum")

Inside Scoop

ONE IOWA FARM FAMILY grows enough food annually to sustain 279 people for a year.

THE STATE'S NICKNAME, the Hawkeye State, is in honor of the courage of Chief Black Hawk. He tried to keep Sauk Indian land from being taken over by the U.S. government.

PARIS, FRANCE, and Cedar Rapids, Iowa, are the only two cities in the world with government buildings on an island in each city's center.

CHARLES RINGLING, born in McGregor, started his circus in 1884 with four of his brothers and two trained animals—a horse and a dancing bear. Their efforts eventually grew into the Ringling Bros. and Barnum & Bailey Circus®—The Greatest Show on Earth®.

A 12-YEAR-OLD from Newton started an organization called Care Bags Foundation that fills handsewn "care bags" with toys, books, toothbrushes, shampoo, and other personal items. The bags are distributed to children in need. The group's founder was named a National Honoree winner in 2001 by the Prudential Spirit of Community Award program.

TIMELINE

1673 Father Jacques Marquette, a French missionary, and Louis Jolliet, a French-Canadian explorer, are the first Europeans to see the area.

1682 René-Robert Cavelier, Sieur de la Salle, claims the region for France.

1803 The United States acquires Iowa through the Louisiana Purchase.

1832 At the end of the Black Hawk War, the United States buys the eastern portion of Iowa from the Sauk Indians.

1891 George Washington Carver becomes the first African-American to attend Iowa State Agricultural College. He earns a master's degree in agriculture in 1896 and goes on to become one of America's greatest scientists.

1928 Herbert Hoover, born in West Branch, is elected the 31st president of the United States.

MINNESOTA

SOUTH DAKOTA

WISCONSIN

NEBRASKA

ILLINOIS

MISSOURI

Sibley • Spirit Lake • Estherville • Milford • Lake Mills • Northwood • Cresco • Decorah • Spillville • Waukon
Sioux Center • Sheldon • Spencer • Forest City • Osage • New Hampton • McGregor • EFFIGY MOUNDS NM
Orange City • Hawarden • Algona • Britt • Garner • Mason City • Charles City • Sumner • West Union • Guttenberg
Le Mars • Cherokee • Pocahontas • Belmond • Hampton • Waverly • Oelwein
Storm Lake • Dakota City • Cedar Falls • Waterloo • Dubuque
Sioux City • Sergeant Bluff • Sac City • Fort Dodge • Webster City • Eldora • Hudson • La Porte City • Dyersville
Ida Grove • Story City • Monticello • Bellevue
Onawa • Denison • Carroll • Jefferson • Ames • Nevada • Marshalltown • Vinton • Anamosa • Maquoketa
Harlan • Audubon • Madrid • Tama • Cedar Rapids • Marion • Clinton
Missouri Valley • Altoona • Newton • Grinnell • Amana Colonies • Iowa City • Eldridge • Park View
Urbandale • ★ DES MOINES • Williamsburg • West Branch • Wilton • Davenport • Bettendorf
Carter Lake • Atlantic • Norwalk • Pella • Muscatine
Council Bluffs • Winterset • Greenfield • Indianola • Knoxville • Oskaloosa • Washington • Wapello
Red Oak • Creston • Osceola • Chariton • Albia • Ottumwa • Fairfield • New London
Shenandoah • Clarinda • Leon • Centerville • Bloomfield • Mount Pleasant • Burlington • Fort Madison
Lamoni • Keokuk

0   50 Miles
0   50 Kilometers

▲◆ AAA GEMS:
Selected Must-See Points of Interest

ADVENTURELAND (Altoona) – This theme park set in the late 1800s and early 1900s features a Main Street, Last Frontier, River City, roller coasters, flume rides, Ferris wheels, and live shows.

AMANA COLONIES – The quaint villages of this former religious community include a woolen mill whose 150-year-old looms are still clacking, a working furniture shop, and many exhibits of daily life in the late 1800s.

BILY CLOCK MUSEUM AND ANTONIN DVORAK EXHIBIT (Spillville) – The Czechoslovakian composer Antonin Dvorak lived in this house in the summer of 1893 while finishing his "New World Symphony." The museum displays hand-carved clocks.

DES MOINES ART CENTER – View masterpieces of modern art, the museum's specialty. The building itself has won praise for its architectural design.

LIVING HISTORY FARMS (Urbandale) – Trace the story of the Midwest from Indian villages to farms, and from frontier towns to mechanized farms as you walk through each re-created example.

At the Family Museum of Arts and Science in Bettendorf, you can touch a 10-foot (3-meter) tornado and watch a miniature landscape change as the wind blows.

Des Moines, Iowa's capital city, is the state's government, business, and arts and entertainment center.

1988 The baseball movie "Field of Dreams" is filmed on the Lansing farm in Dyersville.

1930 Grant Wood, born near Anamosa, finishes his most famous painting, "American Gothic."

1939 John Atanasoff and Clifford Berry, of Iowa State University, build the first digital computer. Atanasoff receives the National Medal of Technology in 1990 for his work.

Iowa farms number 95,000. *2000* Only Texas and Missouri have more.

Kansas

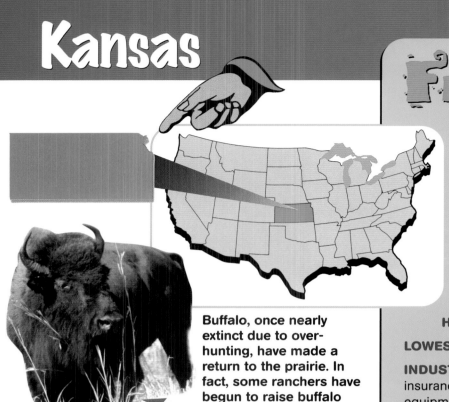

Buffalo, once nearly extinct due to over-hunting, have made a return to the prairie. In fact, some ranchers have begun to raise buffalo rather than cattle.

Inside Scoop

A MARKER in Lebanon shows the exact geographical center of the lower 48 states.

THE SHAWNEE SUN, published in Kansas in 1835, was the first newspaper to be printed entirely in an American Indian language (Algonquian).

KANSAS is known for its tornadoes, such as the one in "The Wizard of Oz."

ONLY A BOULEVARD separates Kansas City, Kan., and Kansas City, Mo.

KANSAS PRODUCES enough wheat each year to make 35 billion loaves of bread—enough to give every person on Earth six loaves.

A SPINACH FEST is held every September in Lenexa. The town mixes the world's largest spinach salad (500 pounds; 226 kilograms) and also makes spinach tortillas and milkshakes.

AN EIGHTH GRADER from Haviland won a Young Inventors Award in 2001 for his Roofer's Helper, which improves the way old roof shingles are torn off. The award is sponsored by the Craftsman/National Science Teachers Association.

FRESH FACTS

NAME From the French spelling of "Kanse," the Kansa Indian word meaning "south wind" or "people of the south wind."

ABBREVIATION Kan.

CAPITAL Topeka

NICKNAME Sunflower State

AREA 82,277 square miles (213,097 square kilometers)

POPULATION 2,688,418

STATEHOOD Jan. 29, 1861 (34th state)

HIGHEST POINT Mount Sunflower (4,039 feet; 1,231 meters)

LOWEST POINT Verdigris River (680 feet; 207 meters)

INDUSTRIES Chemicals, farm equipment, finance, food products, insurance, machinery, publishing, real estate, transportation equipment

AGRICULTURE Cattle, corn, hay, hogs, sorghum, wheat

MOTTO To the stars through difficulty.

FLAG The state seal shows a rising sun, symbolizing that the state's settlers came from the east. The farmer and cabin show the importance of agriculture. The 34 stars represent Kansas as the 34th state in the Union. Above the seal is a sunflower, the state flower, and a twirled bar symbolizing the Louisiana Purchase. The flag was adopted in 1927. The state name was added in 1961.

BIRD The **Western meadowlark,** chosen in 1937, lives on the open prairie. This songbird builds its nest on the ground and hides it under a hollow mound woven from blades of grass and stems.

FLOWER The **sunflower,** adopted in 1903, always turns its "face" toward the sun. It is thought that the first sunflower seeds reached Kansas on the wheels of wagons coming from the Southwest on the Santa Fe Trail.

TREE The **cottonwood** has been called the "Pioneer Tree" because it gave shade and shelter to early homesteaders and indicated that a source of water was nearby. The tree was adopted in 1937.

SONG "Home on the Range" (words by Dr. Brewster Higby; music by Daniel Kelly)

TIMELINE

1541 Spanish explorer Francisco Vasquez de Coronado is the first European to enter the state. Explorer René-Robert Cavelier, Sieur de la Salle, claims the area for France.

1803 Kansas becomes a U.S. territory as part of the Louisiana Purchase.

1827 Fort Leavenworth is the first permanent European settlement in the state.

1854 The Kansas-Nebraska Act opens the area to pioneers.

1862 The Homestead Act offers settlers 160 acres (65 hectares) of land each if they agree to farm it for five years.

NEBRASKA

MISSOURI

COLORADO

Goodland · Colby · Levant · Oakley · Oberlin · Norton · Phillipsburg · Smith Center · Lebanon · Belleville · Marysville · Sabetha · Seneca · Hiawatha · Horton · Atchison · Concordia · Osborne · Beloit · Solomon · Clay Center · Holton · Wamego · Leavenworth · Hill City · Plainville · Minneapolis · Manhattan · Fort Riley North · Junction City · Tuttle Creek Lake · TOPEKA · Kansas City · Merriam · Lenexa · Wa Keeney · Ellis · Hays · Russell · Smoky · Hill · River · Ellsworth · Abilene · Salina · Saline · Lawrence · Osage City · Ottawa · Paola · Osawatomie · Scott City · Hoisington · Herington · Lindsborg · Council Grove · Emporia · Garnett · Great Bend · Ellinwood · McPherson · Hillsboro · Burlington · Larned · Sterling · Hesston · Newton · Arkansas · River · Garden City · Kinsley · Arkansas · Hutchinson · Park City · El Dorado · Eureka · Iola · Fort Scott · Dodge City · Wichita · Derby · Humboldt · Chanute · Ulysses · Pratt · Kingman · Haysville · Fredonia · Frontenac · Pittsburg · Haviland · Neodesha · Parsons · Hugoton · Medicine Lodge · Mulvane · Wellington · Winfield · Independence · Cherryvale · Oswego · Coffeyville · Elkhart · Liberal · Anthony · Arkansas City · Caney

0 _____ 100 Miles
0 _____ 100 Kilometers

OKLAHOMA

AAA GEMS:
Selected Must-See Points of Interest

EISENHOWER CENTER (Abilene) – Learn about the life and career of Dwight D. Eisenhower, our 34th president, who grew up in Abilene and is buried here. Tour Eisenhower's home and visit the Presidential Library.

FRONTIER ARMY MUSEUM (Leavenworth) – Exhibits tell about the frontier army during the Civil, Mexican, and Indian wars and the people who lived here. See the carriage in which Abraham Lincoln rode while visiting the town.

KANSAS COSMOSPHERE AND SPACE CENTER (Hutchinson) – View the Mercury, Gemini, and Apollo spacecraft, and a large variety of space suits.

NATURAL HISTORY MUSEUM AND BIODIVERSITY RESEARCH CENTER (Lawrence) – The museum features fossils and mounted animals as well as live snakes, bees, and fish.

SEDGWICK COUNTY ZOO (Wichita) – Check out the zoo's North American Prairie area where grizzly bears, wolves, and sandhill cranes live, and take a peek at the pink flamingos.

Actors in Larned re-create army life during the Indian wars of the late 1800s. Fort Larned was built in 1859.

In 1996, artist Stan Herd created a one-acre (40-hectare) portrait of pilot Amelia Earhart out of living plants, rocks and other natural materials. She was born in Atchison.

1970 The largest hailstone in the world—17.5 inches (44 centimeters) round and weighing 1.66 pounds (.75 kilograms)—lands in Coffeyville.

1874 Mennonites, a religious group from Russia, bring the first Turkey Red wheat to the United States. Today, Kansas is the leading wheat-producing state in the country.

1954 The U.S. Supreme Court ends public school segregation in the case of Brown vs. Board of Education of Topeka.

Buffalo Soldiers National Monument is 1992 dedicated in Leavenworth to honor the all-black 9th and 10th Cavalry, whose soldiers fought in the Civil War.

Kentucky

The history of the Corvette, one of America's best known sports cars, is celebrated at the National Corvette Museum in Bowling Green.

The Kentucky Derby, run each year at Churchill Downs in Louisville, is the most famous horse race in the world.

Inside Scoop

MILDRED AND PATRICIA HALL, two sisters from Louisville, wrote "Happy Birthday to You," which is sung more often than any other song except the national anthem.

BLUEGRASS is not blue. It's green. However, its buds are bluish, which gives a blue hue to fields and valleys in the spring.

CUMBERLAND FALLS is the only place in the nation where you can see a moonbow—a rainbow caused by light from a full moon striking drops of water.

MAN O' WAR, a chestnut thorough-bred born near Lexington in 1917, lost only one of the 21 races in his career. When he died in 1947, more than 1,000 people attended his funeral.

BOTH ABRAHAM LINCOLN and Jefferson Davis, opposing presidents during the Civil War, were born in Kentucky—about 100 miles (160 kilometers) and eight months apart.

A 17-YEAR-OLD from Elizabethtown won the world championship title in the Open Seventeen-Year-Old Equitation Class at the State Fair in 2002. The blue-ribbon winner paid for her horse, lessons, and shows by working in her father's business and other jobs in her spare time.

TIMELINE

1750 Thomas Walker, working for a Virginia company, explores the eastern part of Kentucky.

1774 The state's first permanent European settlement is established at Harrodsburg.

1775 Daniel Boone blazes the Wilderness Trail (Kentucky's first road) through the Cumberland Gap and builds Fort Boonesborough.

1845 Cassius Marcellus Clay starts an anti-slavery newspaper, "True American," in Lexington.

1866 One of the country's earliest suspension bridges is built across the Ohio River, connecting Covington, Ky., and Cincinnati, Ohio.

1875 The first Kentucky Derby is held in Louisville. The race is called the "Run for the Roses" because a blanket of roses is placed over the winning horse.

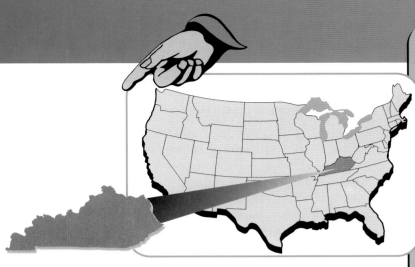

AAA GEMS:
Selected Must-See Points of Interest

CUMBERLAND GAP NATIONAL HISTORICAL PARK – Retrace the footsteps of American Indians and such pioneers as Daniel Boone as they traveled west on this route through the Appalachian Mountains.

KENTUCKY DOWN UNDER/KENTUCKY CAVERNS (Horse Cave) – Roam among kangaroos, feed exotic birds, toss a boomerang, and learn an Aboriginal dance in this interactive nature park that is home to Australian wildlife and a cave with unusual onyx formations.

KENTUCKY HORSE PARK (Lexington) – Learn all about the history of racehorses. Watch a film, tour a horse farm, ride a horse, visit the museum, watch a harness maker, and admire more than 40 breeds of horses.

LOUISVILLE SCIENCE CENTER – Find out how math and science affect everyday life, and discover fascinating facts about outer space, ancient Egypt, and the human body.

MAMMOTH CAVE NATIONAL PARK – Guided tours take you through the world's largest cave system, past underground lakes, rivers, and such awesome rock formations as Frozen Niagara, which looks just like its name. Above ground, drive or hike scenic trails to view rugged bluffs and beautiful valleys.

FRESH FACTS

NAME Based on the Iroquoian Indian word "Ken-tah-the," meaning "land of tomorrow" or "meadow land."

ABBREVIATION Ky.

CAPITAL Frankfort

NICKNAME Bluegrass State

AREA 40,409 square miles (104,660 square kilometers)

POPULATION 4,041,769

STATEHOOD June 1, 1792 (15th state)

HIGHEST POINT Black Mountain (4,145 feet; 1,263 meters)

LOWEST POINT Mississippi River (257 feet; 78 meters)

INDUSTRIES Chemicals, electrical and electronic equipment, finance, food products, insurance, machinery, printed materials, real estate, trade, transportation equipment

AGRICULTURE Cattle, corn, hay, horses, milk, tobacco

MOTTO United we stand, divided we fall.

FLAG The state seal shows a frontiersman and a government official shaking hands. The state motto encircles them. Two branches of goldenrod, the state flower, are below the seal. The flag was adopted in 1918.

BIRD The **cardinal** lives in the state all year long. Chosen in 1926, it has a melodious song that can be heard in woods and fields throughout Kentucky.

FLOWER Thirty different kinds of **goldenrod** grow in Kentucky. It was adopted in 1926.

TREE Chosen in 1994, the **tulip poplar** can live to be 200 years old. Its yellow-green flowers are shaped like tulips and bloom in May.

SONG "My Old Kentucky Home" (words and music by Stephen C. Foster)

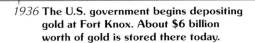 White fences divide many of Kentucky's rolling hills and meadows into horse farms.

1964 Cassius Clay, a native of Louisville, becomes heavyweight boxing champion of the world and changes his name to Muhammad Ali.

1936 The U.S. government begins depositing gold at Fort Knox. About $6 billion worth of gold is stored there today.

1955 Kentucky lowers the voting age from 21 to 18 years.

1996 The Louisville Slugger Museum opens. Visitors can tour the factory where the famous baseball bats have been made for more than 100 years.

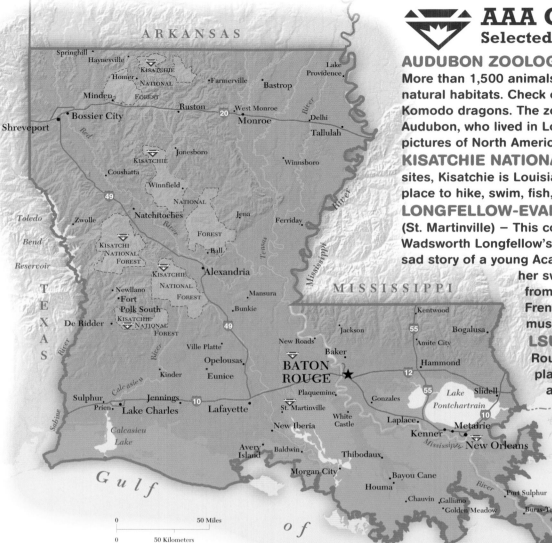

AAA GEMS:
Selected Must-See Points of Interest

AUDUBON ZOOLOGICAL GARDEN (New Orleans) — More than 1,500 animals, many endangered, live here in their natural habitats. Check out the rare white alligators and the Komodo dragons. The zoo is named after John James Audubon, who lived in Louisiana while he painted his famous pictures of North American birds.

KISATCHIE NATIONAL FOREST — Located at six different sites, Kisatchie is Louisiana's only national forest. It's a great place to hike, swim, fish, and camp.

LONGFELLOW-EVANGELINE STATE HISTORIC SITE (St. Martinville) — This could have been the setting for Henry Wadsworth Longfellow's poem "Evangeline," which tells the sad story of a young Acadian girl who became separated from her sweetheart when they were expelled from Canada. Learn more about these French settlers from storytellers and the museum's displays.

LSU RURAL LIFE MUSEUM (Baton Rouge) — Visit a re-created Louisiana plantation from the 1800s, complete with an overseer's house, blacksmith shop, open-kettle sugar mill, plantation store, and church.

MUSÉE CONTI WAX MUSEUM (New Orleans) — See lifelike wax figures of famous people in Louisiana history, such as Napoleon, the pirate Jean Lafitte, jazz musician Louis Armstrong, and many others. There's also a miniature scene of a Mardi Gras parade and an exhibit of monsters and other scary creatures.

The people of New Orleans let the good times roll each year at Mardi Gras, America's best-known festival. Beautiful floats are the highlight of the Mardi Gras Parade.

The Preservation Hall Jazz Band plays nightly in a tiny one-room building in the French Quarter of New Orleans, where jazz music was born.

TIMELINE

1541 Hernando de Soto discovers the Mississippi River.

1682 René-Robert Cavelier, Sieur de la Salle, claims the region for France.

1718 New Orleans is founded by French settlers and named after the Duke of Orleans in France.

1764 About 4,000 Acadians (French settlers, also called Cajuns) arrive after being driven out of Canada by the British.

1803 The United States purchases Louisiana from France as part of the Louisiana Purchase.

1815 Andrew Jackson defeats the British in the Battle of New Orleans. He had not heard that the War of 1812 ended two weeks earlier.

1879 James B. Eads deepens the mouth of the Mississippi River, enabling ocean-going ships to reach New Orleans.

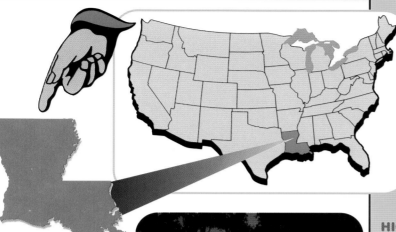

Much of southern Louisiana is swampland, or bayou, as it is called by the French-speaking Cajuns who live in the area.

FRESH FACTS

NAME Named in honor of King Louis XIV of France by René-Robert Cavelier, Sieur de la Salle.

ABBREVIATION La.

CAPITAL Baton Rouge

NICKNAME Pelican State

AREA 51,840 square miles (134,266 square kilometers)

POPULATION 4,468,976

STATEHOOD April 30, 1812 (18th state)

HIGHEST POINT Driskill Mountain (535 feet; 163 meters)

LOWEST POINT New Orleans (5 feet; 1.5 meters below sea level)

INDUSTRIES Chemicals, communication, construction, food products, paper products, petroleum products, tourism, trade, transportation equipment

AGRICULTURE Cattle, chickens, corn, cotton, dairy products, pecans, rice, soybeans, sugar cane, sweet potatoes

MOTTO Union, justice, and confidence.

FLAG The flag shows a mother pelican feeding her three nestlings, symbolizing how the state protects its people and resources. The state motto appears below the birds. The flag was adopted in 1912.

BIRD The **Eastern brown pelican** is a superb diver, plunging 60 to 70 feet (18 to 21 meters) deep into the water. It has a stretchy pouch as part of its lower bill, which expands when the bird scoops up fish. The bird was adopted in 1966.

FLOWER Adopted in 1900, the **magnolia** grows throughout the state. In the summer, thousands of the creamy-white blossoms perfume the air with their fragrant aroma.

TREE Wood from the **bald cypress** is used for boats, railroad ties, and bridges. Many Louisiana houses built with cypress wood more than 100 years ago are still in good condition. The tree was adopted in 1963.

SONGS "Give Me Louisiana" (words and music by Doralice Fontane; music arranged by John W. Schaum). "You Are My Sunshine" (words and music by Jimmy H. Davis and Charles Mitchell).

Inside Scoop

EVERY YEAR, more than 1 million people attend Mardi Gras, French for "Fat Tuesday." Parades with jazz bands, floats, and masqueraders march in New Orleans on the day before Lent begins (40 days before Easter).

LOUISIANA is the only state divided into parishes, not counties.

TABASCO SAUCE was first made on Avery Island by Edmund McIlhenny in 1868. The next year McIlhenny sold his first 658 bottles. Today, the McIlhenny Company sells the spicy sauce in more than 100 countries and territories.

LOUISIANA'S STATE CAPITOL building, completed in 1932, is the tallest in the country. It is 450 feet (137 meters) high and has 34 floors.

THE WORLD'S MOST FAMOUS jazz musician, Louis Armstrong, was born in New Orleans in 1900.

WITH SUPPORT from his schoolmates and his 4-H club, a West Monroe 12-year-old collected hats for young cancer patients whose hair had fallen out from radiation or chemotherapy treatments. The boy received Prudential's Louisiana Spirit of Community Award in 2001.

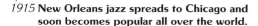

1975 The Louisiana Superdome, an indoor stadium that is 27 stories high and seats more than 95,000, is completed in New Orleans.

1984 The Louisiana World Exposition is held in New Orleans.

1915 New Orleans jazz spreads to Chicago and soon becomes popular all over the world.

Francofête '99 opens. It is a yearlong celebration 1999 of the 300th anniversary of New Orleans, Louisiana's first permanent colony.

AAA GEMS:
Selected Must-See Points of Interest

ACADIA NATIONAL PARK (Mount Desert Island) — Hike, bike, swim, canoe, cross-country ski and marvel at the sweeping ocean and mountain views. Check out Somes Sound, the only fjord in the continental United States, and Thunder Hole, where crashing waves roar.

COLE LAND TRANSPORTATION MUSEUM (Bangor) — Follow the development of vehicles — from wagons to 18-wheelers at this museum. An 1840s covered bridge helps carry out the theme.

MAINE MARITIME MUSEUM (Bath) — On the banks of the Kennebec River, this museum traces Maine's seafaring history. Tour the 1800s shipyard and watch boats being built.

MAINE STATE MUSEUM (Augusta) — Learn all about Maine — from the earliest people who lived here to the more than 1,000 products manufactured in the state.

MUSICAL WONDER HOUSE (Wiscasset) — Listen to antique mechanical musical instruments made in America and Europe.

Mount Katahdin marks the northern end of the Appalachian Trail, which runs more than 2,160 miles (3,476 kilometers) from Maine to Georgia. Although several thousand people try to hike the whole trail each year, only about one in seven finishes.

Locals often take visitors on demonstration cruises to teach them about traditional lobster fishing. This captain may be telling his guest how lobsters smell with their leg hairs!

TIMELINE

c. 1000 Vikings from Norway land on the coast.

1604 French explorer Samuel de Champlain discovers Mount Desert Island, now the site of Acadia National Park.

1622 England gives Maine land to Sir Ferdinando Gorges, a wealthy Englishman who favors building colonies in the New World.

1628 A trading post is established by the Plymouth Colony at what is now Augusta.

1677 Massachusetts buys Maine from the Gorges family.

1819 Maine residents vote to separate from Massachusetts. Maine officially becomes a state in 1820.

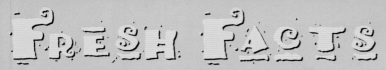

FRESH FACTS

NAME Named after Mayne, a French province, or to identify the land as the mainland, separate from the nearby islands.

ABBREVIATION None

CAPITAL Augusta

NICKNAME Pine Tree State

AREA 35,385 square miles (91,647 square kilometers)

POPULATION 1,274,923

STATEHOOD March 15, 1820 (23rd state)

HIGHEST POINT Mount Katahdin (5,268 feet; 1,606 meters)

LOWEST POINT Sea level

INDUSTRIES Finance, food products, leather products, lumber, paper, tourism, trade, transportation equipment, wood products

AGRICULTURE Apples, blueberries, cattle, chickens, dairy products, potatoes, seafood

MOTTO I direct.

FLAG A moose and a pine tree on the shield in the center represent wildlife. Holding the shield is a farmer and a fisherman who stand for agriculture and fishing. The North Star symbolizes that Maine is the most northerly of the northeastern states. The flag was adopted in 1909.

BIRD The **black-capped chickadee** is named for the black feathers, resembling a cap, on its head. It was adopted as the state bird in 1927.

FLOWER In 1894, Maine residents were asked to vote for an official flower. The winner wasn't a flower. It was the **white pine cone and tassel**, probably because the pine tree was so important to the state's economic growth. The pine cone and tassel were adopted in 1895.

TREE The **Eastern white pine,** adopted in 1945, is the largest conifer in the Northeast.

SONG "State of Maine Song" (words and music by Roger Vinton Snow)

Inside Scoop

A PLAQUE OUTSIDE of Hanson Gregory's house in Rockland honors him as the inventor of the doughnut. As a young boy in 1847, he gave the hole idea to his mother.

MAINE is the only state in the continental United States that borders just one other state: New Hampshire.

MAINE IS SOMETIMES called the "Down East State," because ships that sailed from Boston to Maine's ports traveled downwind and east to get there.

CADILLAC MOUNTAIN, in Acadia National Park, is the first place the sun's light shines upon each day in America.

IN 1858, 15-year-old Chester Greenwood of Farmington invented ear muffs and later started a factory to manufacture them. He also patented over 100 other ideas. The Smithsonian Institution in Washington, D.C., lists him as one of America's 15 most outstanding inventors.

Kayakers enjoy the waters of beautiful Acadia National Park.

1868 The University of Maine opens with 12 students and two teachers. About 10,000 students are enrolled today.

1947 The first Lobster Festival, now an annual event, is held in Rockland.

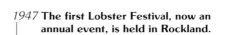

1851 Harriet Beecher Stowe writes "Uncle Tom's Cabin" in Brunswick.

1980 President Jimmy Carter signs the Indian Land Claims Agreement, which pays the Passamaquoddy and Penobscot Indians for the land taken from them in the 1700s.

Maryland

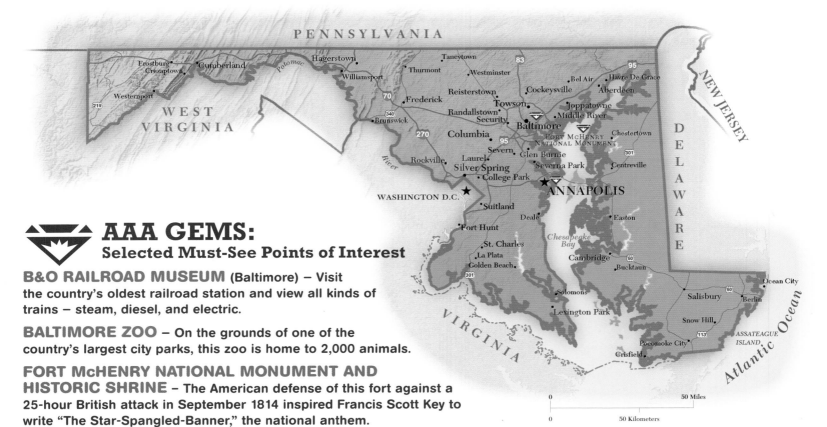

◆ AAA GEMS:
Selected Must-See Points of Interest

B&O RAILROAD MUSEUM (Baltimore) – Visit the country's oldest railroad station and view all kinds of trains – steam, diesel, and electric.

BALTIMORE ZOO – On the grounds of one of the country's largest city parks, this zoo is home to 2,000 animals.

FORT McHENRY NATIONAL MONUMENT AND HISTORIC SHRINE – The American defense of this fort against a 25-hour British attack in September 1814 inspired Francis Scott Key to write "The Star-Spangled-Banner," the national anthem.

MARYLAND SCIENCE CENTER, IMAX THEATER, AND DAVIS PLANETARIUM (Baltimore) – Fun exhibits let you discover science for yourself. Check out the Visible Human exhibit, the science arcade, and the strolling exhibitors.

NATIONAL AQUARIUM IN BALTIMORE – See sharks, stingrays, puffins, and a giant Pacific octopus as well as re-created sections of the Amazon River forest, and an Atlantic coral reef.

U.S. NAVAL ACADEMY (Annapolis) – Ogle Hall, completed in 1739, echoes with the footsteps of George Washington. See the award-winning film "To Lead and to Serve" and find out about our country's naval history and traditions.

Chesapeake Bay is famous for its blue crabs. Crab traps are carried on top of this fishing boat.

Baltimore's glittering harbor is home to the National Aquarium, the triangle-shaped building in the upper right of this picture.

TIMELINE

1632 Lord Baltimore receives Maryland's charter from King Charles I.

1729 Baltimore Town is established.

1784 The 1783 Treaty of Paris is ratified at Annapolis, ending the Revolutionary War and establishing the United States as an independent country.

1791 Maryland gives up land for the District of Columbia.

1814 "The Star-Spangled Banner" is written by Francis Scott Key after American forces successfully defend Fort McHenry against a British attack.

1818 The first road built with federal funds is completed — from Cumberland, Md., to Wheeling, W.Va.

FRESH FACTS

NAME Named in honor of Queen Henrietta Maria (Queen Mary), the wife of King Charles I of England.

ABBREVIATION Md.

CAPITAL Annapolis

NICKNAME Old Line State (also Free State)

AREA 12,407 square miles (32,134 square kilometers)

POPULATION 5,296,486

STATEHOOD April 28, 1788 (7th state)

HIGHEST POINT Backbone Mountain (3,360 feet; 1,024 meters)

LOWEST POINT Sea level

INDUSTRIES Biotechnology, chemical products, electrical and electronic equipment, food processing, information technology, printing and publishing, tourism

AGRICULTURE Chickens, corn, dairy products, seafood, soybeans

MOTTO Manly deeds, womanly words.

FLAG Two family crests are shown on the flag, adopted in 1904. The black and gold represents the Calvert family; the red and white stands for the Crossland family. Lord Baltimore, Maryland's founder, was related to both families.

BIRD The **Baltimore oriole** is named after Lord Baltimore, who liked the jaunty bird and used its orange and black colors for his family's coat of arms. The Baltimore Orioles baseball team was named after the bird and adopted its colors. The bird was adopted in 1947.

FLOWER The **black-eyed Susan** used to grow only east of the Rocky Mountains, but so many gardeners west of the Rockies planted it that the flower can now be seen throughout the United States. Maryland adopted it in 1918.

TREE The **white oak,** adopted in 1941, is named for its whitish bark. American Indians ground the white oaks' acorns into flour and taught the settlers to do this too.

SONG "Maryland, My Maryland" (words by James Ryder Randall; music to the tune of "Lauriger Horatius")

Inside Scoop

IN 1774, five months after the Boston Tea Party, the townspeople of Chestertown held their own protest and tossed a cargo of tea from a British ship into the river. Every May, Chestertown stages a re-enactment as part of its Tea Party Festival.

ORIOLE PARK'S center field was built on the site of Babe Ruth's boyhood home.

HARRIET TUBMAN, the most famous "conductor" on the Underground Railroad, was born a slave in Bucktown around 1820. She helped 300 slaves reach freedom.

AMERICA'S FIRST UMBRELLA FACTORY opened in Baltimore in 1828. Its slogan was "Born in Baltimore, raised everywhere."

A 13-YEAR-OLD rhythmic gymnast from Rockville won the 1996 Junior Pan American Championship.

Wild ponies have lived on Assateague Island since the 1600s. Legend says the first ponies swam there from a shipwrecked Spanish galleon.

1845 The U.S. Naval Academy is founded at Annapolis.

1893 The Johns Hopkins University School of Medicine opens in Baltimore.

1962 Jousting becomes the official state sport. A tournament is held in Calvert County every August.

1967 Thurgood Marshall, from Baltimore, becomes the first African-American justice on the U.S. Supreme Court.

1992 Oriole Park, the new baseball stadium at Camden Yards, opens in Baltimore.

1993 All counties agree to reduce pollution into the Chesapeake Bay.

1998 Cal Ripken, Jr., of the Baltimore Orioles, sets the record for consecutive baseball games played at 2,632.

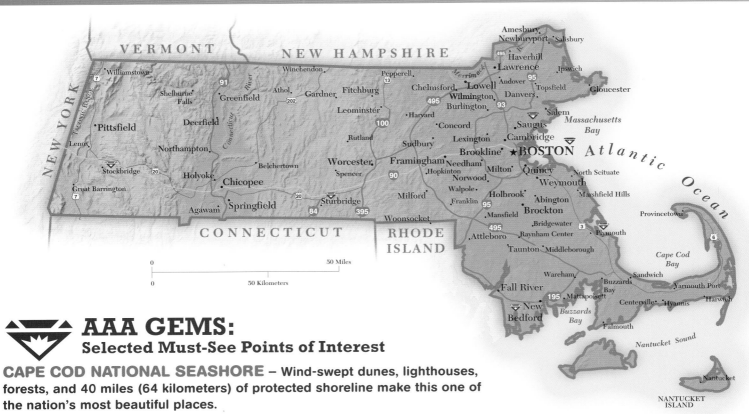

VERMONT   NEW HAMPSHIRE

NEW YORK

Williamstown
Shelburne Falls
Greenfield
Deerfield
Pittsfield
Northampton
Lenox
Stockbridge
Great Barrington
Agawam
Holyoke
Chicopee
Springfield
Belchertown
Spencer
Worcester
Rutland
Athol
Gardner
Fitchburg
Leominster
Sudbury
Framingham
Hopkinton
Milford
Sturbridge
Woonsocket

Winchendon
Pepperell
Chelmsford
Harvard
Concord
Lexington
Needham
Norwood
Walpole
Franklin
Mansfield
Attleboro
Taunton
Middleborough
Raynham Center

Amesbury
Newburyport
Salisbury
Haverhill
Lawrence
Andover
Ipswich
Topsfield
Wilmington
Burlington
Danvers
Saugus
Salem
Gloucester
Cambridge
Brookline
★BOSTON
Milton
Quincy
Weymouth
Holbrook
Abington
Brockton
Bridgewater
Plymouth
North Scituate
Marshfield Hills
Provincetown
Wareham
Buzzards Bay
Sandwich
Fall River
New Bedford
Mattapoisett
Centerville
Hyannis
Yarmouth Port
Harwich
Falmouth
Nantucket

Massachusetts Bay
Atlantic Ocean
Cape Cod Bay
Buzzards Bay
Nantucket Sound
NANTUCKET ISLAND

CONNECTICUT   RHODE ISLAND

0   50 Miles
0   50 Kilometers

AAA GEMS:
Selected Must-See Points of Interest

CAPE COD NATIONAL SEASHORE – Wind-swept dunes, lighthouses, forests, and 40 miles (64 kilometers) of protected shoreline make this one of the nation's most beautiful places.

MUSEUM AT THE JOHN FITZGERALD KENNEDY LIBRARY (Boston) – The life and legacy of President John F. Kennedy are portrayed here.

MUSEUM OF SCIENCE (Boston) – Teens will have fun with the hands-on exhibits dealing with ecology, astronomy, and optical illusions.

NEW BEDFORD WHALING MUSEUM – Learn the history of Herman Melville's classic "Moby-Dick," scrutinize scrimshaw, view a fully equipped whale boat or marvel at the size of a humpback whale skeleton.

NORMAN ROCKWELL MUSEUM AT STOCKBRIDGE – This museum houses Rockwell's studio along with many of his original paintings.

OLD NORTH CHURCH (Boston) – A lantern in the steeple of the church signaled the arrival of British troops in 1775.

OLD STURBRIDGE VILLAGE – Rural New England life of the 1830s is re-created at this living history museum.

PLIMOTH PLANTATION (Plymouth) – Costumed actors re-create a Pilgrim village of the 1600s. Climb aboard a replica of the Mayflower moored at the State Pier.

SAUGUS IRON WORKS NATIONAL HISTORIC SITE – This restored 1646 water-powered ironworks was the first in North America to encompass all phases of iron production.

THE USS CONSTITUTION (Boston) – Nicknamed Old Ironsides during the War of 1812, this 1797 frigate withstood British cannons and stopped French privateers. On July 21, 1997, the ship sailed for the first time in 116 years.

A model of the Pilgrim ship Mayflower complete with costumed tour guides is docked in Plymouth harbor.

TIMELINE

1602 English explorer Bartholomew Gosnold names Cape Cod after the many codfish in the water.

1630 Boston is founded by Puritans from England.

1692 Twenty people were executed as a result of witchcraft trials in Salem.

1826 The first American railroad is built in Quincy.

1620 The Pilgrims, seeking religious freedom, arrive at Plymouth aboard the Mayflower.

1636 Harvard University, the nation's oldest university, is founded in Cambridge.

1773 Protesting British taxes, colonists throw British tea into Boston Harbor.

1775 The first battles of the American Revolution are fought at Lexington and Concord.

FRESH FACTS

NAME Based on an Algonquian Indian word meaning "the large hill place" or "great mountain."

ABBREVIATION Mass.

CAPITAL Boston

NICKNAME Bay State

AREA 10,555 square miles (27,337 square kilometers)

POPULATION 6,349,097

STATEHOOD Feb. 6, 1788 (6th state)

HIGHEST POINT Mount Greylock (3,491 feet; 1,064 meters)

LOWEST POINT Sea level

INDUSTRIES Electrical and electronic equipment, machinery, metal products, printed materials and publishing, scientific instruments, trade

AGRICULTURE Chickens, cranberries, eggs, milk, seafood, vegetables, young plants

MOTTO By the sword we seek peace, but peace only under liberty.

FLAG The shield shows an American Indian holding a bow in one hand and an arrow pointing down in the other, symbolizing peace. The star means the state was one of the original 13 colonies. Above the shield, an arm holds a sword, illustrating the state's motto. The flag was adopted in 1971.

BIRD The **black-capped chickadee** is named after the black feathers on the top of its head and the sound of its call, chick-a-dee. It was adopted in 1941.

FLOWER School children voted in 1918 for the **mayflower** to be the state's flower over the lily. It was adopted the same year.

TREE A specific **American elm** in Boston, nicknamed the Liberty Tree, was a gathering spot and symbol for patriots during the American Revolution. Today, scientists are trying to save these stately trees from the deadly Dutch elm disease. The American elm was adopted in 1941.

SONG "All Hail to Massachusetts" (words and music by Arthur J. Marsh)

Almost half of all cranberries grown in the United States come from Massachusetts. These men are collecting berries in one of the state's 1,400 cranberry bogs.

Inside Scoop

THE FIRST BASKETBALL GAME was played in Springfield and the first volleyball game in Holyoke.

THE PILGRIMS LIKED POPCORN so much that they ate it as a breakfast cereal with milk.

BOSTON IS HOME to the first public park and the first public school.

A WOODEN CODFISH, called the "Sacred Cod," hangs from the ceiling in the statehouse in Boston as a tribute to the state's oldest industry, fishing. Its kin, the "Holy Mackerel," hangs in the state senate.

IN 1983, Deborah Samson was officially declared the state heroine. Disguised as a man, she fought for a year in the Continental Army in the Revolutionary War before she was discovered. She was the first female to receive a military pension.

A SMALL GROUP OF TEEN GIRLS in Walpole have developed "A Video Quilt," a video patchwork of the lives of local senior citizens that will be shown in schools. The group has also produced community-access television shows about important teen issues.

During the mid-1800s, New Bedford was one of the biggest whaling ports in the world. Two full-sized whale skeletons hang in the New Bedford Whaling Museum.

1944 Howard Aiken and Grace Hopper of Harvard University build the Mark 1, the first computer put to practical use.

1876 Alexander Graham Bell invents the telephone in Boston.

1898 The nation's first subway begins service in Boston.

1996 The Boston Marathon celebrates its 100th anniversary; more than 37,000 people representing 84 countries participate in the race.

The Mackinac Bridge connects the upper and lower peninsulas of Michigan.

AAA GEMS:
Selected Must-See Points of Interest

BINDER PARK ZOO (Battle Creek) – Take a train ride through an African safari-style habitat and ride a camel.

FORT MACKINAC (Mackinac Island) – Tour the original buildings and battlements built in the 1700s and 1800s that guarded the Straits of Mackinac for 115 years. Costumed guides re-enact events and fire cannons and rifles.

HENRY FORD MUSEUM & GREENFIELD VILLAGE (Dearborn) – Discover how the automobile changed life in America, trace the history of American industry, see items used by American presidents, tour houses of famous people, ride a steam train or a steamboat, watch craft demonstrations, and more.

ISLE ROYALE NATIONAL PARK – A densely forested island in Lake Superior is home to moose, foxes, wolves, snowshoe hares, loons, and other wildlife.

MICHIGAN SPACE AND SCIENCE CENTER (Jackson) – See the Apollo 9 command module, a model of the Hubble Space Telescope, a Mars Pathfinder exhibit, and climb into a space capsule.

SOO LOCKS BOAT TOURS (Sault Ste. Marie) – Experience the gradual rising and lowering of the water under your tour boat as you travel through the locks like the giant ships and tankers do.

Although the Presque Island lighthouse closed in 1870 when a taller lighthouse replaced it, a light has been seen coming from the tower. Some say the lighhouse, now used as a museum, is haunted!

TIMELINE

1668 Father Jacques Marquette, a French missionary, founds the first European permanent settlement at Sault Ste. Marie.

1701 French commander Antoine Cadillac builds the first fort at present-day Detroit.

1763 France gives up Michigan to England as part of the Treaty of Paris, which ends the French and Indian War.

1783 England surrenders Michigan to the United States as part of the Treaty of Paris.

1855 The Soo Locks are opened, allowing ships to navigate the rapids between lakes Superior and Huron.

1894 The Kellogg brothers in Battle Creek develop a flake cereal. Today, Battle Creek is the "Cereal Capital of the World."

FRESH FACTS

NAME From the Chippewa Indian word "majigan," meaning "clearing."

ABBREVIATION Mich.

CAPITAL Lansing

NICKNAME Wolverine State (also, Great Lakes State)

AREA 96,716 square miles (250,494 square kilometers)

POPULATION 9,938,444

STATEHOOD Jan. 26, 1837 (26th state)

HIGHEST POINT Mount Curwood (1,980 feet; 604 meters)

LOWEST POINT Lake Erie (572 feet; 174 meters)

INDUSTRIES Chemicals, food products, lumber and wood products, machinery, metal products, motor vehicles and parts, plastic, tourism

AGRICULTURE Apples, beans, cattle, cherries, corn, dairy products, hay, potatoes, soybeans, wheat, young plants

MOTTO If you seek a pleasant peninsula, look about you.

FLAG Adopted in 1911, the flag has the state's coat of arms at its center. The blue shield shows a sun rising at a lake and a pioneer standing on a peninsula. An elk and a moose, symbolizing the state's wildlife, hold the shield. A bald eagle represents the United States. Three mottoes appear in Latin. They mean "From many, one"; "I will defend"; and the state's motto (see above).

BIRD When the **American robin** was adopted in 1931, the state's legislators said it was "the best known and best loved of all the birds in the state of Michigan."

FLOWER The **apple blossom** was adopted in 1897 in honor of the state's apple trees. Michigan produces more than 800 million pounds of apples a year.

TREE Adopted in 1955, the **white pine** symbolizes the importance of the state's lumber industry. In the 1800s, Michigan produced the most lumber in the nation.

SONG "My Michigan" (words by Giles Kavanagh; music by H. O'Reilly Clint)

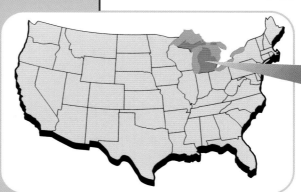

Inside Scoop

MICHIGAN is the only state made up of two peninsulas, the Upper and Lower, now connected by the Mackinac Bridge.

MICHIGAN MANUFACTURES more cars than any other state.

ALTHOUGH MICHIGAN is called the Wolverine State, no one has seen this animal in the wild in Michigan for 100 years or more. Scientists debate whether wolverines ever lived in the state.

TRAVERSE CITY is the Cherry Capital of the World. Try the cherry pie.

MICHIGAN'S BORDERS TOUCH four of the five Great Lakes, making it the state with the most freshwater shoreline.

DETROIT'S NICKNAME is "Motown," a shortened version of "Motor Town."

A 13-YEAR-OLD from Blissfield, along with some friends, recruited hundreds of volunteers to collect supplies for painting and wallpapering a homeless shelter.

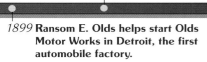

Snowmobile fans love Michigan's chilly winters.

1899 Ransom E. Olds helps start Olds Motor Works in Detroit, the first automobile factory.

1908 The General Motors Company in Flint buys the Olds Motor Works, the first of several automobile manufacturer purchases. Henry Ford introduces the Model T.

1957 The Mackinac Bridge is built over the Straits of Mackinac, connecting the state's Upper and Lower peninsulas.

1984 The Detroit Tigers baseball team wins the World Series.

1997 The largest museum of African-American history opens in Detroit.

Minnesota

CANADA

MANITOBA

ONTARIO

The Great Lakes Aquarium in Duluth is North America's only freshwater aquarium.

◆ AAA GEMS:
Selected Must-See Points of Interest

FOREST HISTORY CENTER (Grand Rapids) — Costumed guides bring to life the work of lumberjacks at a logging camp in 1900. Check out the cookhouse, outhouse, and the scenic view from the tall fire tower.

RUNESTONE MUSEUM (Alexandria) — Carvings on the Kensington Runestone tell the tragic story of a band of Vikings from 1362. However, not everyone agrees the runestone is authentic. There are also displays of Viking tools, wildlife, and an American Indian exhibit.

SCIENCE MUSEUM OF MINNESOTA (St. Paul) — Hands-on exhibits let visitors touch a tornado, walk under a dinosaur, and climb onto a Mississippi River tugboat. Check out the Egyptian mummy, the human body gallery, and the IMAX theater where films and 3-D laser shows bring science adventures up very close.

VOYAGEURS NATIONAL PARK (International Falls) — This is a great place for canoeing, kayaking, and hiking. In the 1700s and 1800s, French-Canadians called "voyageurs" traveled these waterways in canoes filled with furs and goods to trade. Every summer, one group of voyageurs from Montreal in eastern Canada and one group from northwest Canada would meet in the middle at trading posts in Minnesota to exchange goods.

Opened in Bloomington in 1992, the Mall of America is the nation's largest, with more than 500 stores and restaurants. It also has the nation's largest indoor theme park — with a roller coaster, flume ride, and 3-D movie — a bi-level mini-golf course, an aquarium with a submarine ride, and much more.

TIMELINE

c.1660 French fur traders Pierre Radisson and Médard Chouart, Sieur des Groseilliers, explore the area.

1679 Daniel Greysolon, Sieur Duluth, claims much of Minnesota for France.

1783 England surrenders Minnesota land east of the Mississippi River to the United States under the Treaty of Paris, ending the Revolutionary War.

1803 The United States buys Minnesota land west of the Mississippi River from France as part of the Louisiana Purchase.

1819 Fort Snelling, near present-day St. Paul, is built. It is Minnesota's first permanent white settlement.

1832 Henry Rowe Schoolcraft discovers the source of the Mississippi River at Lake Itasca.

FRESH FACTS

NAME From the Dakota Sioux Indian word "mnishota," meaning "cloudy water," which described the water of the Minnesota River.

ABBREVIATION Minn.

CAPITAL St. Paul

NICKNAME The North Star State (also, Gopher State)

AREA 86,939 square miles (225,172 square kilometers)

POPULATION 4,919,479

STATEHOOD May 11, 1858 (32nd state)

HIGHEST POINT Eagle Mountain (2,301 feet; 701 meters)

LOWEST POINT Lake Superior (602 feet; 83 meters)

INDUSTRIES Chemical products, electrical and electronic equipment, food products, lumber, machinery, metal products, mining, printed materials, tourism, wood products

AGRICULTURE Cattle, chickens, corn, dairy products, hogs, soybeans, sugar beets, wheat, wild rice

MOTTO The star of the north.

FLAG Three dates appear on the wreath of pink-and-white-lady's slippers (the state flower) that encircles the state seal. The year 1819 is when Fort Snelling was built; 1858 is when Minnesota became a state; and 1893 is when the original flag was adopted. The 19 stars around the wreath show that Minnesota was the 19th state in the Union after the first 13 colonies became states. The flag was adopted in 1957.

BIRD The **common loon** gets its name from a Norwegian word meaning "loud, sad cry," which can be heard on summer nights. Loons are expert divers and underwater swimmers, but they are clumsy on land. Loons can take flight only from water. The bird was adopted in 1961.

FLOWER The delicate **pink-and-white lady's slipper** (also called showy lady's slipper) is such a rare wildflower that it has been protected by law in Minnesota for more than 75 years. It was adopted in 1902.

TREE The **Norway pine,** adopted in 1953, is also known as the red pine because of its reddish-brown bark. The tallest Norway pine (120 feet; 36.5 meters) is in Itasca State Park.

SONG "Hail! Minnesota" (first verse and music by Truman E. Rickard; second verse by Arthur E. Upson)

You can find out how SPAM® is made and how it helped feed Allied soldiers during World War II at the SPAM Museum in Austin.

Inside Scoop

EVELETH is the home of the U.S. Hockey Hall of Fame.

YOU CAN WADE across the Mississippi River at its source at Itasca State Park.

ACCORDING TO AN American Indian legend, a white bison turned the stone red at what is now called Pipestone National Monument. The sacred red stone was carved into ceremonial pipes.

IN-LINE SKATES were developed in Minneapolis by the Olson brothers in 1980 so that hockey players could practice off-season on pavement. Their company became Rollerblade®, Inc.

LAURA INGALLS WILDER, who wrote the book series "Little House," lived near Walnut Grove as a child. Some sites she described in "On the Banks of Plum Creek" look just the same today.

A 13-YEAR-OLD from Anoka won the Scripps-Howard National Spelling Bee in 2001. A total of 248 contestants participated.

1889 Dr. William Mayo and two sons start the Mayo Clinic in Rochester, now one of the world's largest and finest medical centers.

1930 Sinclair Lewis becomes the first American to win the Nobel Prize for literature. His book "Main Street" is based on his Minnesota hometown, Sauk Centre.

1987 The Minnesota Twins win the World Series.

1996 The temperature in Tower plunges to −60° F (-51° C) on Feb. 2, the coldest day ever recorded in the state.

1998 Former professional wrestler, mayor, and radio talk-show host Jesse Ventura, a Minneapolis native, is elected governor for a four-year term.

Mississippi

FRESH FACTS

NAME From the Chippewa Indian words "mici zibi," meaning "large river."

ABBREVIATION Miss.

CAPITAL Jackson

NICKNAME Magnolia State

AREA 47,695 square miles (123,530 square kilometers)

POPULATION 2,844,658

STATEHOOD Dec.10, 1817 (20th state)

HIGHEST POINT Woodall Mountain (806 feet; 246 meters)

LOWEST POINT Sea level

INDUSTRIES Chemicals, food products, lumber and wood products, machinery, natural gas, petroleum, trade, transportation equipment

AGRICULTURE Catfish, cattle, cotton, poultry, rice, soybeans

MOTTO By valor and arms.

FLAG Adopted in 1894, the flag reflects Mississippi's loyalty to the Confederacy and the United States. In the upper-left corner is a replica of the Confederate flag with 13 stars representing the 13 original states. The red, white, and blue colors are the colors of the U.S. flag.

BIRD The **mockingbird,** chosen in 1929, is a cheerful songbird that can be heard night and day. It likes to mimic other birds and sometimes the sounds of other animals with its songs.

FLOWER Although 23,278 school children voted overwhelmingly in 1900 for the **magnolia** to be the state flower, it was not officially adopted until 1952.

TREE School children also chose the **magnolia** to be the state tree. It was adopted in 1938.

SONG "Go, Mississippi" (words and music by Houston Davis)

Inside Scoop

WHILE ON A HUNTING TRIP in Sharkey County in 1902, President Teddy Roosevelt refused to shoot a captured bear. Shortly afterward, a candy-store owner in Brooklyn, N.Y., made a stuffed toy bear in the president's honor and put it up for sale. The teddy bear has been beloved ever since.

CAPT. ISAAC ROSS, a plantation owner in Lorman, freed his slaves in 1834. They sailed to Africa and were among those who established the nation of Liberia.

THE INTERNATIONAL CHECKERS Hall of Fame is located in Petal.

A FAMOUS SONG tells the story of Casey Jones, a railroad engineer. In 1900 he could not prevent his train from colliding with a freight train at Vaughn. He told his assistant to jump off while he stayed at the wheel and died. Casey became a folk hero.

A BRANDON NATIVE who won the Miss Teen All-American competition in 1999 started a Queen for a Day program to bring cheer to seriously ill girls in hospitals and cancer centers. The royal treatment included a manicure and make-up as well as a glittering crown donated by beauty queens around the country.

Colorful American Indian costumes are worn at this traditional powwow in Philadelphia.

TIMELINE

1541 Hernando de Soto is the first European to see the Mississippi River.

1719 French settlers bring the first African slaves to work on rice plantations.

1699 Pierre le Moyne, Sieur d'Iberville, establishes the state's first permanent white settlement at Old Biloxi.

1863 Gen. Ulysses S. Grant takes Vicksburg in the Civil War after a 47-day siege. The North gains control of the Mississippi River.

1870 Hiram R. Revels, from Natchez, becomes the first African-American to serve in the U.S. Senate. He completes the term of Jefferson Davis, who had been president of the Confederacy.

AAA GEMS:
Selected Must-See Points of Interest

DESOTO NATIONAL FOREST – This is the largest of Mississippi's national forests, a great place for hiking, horseback riding, fishing, canoeing, watching wildlife, camping, and mountain biking.

FLOREWOOD RIVER PLANTATION STATE PARK (Greenwood) – Costumed guides describe plantation life of the 1850s and demonstrate the trades and crafts of the 1800s. Visitors in late summer can pick cotton.

JEFFERSON DAVIS HOME (Biloxi) – Tour the last home of Jefferson Davis, president of the Confederate States of America. Visit the Confederate museum, the Jefferson Davis Presidential Library, and stroll the beautiful grounds.

MISSISSIPPI MUSEUM OF NATURAL SCIENCE (Jackson) – Indoor exhibits and outdoor habitats focus on Mississippi's plants and animals. There's a huge aquarium, a greenhouse with alligators and turtles, and nature trails.

VICKSBURG NATIONAL MILITARY PARK – Known as "The Gibraltar of the Confederacy," Vicksburg guarded the Mississippi River during the Civil War. The battlefield has 1,235 historic markers and monuments and 144 cannons. A restored Union gunboat can also be viewed.

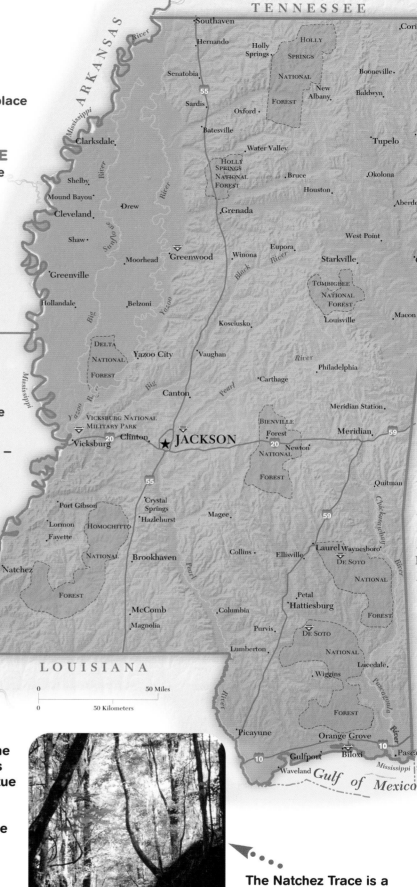

The Mississippi Delta area was the birthplace of blues music. This wax statue is of singer Muddy Waters, who was born in Clarksdale. Today, Clarksdale is home to the Delta Blues Museum.

The Natchez Trace is a 440-mile (708-kilometer) trail first used by Indians, and then by European and American explorers.

1935 Rock 'n' roll star Elvis Presley is born in Tupelo.

1962 James Meredith, born in Kosciusko, becomes the first African-American in the state to attend a white public college, the University of Mississippi.

1949 Mississippi author William Faulkner, from Oxford, wins the Nobel Prize for literature.

1964 Three civil rights workers are killed in a riot near Philadelphia. The state's first public schools are integrated.

1991 Residents can register to vote by mail. Mississippi is the 21st state to allow this.

Missouri

The Gateway Arch in St. Louis, completed in 1965, stands 630 feet (192 meters) high and weighs 16,878 tons. Despite its weight, it was built to sway by as much as an inch (2.5 centimeter) in a 20-mph (32-kph) wind.

One of Missouri's most famous citizens was Samuel Clemens, better known as Mark Twain. His books include "The Adventures of Tom Sawyer" and "The Adventures of Huckleberry Finn," both of which take place in Missouri.

AAA GEMS:
Selected Must-See Points of Interest

ARABIA STEAMBOAT MUSEUM (Kansas City) – A guided tour of this sunken steamship that was recovered from watery depths reveals what pioneers going west carried: medicine, clothing and shoes, guns, jewelry, and perfume.

GATEWAY ARCH (St. Louis) – This gleaming, stainless steel structure is a symbol of America's pioneer spirit. View a film about the arch and the pioneers who passed through St. Louis on their way west. Then take the tram to the top for a panoramic view of the city.

MERAMEC CAVERNS (Stanton) – This fascinating cave has five levels of spectacular rock formations, including one called the "Stage Curtain," which is 70 feet (21 meters) high. The cave served as a hideout for escaping slaves and for outlaw Jesse James.

SILVER DOLLAR CITY (Branson) – Crafts, rides, and family entertainment are on tap at this 1880s-style amusement park. Blacksmithing, woodcarving, and glassblowing are just some of the skills demonstrated by more than 100 artisans. Flume, raft, and coaster rides offer plenty of thrills.

ST. LOUIS ZOO – Step aboard the Zooline Railroad and ride past the zoo's favorite attractions. Then visit River's Edge, the home of Asian elephants, cheetahs, and hyenas; Big Cat Country where big felines stroll by rocky dens, pools, and waterfalls; and Jungle of the Apes, a tropical rain forest, with gorillas, chimpanzees, and orangutans.

TIMELINE

1673 Father Jacques Marquette, a French missionary, and Louis Jolliet, a French-Canadian explorer, are the first white men to see the mouth of the Missouri River.

c. 1735 Ste. Genevieve, the state's oldest permanent settlement, is established by French settlers.

1804 Explorers Meriwether Lewis and William Clark leave St. Louis to start their expedition to the Pacific coast.

1682 René-Robert Cavelier, Sieur de la Salle, claims the area for France.

1764 St. Louis is founded by 15-year-old René Auguste Chouteau and his stepfather, Pierre Laclede. It becomes an important fur trading post.

1811–12 Three of the nation's most powerful earthquakes shake southeast Missouri near Madrid. One causes the Mississippi River to flow backward temporarily.

FRESH FACTS

NAME From a Missouri Indian term meaning "people of the big canoes," referring to the natives who traveled on the Mississippi River.

ABBREVIATION Mo.

CAPITAL Jefferson City

NICKNAME Show Me State

AREA 69,709 square miles (180,546 square kilometers)

POPULATION 5,595,211

STATEHOOD Aug. 10, 1821 (24th state)

HIGHEST POINT Taum Sauk Mountain (1,772 feet; 540 meters)

LOWEST POINT St. Francis River (230 feet; 70 meters)

INDUSTRIES Chemicals, electrical and electronic equipment, food products, machinery, printed materials, tourism, transportation equipment

AGRICULTURE Cattle, chickens, corn, eggs, hay, hogs, soybeans, wheat

MOTTO The welfare of the people shall be the supreme law.

FLAG The flag, adopted in 1913, was designed by Marie Elizabeth Watkins Oliver, wife of a state senator, and Mary Kochtitzky. The state seal in the center is surrounded by 24 stars, showing that Missouri was the 24th state to enter the Union. The grizzly bears in the seal represent courage and strength.

BIRD The **bluebird,** adopted in 1927, is thought to be a symbol of happiness. Its sweet song can be heard in Missouri from spring to November.

FLOWER The **white hawthorn** was adopted in 1923. In England, the hawthorn is called mayflower. The Pilgrims named their ship Mayflower for this flower.

TREE The roots of the flowering **dogwood** tree were made into a medicine by American Indians to treat fevers. Early settlers split the ends of small branches, which they used for cleaning their teeth. The tree was adopted in 1955.

SONG "Missouri Waltz" (words by James R. Shannon; music by John V. Eppel)

Inside Scoop

THE FIRST ICE CREAM CONES were served at the 1904 World's Fair in St. Louis.

MISSOURI'S NICKNAME, which means the same as "seeing is believing," most likely comes from a speech made in 1899 by Congressman Willard Duncan Vandiver in which he said, "Frothy eloquence neither convinces me nor satisfies me. I am from Missouri. You have to show me."

CHARLES LINDBERGH was the first person to fly solo across the Atlantic in 1927. He named his plane "The Spirit of St. Louis" in honor of the St. Louis businessmen who sponsored him.

BEFORE BECOMING THE 33RD PRESIDENT of the United States, Harry S. Truman, a native of Missouri, once worked as a Kansas City salesman for AAA (American Automobile Association).

A 15-YEAR-OLD from St. Charles, who has had heart problems since birth, served as an inspirational co-chairman of the American HeartWalk in 2000, which raised money for the American Heart Association. More than 1,600 people participated in the fundraiser.

There are lots of fun and games at Kansas City's annual Pumpkin Patch at the Crowne Center Plaza. • • • •

1965 The Gateway Arch in St. Louis is completed. The 630-foot (192-meter) steel arch is the nation's tallest man-made monument.

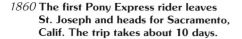

1860 The first Pony Express rider leaves St. Joseph and heads for Sacramento, Calif. The trip takes about 10 days.

1904 About 20 million people attend the St. Louis World's Fair to celebrate the 100th anniversary of the Louisiana Purchase in 1803.

1998 St. Louis Cardinal Mark McGwire hits 70 home runs in a regular season, a record that stands until 2001.

Montana

FRESH FACTS

NAME From the Spanish word "montana," meaning "mountainous."

ABBREVIATION Mont.

CAPITAL Helena

NICKNAME Treasure State (also, Big Sky Country)

AREA 147,046 square miles (380,848 square kilometers)

POPULATION 902,195

STATEHOOD Nov. 8, 1889 (41st state)

HIGHEST POINT Granite Peak (12,799 feet; 3,901 meters)

LOWEST POINT Kootenai River (1,800 feet; 549 meters)

INDUSTRIES Food products, lumber and wood products, mining, natural gas, oil, printed materials, tourism

AGRICULTURE Barley, cattle, hay, oats, sugar beets, wheat

MOTTO Gold and silver.

FLAG The state seal in the center shows Montana's mountains and a rising sun. The miner's pick and shovel and the farmer's plow honor the work of pioneers. The state motto appears in Spanish. Before it was adopted in 1905, the flag was carried by the Montana Volunteers in the Spanish-American War of 1898.

BIRD The **Western meadowlark** was first described in the journal of explorers Meriwether Lewis and William Clark. They saw the bird often on their voyage up the Missouri River and heard its "curious notes," which are flute-like. The songbird was adopted in 1931.

FLOWER The pink, daisy-like flowers of the **bitterroot** grow close to the ground on mountain slopes. Bitterroot is also the name of a mountain range, river, valley, and tunnel in Montana. The plant was adopted in 1895.

TREE The **Ponderosa pine,** adopted in 1949, is a tall, straight tree whose wood was used for dugout canoes, furniture, and homes. Its resin was used for waterproofing and ointments.

SONG "Montana" (words by Charles C. Cohen; music by Joseph E. Howard)

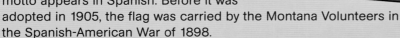

AAA GEMS:
Selected Must-See Points of Interest

GLACIER NATIONAL PARK – Drive up one of the world's most scenic routes, Going-to-the-Sun Road, in this Rocky Mountain park. The 52-mile (83-kilometer) road climbs as high as 6,680 feet (2,036 meters) and crosses the Continental Divide. The park is home to grizzly bears, wolves, mountain lions, 200 kinds of birds, 50 glaciers, waterfalls, and more than 200 lakes and streams.

LAST CHANCE TOUR TRAIN (Helena) – A one-hour train ride takes you on a trip through the capital city that began as a gold mining town. You will see highlights of Helena's past and present.

LEWIS AND CLARK CAVERNS STATE PARK (Cardwell) – A limestone cavern with vaulted rooms, passageways, and multi-colored formations make this one of the nation's most beautiful caves to visit.

LITTLE BIGHORN BATTLEFIELD NATIONAL MONUMENT (southeast of Hardin) – A national cemetery, monuments, and memorials commemorate "Custer's Last Stand." Lt. Col. George Custer and his men of the Seventh Cavalry were defeated here by Sioux and Cheyenne warriors. A museum with maps, dioramas, and photographs tell the story. An audiotape for a car tour of the battlefield is available.

VIRGINIA CITY – Thousands of miners came here after gold was discovered in 1863. Visit restored buildings, including the state's first newspaper office, a pharmacy, a saloon, and general stores. You can also pan for gold, fish, and hunt.

TIMELINE

1743 The Verendrye brothers, French fur traders, explore the region.

1807 American fur trader Manuel Lisa establishes the first trading post at the mouth of the Bighorn River.

1805 Meriwether Lewis and William Clark sail on the Missouri River on their way west.

1862 Gold is found at Grasshopper Creek, and Montana's gold rush begins.

1866 The first longhorn cattle herd arrives from Texas.

1876 Sioux and Cheyenne Indians defeat Lt. Col. George Armstrong Custer's troops at the Battle of Little Bighorn.

Visitors to Montana's Missouri River Country can relive the excitement of the frontier by taking part in a wagon train.

The Blackfeet Indian Nation's reservation is just outside beautiful Glacier National Park.

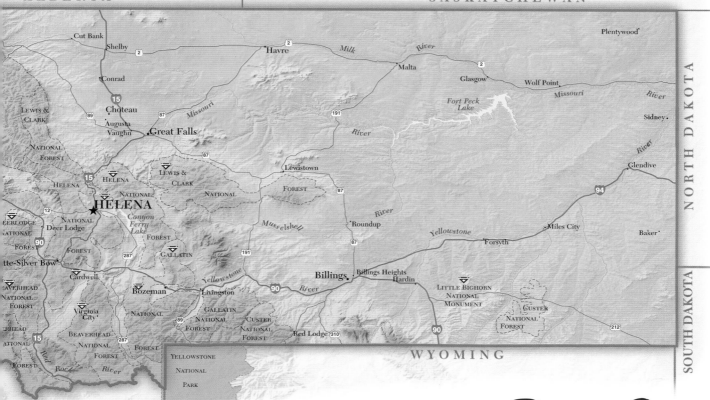

CANADA

ALBERTA · SASKATCHEWAN

Cut Bank · Shelby · Plentywood

Havre · Milk · River

Malta · Glasgow · Wolf Point · Missouri · River · Sidney

Conrad

Choteau · Missouri · Fort Peck Lake

Augusta · Vaughn · Great Falls

LEWIS & CLARK · NATIONAL FOREST

Lewistown · Glendive

HELENA · LEWIS & CLARK NATIONAL FOREST

★ HELENA · NATIONAL FOREST · Canyon Ferry Lake

Deer Lodge · Musselshell River · Roundup · Yellowstone · Miles City · Baker

Butte-Silver Bow · GALLATIN · Forsyth

Cardwell · Bozeman · Livingston · Billings · Billings Heights · Hardin · LITTLE BIGHORN NATIONAL MONUMENT · CUSTER NATIONAL FOREST

BEAVERHEAD NATIONAL FOREST · Virginia City · GALLATIN NATIONAL FOREST · CUSTER NATIONAL FOREST · Red Lodge

NORTH DAKOTA · SOUTH DAKOTA

YELLOWSTONE NATIONAL PARK

WYOMING

Augusta's annual American Legion Rodeo is the largest single-day rodeo in Montana.

Inside Scoop

THE CONTINENTAL DIVIDE cuts through Montana. Rivers to the west of the Divide flow into the Pacific Ocean, and rivers to the east flow into Atlantic Ocean. Raindrops that fall into neighboring Montana rivers end up thousands of miles apart.

GIANT SPRINGS in Great Falls is among the world's largest springs. Each day some 390 million gallons (1.5 billion liters) of water bubble out of the earth.

MINERS ARRIVING in present-day Helena in 1864 believed they had reached their "last chance" to find gold. They did strike it rich, and the city's main street was named Last Chance Gulch.

SWARMS of grasshoppers were trapped long ago in ice. They can still be seen in Grasshopper Glacier near Granite Peak.

MORE GRIZZLY BEARS live in Montana than in any other of the 48 lower states.

A 13-YEAR-OLD from Sidney wrote three poetry books and donated the money she earned from selling them to children's charities.

1910 The U.S. Congress creates Glacier National Park.

1877 Chief Joseph of the Nez Perce tribe surrenders to government troops, ending Montana's Indian wars.

1917 Jeannette Rankin becomes the first woman elected to the U.S. House of Representatives.

1951 Oil is discovered in Williston Basin, and the first wells begin production.

1978 At Egg Mountain near Choteau, John Horner unearths a colony of dinosaur nests. They hold hundreds of eggs and bones of baby dinosaurs.

1989 A two-pound (907-gram) gold nugget, the largest found in 80 years, is discovered south of Butte.

Nebraska

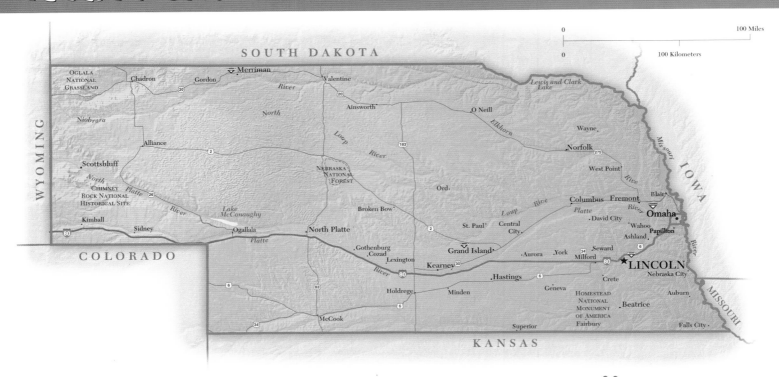

SOUTH DAKOTA

WYOMING

COLORADO

KANSAS

IOWA

MISSOURI

Oglala National Grassland · Chadron · Gordon · Merriman · Valentine
Niobrara River · Ainsworth · O Neill · Lewis and Clark Lake
Alliance · North · Wayne · Norfolk · West Point
Scottsbluff · Loup River · Nebraska National Forest · Ord · Columbus · Fremont · Blair
Chimney Rock National Historical Site · Platte River · Lake McConaughy · Broken Bow · St. Paul · Central City · David City · Omaha
Kimball · Sidney · Ogallala · North Platte · Platte · Grand Island · Aurora · York · Seward · Milford · Wahoo · Ashland · Papillion
Gothenburg · Cozad · Lexington · Kearney · LINCOLN · Nebraska City
Holdrege · Minden · Hastings · Geneva · Crete · Homestead National Monument of America · Auburn
McCook · Superior · Fairbury · Beatrice · Falls City

AAA GEMS:
Selected Must-See Points of Interest

ARTHUR BOWRING SANDHILLS RANCH STATE HISTORICAL PARK (Merriman) – Visitors to this huge working cattle ranch and living-history museum can see ranching firsthand. A film describes the life of a rancher, exhibits offer a history of the area, and a tour of the house is available.

OMAHA'S HENRY DOORLY ZOO – Among the 2,500 animals here are the rare white tiger and snow leopard. Don't miss the aquarium and the Lied jungle, the world's largest indoor rain forest, where monkeys, reptiles, and birds live among waterfalls and lush plants.

STUHR MUSEUM OF THE PRAIRIE PIONEER (Grand Island) – If you want to know what an 1860s railroad town was like, this is the place to visit. Sixty buildings were moved here. A film tells you about the site, and the museum offers exhibits about pioneer life.

UNIVERSITY OF NEBRASKA STATE MUSEUM (Lincoln) – See the largest mammoth fossil ever found as well as bones of the huge woolly mammoths, a wildlife diorama you can walk through, Omaha and Sioux Indian artifacts, and the Gallery of Ancient Life.

One of Nebraska's most unusual landmarks is Carhenge, just north of Alliance. Modeled after Stonehenge, England's ancient circle of stones believed to chart the movement of the sun and moon, Carhenge is built entirely from old automobiles.

Chimney Rock is a famous Nebraska landmark that rises about 500 feet (152 meters) above the surrounding flat plains. That's about the height of a 50-story building.

TIMELINE

1682 Explorer René-Robert Cavelier, Sieur de la Salle, claims the region for France.

1854 The Kansas-Nebraska Act makes Nebraska a territory.

1803 The United States buys Nebraska land from France as part of the Louisiana Purchase.

1843 Pioneers on the Oregon Trail begin to pass through Nebraska.

1862 The Homestead Act of the United States offers public land free to settlers if they live on it for five years. Daniel Freeman of Beatrice gets the first parcel of land.

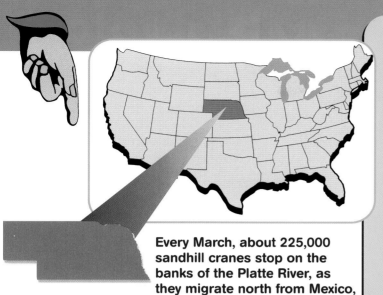

Every March, about 225,000 sandhill cranes stop on the banks of the Platte River, as they migrate north from Mexico, New Mexico, and Texas toward Alaska and Siberia.

FRESH FACTS

NAME Based on the Oto Indian word "nebrathka," which means "flat water" and refers to the Platte River that flows through the state.

ABBREVIATION Neb.

CAPITAL Lincoln

NICKNAME Cornhusker State

AREA 77,354 square miles (200,346 square kilometers)

POPULATION 1,711,263

STATEHOOD March 1, 1867 (37th state)

HIGHEST POINT Kimball County (5,426 feet; 1,654 meters)

LOWEST POINT Richardson County (840 feet; 256 meters)

INDUSTRIES Chemicals, electrical and electronic equipment, food products, machinery, metal products, printing, transportation equipment

AGRICULTURE Cattle, chickens, corn, hay, hogs, sorghum, soybeans, wheat

MOTTO Equality before the law.

FLAG In the center of the flag, which was adopted in 1925, is the state seal. It shows a blacksmith, wheat, and a cabin as reminders of the state's pioneer days. A steamboat and train represent transportation. The state motto appears over the Rocky Mountains in the background.

BIRD The **Western meadowlark** lives on the open plains and builds its nest on the ground near clumps of grass. Its song is loud and rapid. It became the official bird in 1929.

FLOWER The **goldenrod,** adopted in 1895, grows alongside roads and in fields and prairies throughout the state. Many people mistakenly blame it for causing hay fever and other allergies, but its pollen is too heavy to be carried by the wind.

TREE Pioneers planted quick-growing **cottonwoods** because they are good shade trees, they slow erosion at riverbanks, and they serve as windbreaks during storms. The cottonwood was adopted in 1972.

SONG "Beautiful Nebraska" (words and music by Jim Fras)

Inside Scoop

NEBRASKA'S PIONEERS built their houses from blocks of sod, or tough ground, because of the lack of trees on the Plains. The houses were called "soddies," and the blocks were nicknamed "Nebraska marble."

AK-SAR-BEN, which is Nebraska spelled backward, is the name of an aquarium, a coliseum, a rodeo, a former racetrack, and a group of businessmen, among others.

AT THE NATIONAL MUSEUM of Roller Skating in Lincoln, exhibits tell the story of the sport from its beginning in 1819 to the present.

AN ELLSWORTH TEEN started his own consulting and Web-design company while still in high school. He received several entrepreneurial awards, and Nebraska named an annual award after him. The award will be given to a youth who shows "a strong commitment to his community and state."

1872 The nation's first Arbor Day is held in Nebraska City. One million trees are planted on the dusty plains.

1874–77 Huge swarms of grasshoppers invade the state and devastate crops.

1882 Buffalo Bill Cody hosts the first Wild West Show in North Platte.

1917 Father Edward Flanagan starts a home called Boys Town in Omaha for boys who are homeless or in trouble. Today, it is called Girls and Boys Town and has grown into a community with campuses in various states.

1986 The race for governor is the first in the nation in which both candidates are women.

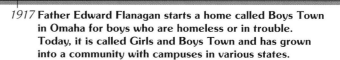

Nevada

AAA GEMS:
Selected Must-See Points of Interest

FLEISCHMANN PLANETARIUM (Reno) – Realistic images projected on the domed screen take viewers on a trip to the stars.

GREAT BASIN NATIONAL PARK – Sightseers can travel upward from the desert floor with its cacti and jackrabbits to thick mountain forests and end high up at a small glacier.

LAKE MEAD NATIONAL RECREATION AREA – Three different types of desert ecosystems meet in this year-round park. Visitors can fish, do water sports, and see wildlife. Take a "hard-hat" tour behind the scenes for a close-up look at the inner workings of the Hoover Dam.

LEHMAN CAVES (Great Basin National Park) – Take a guided tour through colorful marble and limestone passageways at this cave at Wheeler Peak.

NATIONAL AUTOMOBILE MUSEUM (Reno) – Many of the cars displayed here were used in movies. Check out the multimedia presentation, antique clothing, and re-created street scenes.

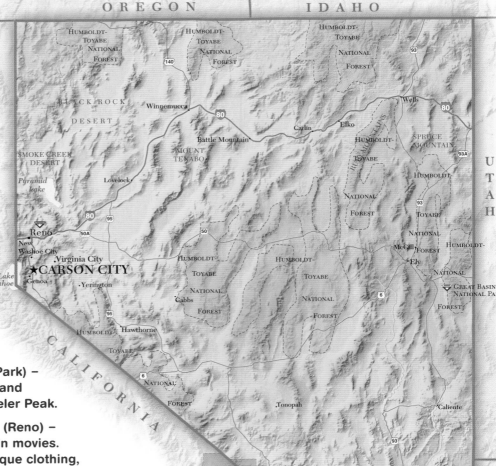

Look closely and you'll see a cow having a close encounter with this UFO along Nevada's Highway 375. Believe it or not, Nevada really did rename the road "the Extraterrestrial Highway" in 1996.

Nevada's rugged, wide-open spaces make the state perfect for hang-gliding fans.

TIMELINE

1826–27 Explorer Jedediah Smith and his group pass through Nevada on their way west to California.

1843–45 Lt. John C. Fremont explores the Great Basin and the Sierra Nevada and provides accurate maps of the region.

1848 Mexico surrenders Nevada land to the United States under the Treaty of Guadeloupe Hidalgo.

1849 Mormon Station, now named Genoa, becomes the state's first permanent white settlement.

1900 New sources of silver, gold, and copper are discovered.

1859 Miners near present-day Reno discover the Comstock Lode, a rich source of gold and silver that lures many people to the area.

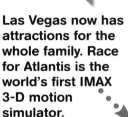

Las Vegas now has attractions for the whole family. Race for Atlantis is the world's first IMAX 3-D motion simulator.

Inside Scoop

NEVADA gets the least amount of rain of any state in the country.

THE GUINNESS World Records Museum is located in Las Vegas.

A JET-POWERED CAR went faster than the speed of sound at Black Rock Desert in 1997. Driven by Andy Green, a British air force pilot, the car set a land-speed record.

LAKE MEAD, formed by Hoover Dam, is one of the world's largest artificially created lakes.

A 13-YEAR-OLD was the youngest (and the only teen) player to reach the finals in the National Monopoly Game Championship held in Las Vegas in 1999.

FRESH FACTS

NAME From the Spanish word "nevada," meaning "snow" or "snowy," describing the Sierra Nevada.

ABBREVIATION Nev.

CAPITAL Carson City

NICKNAME Sagebrush State (also, Battle Born State and Silver State)

AREA 110,561 square miles (286,352 square kilometers)

POPULATION 1,998,257

STATEHOOD Oct. 31, 1864 (36th state)

HIGHEST POINT Boundary Peak, White Mountains (13,140 feet; 4,005 meters)

LOWEST POINT Colorado River (470 feet; 143 meters)

INDUSTRIES Aerospace products, chemicals, food products, gambling, gold and silver mining, plastics, printing and publishing, tourism, trade

AGRICULTURE Alfalfa seed, cattle ranching, dairy cows, hay, potatoes

MOTTO All for our country.

FLAG The five-point star in the upper-left corner represents silver, the state mineral. Above it, "Battle Born" refers to Nevada joining the Union during the Civil War. Two sprays of sagebrush, the state flower, appear on the sides. The flag was adopted in 1929.

BIRD Adopted in 1967, the **mountain bluebird** lives high up in western mountain forests but flies down to the desert in winter to look for food.

FLOWER Sagebrush, a sweet-smelling, silvery-green bush, blooms with small yellow and white flowers. It grows abundantly on Nevada's dry plains. American Indians used its wood to weave mats. It was adopted in 1967.

TREE Nevada has two state trees. The **single-leaf piñon** was adopted in 1953, and the **bristlecone pine** was adopted in 1987. Bristlecones are known for their long lives: some bristlecones are 4,000 years old.

SONG "Home Means Nevada" (words and music by Mrs. Bertha Raffetto)

single-leaf piñon

bristlecone pine

1936 The Hoover Dam is completed, providing water and electrical power to California and the Southwest.

1931 Gambling is legalized by the state legislature. Nevada's population booms as Las Vegas is built.

1980 New conservation laws are passed by the state legislature to protect Lake Tahoe.

1986 Great Basin National Park, the first national park in the state, is established.

1996 The new Las Vegas Motor Speedway hosts its first NASCAR race.

AAA GEMS:
Selected Must-See Points of Interest

CANTERBURY SHAKER VILLAGE – Tour the 25 restored buildings of this Shaker village and watch crafts people make such traditional Shaker products as brooms, furniture, and woven fabrics. Check out the herb garden, and the ponds the Shakers designed to maximize water usage more than 200 years ago.

FRANCONIA NOTCH – This gap between two mountain ranges offers several scenic adventures: a ride up on the Cannon Mountain Aerial Tramway for a spectacular view; a walk along the boardwalk at The Flume, a gorge with waterfalls and glacial boulders; and a view of The Profile, a natural stone formation that looks like its name: Old Man of the Mountain.

THE CURRIER GALLERY OF ART (Manchester) – Housed in a building that looks like a palace, the museum's collection includes works by such famous artists as Winslow Homer, Claude Monet, Pablo Picasso, Andrew Wyeth, and Georgia O'Keeffe. New Hampshire artists are also featured.

WHITE MOUNTAINS AND WHITE MOUNTAIN NATIONAL FOREST – The highest mountain peaks in the Northeast are located here in the President Range, including Mounts Washington, Adams, Jefferson, Monroe, and Madison. Ski in the winter. Hike on the Appalachian Trail, fish, camp out, and enjoy some of nature's best scenery in warmer weather.

Cathedral Ledge in the White Mountains attracts rock climbers from around the world.

Participants in New Hampshire's annual Wildman Biathlon run 6.2 miles (10 kilometers), bike 22.3 miles (36 kilometers), then run uphill 3 miles (5 kilometers)!

TIMELINE

1603 Martin Pring, an English sea captain, is the first European to explore New Hampshire.

1641 New Hampshire becomes part of Massachusetts.

1776 New Hampshire is the first colony to adopt a provisional constitution and declare independence from England.

1623 The first permanent European settlements are established at what is now Dover and Rye.

1680 England makes New Hampshire its own colony, separate from Massachusetts.

1769 Dartmouth College is founded in Hanover.

1852 Franklin Pierce, born in Hillsboro, is elected 14th president of the United States.

FRESH FACTS

NAME For the county of Hampshire in England.

ABBREVIATION N.H.

CAPITAL Concord

NICKNAME Granite State

AREA 9,350 square miles (24,216 square kilometers)

POPULATION 1,235,786

STATEHOOD June 21, 1788 (9th state)

HIGHEST POINT Mount Washington (6,288 feet; 1,917 meters)

LOWEST POINT Sea level

INDUSTRIES Computers, electrical and electronic equipment, furniture, machinery, metal products, paper, plastic products, rubber products, tourism, trade

AGRICULTURE Dairy products, fruit, hay, maple syrup, vegetables, young plants

MOTTO Live free or die.

FLAG In the center is the state seal surrounded by a wreath of laurel leaves and nine stars, showing that New Hampshire was the ninth state to join the Union. The flag was adopted in 1909.

BIRD The **purple finch**, adopted in 1957, is named for the raspberry-red color of the male. The female is brown on top and white with brown streaks underneath.

FLOWER The **purple lilac** was first brought from England and planted in New Hampshire about 1690. Now it blooms all over the state. It was adopted in 1919.

TREE The **white birch** is named after the color of its bark, which was used by American Indians to build their canoes. This graceful tree was adopted in 1947.

SONG "Old New Hampshire" (words by Dr. John F. Holmes; music by Maurice Hoffman)

Inside Scoop

NEW HAMPSHIRE has the shortest coastline among the New England states. It is 13 miles (21 kilometers) long.

THE COG RAILWAY that chugs up and down Mount Washington was the nation's first. It was built in 1869.

THE FIRST POTATO CROP in the United States was planted in Londonderry in 1719.

NEW HAMPSHIRE'S HOUSE OF REPRESENTATIVES, with 400 members, is the largest state legislative body in the United States.

THE CHRISTA MCAULIFFE PLANETARIUM in Concord is dedicated to the New Hampshire teacher who died aboard the Space Shuttle Challenger when it exploded in 1986.

A 13-YEAR-OLD from Merrimack who has Down Syndrome helped collect 1 million names on a petition to the federal government to release all the money approved for educational programs that help children with disabilities.

Sailing is always popular on Lake Sunapee.

1934 **The strongest winds ever recorded in the nation blow across Mount Washington. At 231 mph (371 kph), the winds are faster than those of most hurricanes and tornadoes.**

1944 **The International Monetary Conference at Bretton Woods leads to the formation of the World Bank and the International Monetary Fund.**

1952 **New Hampshire holds the first U.S. presidential primary.**

1961 **Alan B. Shepard Jr., from East Derry, is the first American to blast into space. His flight lasts 15 minutes.**

1964 **New Hampshire holds the nation's first legal lottery sponsored by a state since 1894.**

New Jersey

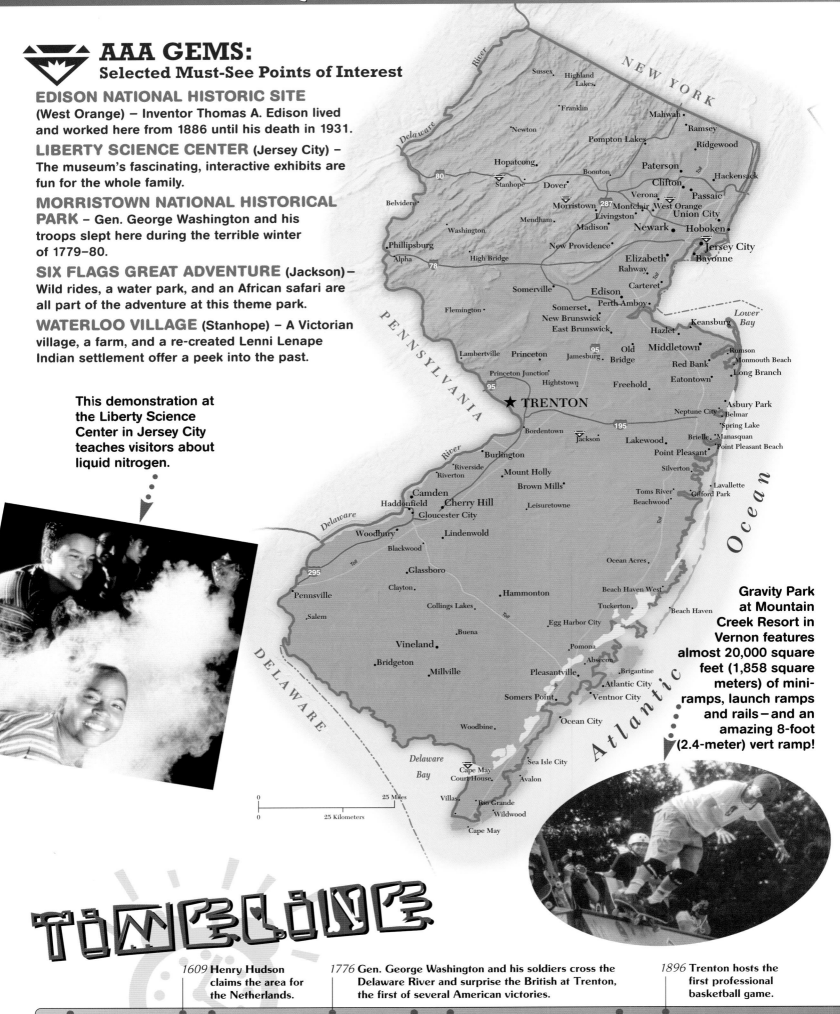

◆ AAA GEMS:
Selected Must-See Points of Interest

EDISON NATIONAL HISTORIC SITE
(West Orange) – Inventor Thomas A. Edison lived and worked here from 1886 until his death in 1931.

LIBERTY SCIENCE CENTER (Jersey City) – The museum's fascinating, interactive exhibits are fun for the whole family.

MORRISTOWN NATIONAL HISTORICAL PARK – Gen. George Washington and his troops slept here during the terrible winter of 1779–80.

SIX FLAGS GREAT ADVENTURE (Jackson) – Wild rides, a water park, and an African safari are all part of the adventure at this theme park.

WATERLOO VILLAGE (Stanhope) – A Victorian village, a farm, and a re-created Lenni Lenape Indian settlement offer a peek into the past.

This demonstration at the Liberty Science Center in Jersey City teaches visitors about liquid nitrogen.

Gravity Park at Mountain Creek Resort in Vernon features almost 20,000 square feet (1,858 square meters) of mini-ramps, launch ramps and rails—and an amazing 8-foot (2.4-meter) vert ramp!

TIMELINE

1609 Henry Hudson claims the area for the Netherlands.

1776 Gen. George Washington and his soldiers cross the Delaware River and surprise the British at Trenton, the first of several American victories.

1896 Trenton hosts the first professional basketball game.

1524 Giovanni da Verrazano explores the coast of New Jersey.

1664 England takes over New Netherland.

Samuel Morse **1837** invents the telegraph in Morristown.

1846 The first organized baseball game is played at Elysian Field in Hoboken on June 19.

1879 Thomas A. Edison invents the electric light bulb in Menlo Park.

FRESH FACTS

NAME After Jersey, a British island in the English Channel.

ABBREVIATION N.J.

CAPITAL Trenton

NICKNAME Garden State

AREA 8,721 square miles (22,587 square kilometers)

POPULATION 8,414,350

STATEHOOD Dec. 18, 1787 (3rd state)

HIGHEST POINT High Point Mountain
(1,801 feet; 549 meters)

LOWEST POINT Sea level

INDUSTRIES Biotechnology, chemical production, electronic equipment, food processing, pharmaceuticals, printing, publishing, telecommunications, tourism

AGRICULTURE Fruits, horses, milk, nuts, vegetables, young plants

MOTTO Liberty and prosperity.

FLAG At the center is the state's coat of arms, with the goddess of liberty to the left and the goddess of agriculture to the right. The three plows symbolize agriculture. The background color represents the uniforms of Gen. George Washington's New Jersey Continental Line troops. The flag was adopted in 1896.

BIRD The **Eastern (American) goldfinch,** adopted in 1935, is a common songbird in the New Jersey–New York region.

FLOWER The **purple violet** was officially adopted in 1971 after the state's garden clubs claimed that the 1913 adoption of the flower was not legal.

TREE The **red oak** was adopted as the state's tree in 1950. Its acorns were an important food source for American Indians.

SONG None

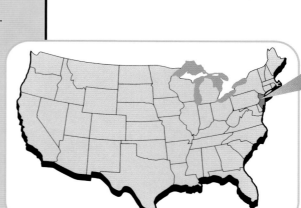

Great beaches help make tourism New Jersey's second largest industry.

Inside Scoop

IN THE BOARD GAME MONOPOLY®, the properties were named after streets in Atlantic City.

TWO-THIRDS OF THE WORLD'S EGGPLANT is grown in New Jersey.

THE FIRST DINOSAUR SKELETON in North America was discovered in Haddonfield in 1858.

RUTGERS BEAT PRINCETON in the first college football game, played in 1869 in New Brunswick.

EVERY SPRING, three teen siblings from Princeton round up support and participants for the annual cystic fibrosis walk. They have seen their efforts pay off with new medicines for their younger brother, who was born with the disease.

1921 **The first Miss America pageant is held in Atlantic City.**

1940 **The solid-body electric guitar is invented by Les Paul of Mahwah.**

The Little League team from *1998* **Toms River wins the Little League World Series.**

1903 **The first commercially successful movie, "The Great Train Robbery," is shot in New Jersey. It is 10 minutes long.**

The U.S. Supreme Court rules that Ellis *1998* **Island is part of New Jersey.**

New Mexico

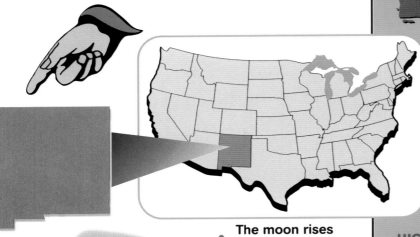

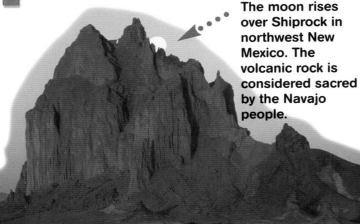

The moon rises over Shiprock in northwest New Mexico. The volcanic rock is considered sacred by the Navajo people.

FRESH FACTS

NAME Named by Spanish explorers for lands north of the Rio Grande in honor of Mexico, the land from which they came.

ABBREVIATION N.M.

CAPITAL Santa Fe

NICKNAME Land of Enchantment

AREA 121,589 square miles (314,916 square kilometers)

POPULATION 1,819,046

STATEHOOD Jan. 6, 1912 (47th state)

HIGHEST POINT Wheeler Peak (13,161 feet; 4,011 meters.)

LOWEST POINT Red Bluff Reservoir (2,817 feet; 859 meters)

INDUSTRIES Clothing, electrical equipment, electronics, food products, lumber, machinery, petroleum, printed materials, semiconductors, trade, transportation equipment

AGRICULTURE Cattle, chili peppers, cotton, dairy products, hay, pecans, young plants

MOTTO It grows as it goes.

FLAG The sun in the center is the ancient symbol of the Zia Pueblo Indians and represents the harmony of all things in the universe. The red and yellow rays were the royal colors of Spain at the time the Spanish explorers came to New Mexico. The flag was adopted in 1925.

BIRD The **chaparral** is nicknamed the roadrunner, because it prefers to run rather than fly. When hungry, it can run as fast as 20 mph (32 kph) in search of food. It became the state bird in 1949.

FLOWER Adopted in 1927, the **yucca** is also called soapweed, because American Indians made soap from its roots.

TREE Spanish explorers found that the small nuts of the **piñon tree** were a popular food among America's native people. Street vendors still sell raw or roasted piñon nuts. It was adopted in 1948.

SONG "O, Fair New Mexico" (words and music by Elizabeth Garrett). "Asi Es Nuevo Mejico" (words and music by Amadeo Lucero)

Inside Scoop

THE OLDEST ROAD in the United States is "El Camino Real," the Royal Highway. It follows an old Indian trail that connects Mexico and New Mexico.

THE NORTHWEST CORNER of New Mexico is the only place in the country where four states meet. If you crouch, you can put your right foot in New Mexico, your left foot in Arizona, your left hand in Utah, and your right hand in Colorado.

DURING WORLD WAR II, the United States sent secret messages coded in the Navajo Indian language, which is so unique that other countries could not decipher it.

A 19-YEAR-OLD from Gallup invented corrective goggles that make it easier for dyslexic kids to read.

TIMELINE

1536 Álvar Núñez Cabeza de Vaca, the first European to arrive in present-day New Mexico, claims the area for Spain.

1540–42 Spanish explorer Francisco Vasquez de Coronado, searching for the legendary golden cities of Cibola, leads an expedition through the region.

1609–10 Santa Fe is founded. At 6,590 feet (2,009 meters) in elevation, it is today the nation's highest state capital.

1680 The Pueblo Indians rebel and drive out the Spanish. Twelve years later, the Spanish recapture the area.

1821 William Becknell brings the first wagons with goods to Santa Fe from the northeast and opens the Santa Fe Trail.

1848 The United States wins the Mexican War and gains New Mexico under the Treaty of Guadeloupe Hidalgo.

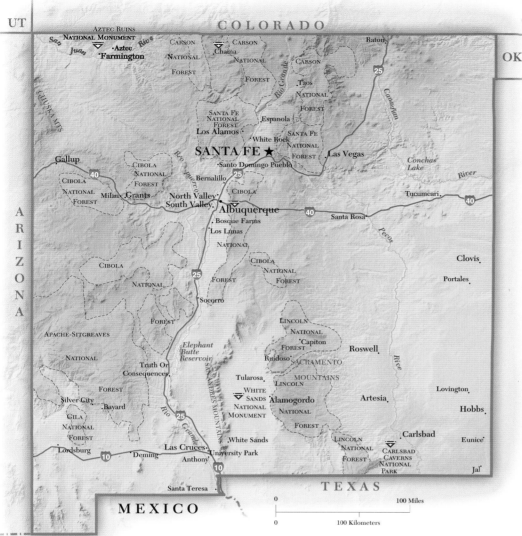

UT

COLORADO

OK

Reports of a crashed UFO (unidentified flying object) at Roswell grabbed the nation's attention in 1947. Some believed that aliens landed there.

ARIZONA

MEXICO

TEXAS

0   100 Miles

0   100 Kilometers

AAA GEMS:
Selected Must-See Points of Interest

AZTEC RUINS NATIONAL MONUMENT – The monument marks one of the largest and best-preserved Anasazi Indian ruins in the Southwest. The original pueblo, or Indian village, had 500 rooms and a great kiva, a round ceremonial room. Early white settlers mistakenly thought the pueblo was the home of the Aztecs of Mexico.

CARLSBAD CAVERNS (Carlsbad Caverns National Park) – Explore underground caves with such names as Whale's Mouth, Christmas Tree, and Frozen Waterfalls that were formed over millions of years. The Big Room is 255 feet (78 meters) high. If you visit at night, you'll witness an incredible sight: thousands of bats flying out of the caverns.

CUMBRES AND TOLTEC SCENIC RAILROAD (Chama) – All aboard this narrow-gauge, coal-burning railroad that travels through spectacular mountain scenery between Chama and Oster, Colo. You may have seen this train in the movie "Indiana Jones and the Last Crusade."

OLD TOWN (Albuquerque) – This small area in modern-day Albuquerque has been preserved to show how the town looked when it was laid out in the early 1700s.

WHITE SANDS NATIONAL MONUMENT (southwest of Alamogordo) – New Mexico's white sand dunes are one of the few landmarks that can be seen from outer space. Drive the 16-mile (25-kilometer) roundtrip route in this white wonderland or climb to the top of the dunes and surf down on a sled.

Albuquerque's first international hot-air balloon festival was held in 1972, and the colorful balloons have floated over the city every October since then.

The burning of Zozobra, or Old Man Gloom, a 50-foot (15-meter) tall puppet, has marked the start of the Fiestas de Santa Fe every year since 1926. It is meant to sweep out hard times and bad luck.

1901 Cowboy Jim White discovers Carlsbad Caverns, which contains the world's largest natural underground room.

1950 Firefighters rescue an orphaned bear cub from a forest fire and name him Smokey Bear after the nation's fire prevention's symbolic bear. The cub becomes the living emblem for fire prevention.

1976 Lovington holds the first World's Greatest Lizard Race on July 4. About 200 lizards of all kinds now compete in this annual event.

1886 Geronimo's surrender ends the fighting between Indians and white settlers in New Mexico.

1945 The United States tests the first atomic bomb at Trinity Site near Alamogordo.

The biggest fire in the state's history forces *2000* 25,000 people, including all residents of Los Alamos, to abandon their homes.

New York

A statue of New York Yankee great Babe Ruth greets visitors at the Baseball Hall of Fame in Cooperstown.

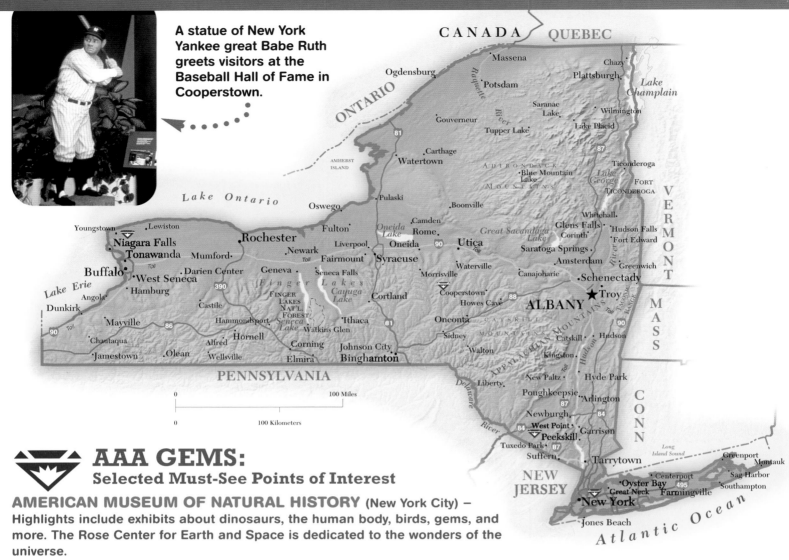

CANADA QUEBEC
ONTARIO
Massena
Ogdensburg
Potsdam
Chazy
Plattsburgh
Lake Champlain
Saranac Lake
Gouverneur
Wilmington
Lake Placid
Carthage
Tupper Lake
Watertown
AMHERST ISLAND
ADIRONDACK MOUNTAINS
Blue Mountain Lake
Ticonderoga
Lake George
FORT TICONDEROGA
VERMONT
Pulaski
Boonville
Lake Ontario
Oswego
Camden
Rome
Whitehall
Glens Falls
Corinth
Hudson Falls
Fort Edward
Youngstown
Lewiston
Fulton
Oneida Lake
Great Sacandaga Lake
Niagara Falls
Tonawanda
Rochester
Newark
Liverpool
Oneida
Utica
Saratoga Springs
Amsterdam
Greenwich
Buffalo
Mumford
Fairmount
Syracuse
Waterville
Canajoharie
Schenectady
West Seneca
Darien Center
Geneva
Seneca Falls
Morrisville
Cooperstown
ALBANY
Troy
MASS
Lake Erie
Hamburg
Finger Lakes
Cayuga Lake
Cortland
Howes Cave
Angola
Castile
FINGER LAKES NAT'L FOREST
Seneca Lake
Ithaca
Oneonta
CATSKILL MOUNTAINS
Catskill
Hudson
Dunkirk
Mayville
Hammondsport
Watkins Glen
Sidney
Walton
Kingston
Chautauqua
Alfred
Hornell
Corning
Johnson City
Liberty
New Paltz
Hyde Park
Jamestown
Olean
Wellsville
Elmira
Binghamton
Poughkeepsie
Arlington
PENNSYLVANIA
Newburgh
West Point
Garrison
0 100 Miles
0 100 Kilometers
Tuxedo Park
Peekskill
Suffern
Long Island Sound
Greenport
Montauk
NEW JERSEY
Oyster Bay
Great Neck
Tarrytown
Centerport
Farmingville
Sag Harbor
Southampton
New York
Atlantic Ocean
Jones Beach

AAA GEMS:
Selected Must-See Points of Interest

AMERICAN MUSEUM OF NATURAL HISTORY (New York City) – Highlights include exhibits about dinosaurs, the human body, birds, gems, and more. The Rose Center for Earth and Space is dedicated to the wonders of the universe.

BRONX ZOO/WILDLIFE CONSERVATION PARK (New York City) – A cable car ride gives a great overview of the zoo where some 4,000 animals live. There's a rain forest, a building for butterflies, another for birds, and a children's zoo.

EMPIRE STATE BUILDING (New York City) – Ride the elevator to the observation deck on the 102nd floor for a panoramic view.

MAID OF THE MIST (Niagara Falls) – Take a boat ride to the front of the Falls or view them from wooden walkways. See a movie about how generators work and another about the daredevils who have challenged the Falls.

NATIONAL BASEBALL HALL OF FAME AND MUSEUM (Cooperstown) – Baseball's legendary heroes are honored at this museum, which traces the history of the sport from its beginnings in the 1800s to the present.

STATUE OF LIBERTY NATIONAL MONUMENT (New York City) – Climb to the top of Lady Liberty, a gift from France in 1884.

UNITED STATES MILITARY ACADEMY (West Point) – Many of America's military heroes attended this school. Its museum covers military history from Revolutionary War days to the present.

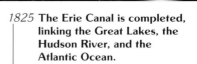

To honor the heroes of the Sept. 11, 2001 tragedy, two huge beams of light glowed over New York City's skies during March and April 2002.

TIMELINE

1524 Giovanni da Verrazano, an Italian navigator, is the first European to enter New York Harbor.

1626 Peter Minuit buys Manhattan Island from resident American Indians for about $24 and establishes the town of New Amsterdam.

1825 The Erie Canal is completed, linking the Great Lakes, the Hudson River, and the Atlantic Ocean.

1609 Samuel Champlain explores northern New York for France; Henry Hudson, sent out by the Netherlands, sails up the Hudson River to Albany. The area is named New Netherland.

1664 The English take New Netherland away from the Dutch and rename it New York.

1789 George Washington is inaugurated as the first president of the United States on the balcony of the Federal Building in New York City.

FRESH FACTS

NAME After the Duke of York and Albany, who was given the land in 1664 by his brother, King Charles II of England.

ABBREVIATION N.Y.

CAPITAL Albany

NICKNAME Empire State

AREA 54,556 square miles (141,299 square kilometers)

POPULATION 18,976,457

STATEHOOD July 26, 1788 (11th state)

HIGHEST POINT Mount Marcy (5,344 feet; 1,629 meters)

LOWEST POINT Sea level

INDUSTRIES Air travel, banking and finance, chemicals, clothing, communications, electronic equipment, machinery, pharmaceuticals, printing and publishing, scientific instruments, tourism, toys

AGRICULTURE Apples, cattle, cherries, chickens, dairy products, grapes, strawberries, vegetables, young plants

MOTTO Ever upward.

FLAG The state's coat of arms shows the figure of Liberty on the left. The crown at her feet symbolizes freedom from England. The figure of Justice on the right holds a set of scales, signifying that everyone is entitled to equal treatment under the law. Above is an eagle atop a globe. The ships in the center represent commerce. The flag was adopted in 1901.

BIRD The **Eastern bluebird** was called blue robin by early settlers because it looks so much like a robin, except for the difference in color. The bird was adopted in 1970.

FLOWER In 1955, all colors and varieties of the **rose** were chosen by the state legislature as the state flower. The rose has been cultivated for many centuries.

TREE In the spring, people collect sweet sap from **sugar maples** to make maple syrup. The tree was adopted in 1956.

SONG None

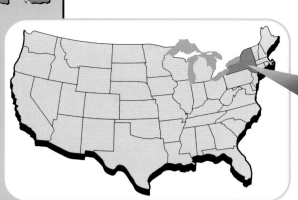

Did you know that Niagara Falls is actually two waterfalls? The larger one, called American Falls, is in New York. It's 10 feet (4 meters) higher than nearby Horseshoe Falls on the Canadian side of the border.

Inside Scoop

EVEN THOUGH Grandma Moses (Anna Moses) of Greenwich did not start to paint until she was in her late 70s, she created about 2,000 landscapes of rural life.

LAKE PLACID has hosted two Winter Olympics (1932 and 1980). Its ski jumps, ice-skating rinks, and bobsled runs serve as training grounds for Olympic hopefuls.

NEW YORK CITY BUILT the nation's longest subway system. If all the tracks were laid end to end, they would reach a distance of 714 miles (1,142 kilometers), almost three times the distance between New York and Washington, D.C.

THE TUXEDO gets its name from Tuxedo Park where it was first introduced in the 1920s by a wealthy man who grew bored with formal dinner clothes.

A 16-YEAR-OLD from New York City paints pictures of celebrities and donates them to organizations that help children. The organizations auction the paintings to raise money for their programs.

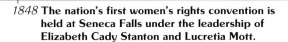

1883 The Brooklyn Bridge, the first suspension bridge to use steel-wire cables, opens.

1848 The nation's first women's rights convention is held at Seneca Falls under the leadership of Elizabeth Cady Stanton and Lucretia Mott.

1923 The New York Yankees play their first game at Yankee Stadium, beating the Boston Red Sox 4-1 on a home run by Babe Ruth.

1952 The United Nations opens its headquarters in New York City.

The Twin Towers of New York City's **2001** World Trade Center collapse when terrorists fly two commercial planes into the buildings, beginning the nation's global war against terrorism.

Sixteen-year-old Sarah **2002** Hughes from Great Neck wins the Olympic gold medal in figure skating.

The Black Mountains, northeast of Asheville, include Mount Mitchell, the tallest mountain east of the Mississippi River.

The Cape Hatteras lighthouse is the tallest in the country. It towers 208 feet (63 meters) above the Atlantic Ocean, about as high as a 20-story building.

AAA GEMS:
Selected Must-See Points of Interest

BATTLESHIP NORTH CAROLINA (Wilmington) — Tour this vessel that won 15 battle stars in World War II. Visit its nine decks, the bridge, the crew's quarters, the gun turrets, and the radio and engine rooms.

CAPE HATTERAS NATIONAL SEASHORE — This area of dunes, beaches, and wetlands on the Outer Banks is a good place to vacation. Swim, fish, bird watch, or climb the 268 steps to the top of the Cape Hatteras lighthouse, which warns ships to stay away from the dangerous Diamond Shoals near the coast.

DISCOVERY PLACE (Charlotte) — Roaring animated dinosaurs are the official greeters at this exciting science center. In addition to the dinosaur exhibit, there's a rain forest, a planetarium, and a space station to explore.

GRANDFATHER MOUNTAIN (Linville) — When seen from the north, the mountain resembles a bearded grandfather gazing toward the sky. Visitors can walk to the summit where, if they dare, they can cross the swinging Mile High suspension bridge that links the mountain's two peaks. Hiking trails give spectacular views of the region.

TWEETSIE RAILROAD (Blowing Rock) — Mock train robbers and Indian attacks lend excitement as you ride on a restored coal-powered train at this Western theme park. Other activities include craft demonstrations, music shows, and a chairlift to a reconstructed mining town.

WRIGHT BROTHERS NATIONAL MEMORIAL (Kitty Hawk) — Visitors can follow markers measuring the distances of the first four airplane flights made by Orville and Wilbur Wright. A replica of the 1903 flier is on display as is the Wright Brothers' reconstructed workshop.

TIMELINE

1524 Giovanni da Verrazano, an Italian navigator working for France, explores the North Carolina coast.

1587 Virginia Dare of Roanoke Island is the first child born to English parents in America.

1775 Under the Mecklenburg Declaration, North Carolina declares its independence from England.

1585 Sir Walter Raleigh establishes North America's first English colony on Roanoke Island.

1650s Virginia colonists establish the first permanent settlement in the Albemarle region.

1718 The greatly feared pirate Edward Teach, better known as Blackbeard, is beheaded by the British on Ocracoke Island. Legend says his ghost still haunts the coast.

FRESH FACTS

NAME Named in honor of England's King Charles I, whose Latin name is Carolus.

ABBREVIATION N.C.

CAPITAL Raleigh

NICKNAME Old North State (also, Tar Heel State)

AREA 52,586 square miles (136,198 square kilometers)

POPULATION 8,049,313

STATEHOOD Nov. 21, 1789 (12th state)

HIGHEST POINT Mount Mitchell (6,684 feet; 2,037 meters)

LOWEST POINT Sea level

INDUSTRIES Chemicals, electrical and electronic equipment, food products, furniture, machinery, textiles, tobacco products, tourism

AGRICULTURE Chickens, corn, cotton, dairy products, hogs, peanuts, soybeans, sweet potatoes, tobacco, young plants

MOTTO To be rather than to seem.

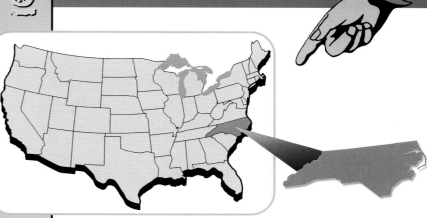

FLAG The two dates above and below the star and the letters N and C are: May 20, 1775, the day the state declared independence from England, and April 12, 1776, the day North Carolinians told their delegates at the Continental Congress to vote for independence. The flag was adopted in 1885.

BIRD The **cardinal** is sometimes called the "winter redbird," because it is the only red bird that remains in North Carolina during the cold and snowy months. It was adopted in 1943.

FLOWER The **dogwood** is a tree flower, and dogwood trees grow throughout North Carolina. The flower was adopted in 1941.

TREE The **pine tree** was adopted in 1963. It is the most common tree in the state and has played an important role in its economy. Before 1900, merchants and shipbuilders depended on this tall tree as a source of lumber, resin, and turpentine.

SONG "The Old North State" (words by William Gaston; music by Mrs. E.E. Randolph)

Benson's annual Mule Days Festival attracts more than 60,000 visitors. In addition to a mule-pulling contest, the weekend features parades, live music, carnival rides, and more.

Inside Scoop

IN 1774, 51 women in Edenton held the Edenton Tea Party, signing a petition that called for a boycott of British goods. It was one of the nation's first protests by women.

THE VENUS FLYTRAP is a plant that grows only in North and South Carolina. It captures insects in its leaves and then devours them.

BUILT BY THE Vanderbilt family, the Biltmore Estate in Asheville contains 250 rooms, including 34 master bedrooms, 43 bathrooms, and 65 fireplaces.

MICHAEL JORDAN, one of the National Basketball Association's greatest players, grew up in Wilmington and played for the University of North Carolina.

A 13-YEAR-OLD volunteer from Topsail Beach helped take care of injured sea turtles. Sea turtles need extra-special care because they are endangered.

1903 At Kitty Hawk, Orville and Wilbur Wright fly the plane they built. The world's first successful airplane flight takes 12 seconds and goes 120 feet (37 meters) in the air.

1960 To protest segregation, four African-American students begin the "sit-in" movement at a lunch counter in Greensboro. They refuse to leave until they are served.

1898 Pepsi-Cola® is first created and served in New Bern. Advertisements say it helps aid digestion.

1914 Babe Ruth's first professional home run is hit during spring training at Fayetteville on March 7.

The Cape Hatteras lighthouse is successfully relocated nearly 3,000 feet (914 meters) from the shore to save it from the encroaching waters of the Atlantic Ocean. *1999*

North Dakota

FRESH FACTS

NAME From the Sioux Indian word "dakota," meaning "friend."

ABBREVIATION N.D.

CAPITAL Bismarck

NICKNAME Peace Garden State (also Flickertail State and Rough Rider State)

AREA 70,074 square miles (183,123 square kilometers)

POPULATION 642,200

STATEHOOD Nov. 2, 1889 (39th state)

HIGHEST POINT White Butte (3,506 feet; 1,069 meters)

LOWEST POINT Red River, Pembina County (750 feet; 229 meters)

INDUSTRIES Farm equipment, food products, machinery, mining, printed materials, telecommunications, tourism, transportation equipment

AGRICULTURE Barley, cattle, flaxseed, hay, milk, oats, potatoes, sugar beets, sunflower seeds, wheat

MOTTO Liberty and union, now and forever, one and inseparable.

FLAG The eagle holds an olive branch for peace in one claw and a bundle of arrows for power in war in the other. On the ribbon in the eagle's beak is written "One nation made up of many states." The fan-shaped design above the eagle with 13 stars and rays of the sun represent the birth of a new nation. The flag was adopted in 1911.

BIRD Named as the official bird in 1947, the **Western meadowlark** usually sings five to seven notes. It is one of more than 300 kinds of birds that live in the state.

FLOWER The wild **prairie rose,** adopted in 1907, adds color to fields and roadsides when it begins to bloom in June. Oils from roses are used in perfumes and medicines.

TREE The graceful **American elm,** adopted in 1947, grows throughout North Dakota. American Indians used its bark for canoes. It can reach a height of 120 feet (37 meters).

SONG "North Dakota Hymn" (words by James W. Foley; music by Dr. C. S. Putnam)

▶ The skeleton of a humongous mosasaur (a prehistoric ocean lizard nicknamed the "Tyrannosaurus Rex of the Sea") hangs from the ceiling at the North Dakota Heritage Center in Bismarck. It is 23 feet (7 meters) long and was discovered in 1995 in Cooperstown.

TIMELINE

1738 **French fur trader Pierre Gaultier de Varennes, Sieur de La Verendrye is the first European to visit the area.**

1812 **Canadian traders establish the first permanent settlement at Pembina.**

1875 **Huge tracts of land, known as bonanza farms, attract many settlers to the Red River Valley.**

1804–05 **The Lewis and Clark expedition spends the winter at Fort Mandan.**

1837 **A smallpox epidemic kills many American Indians.**

1861 **The U.S. Congress creates the Dakota Territory. It is opened to homesteaders two years later.**

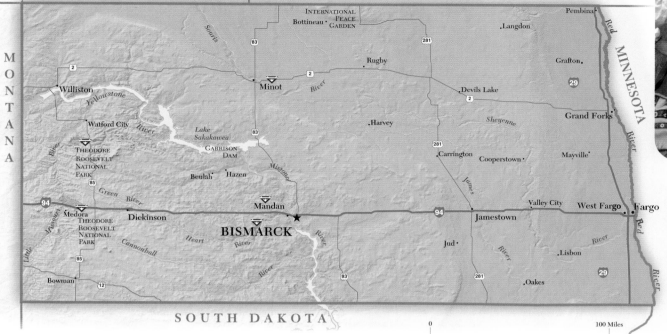

CANADA

SASKATCHEWAN · MANITOBA

MONTANA · MINNESOTA · SOUTH DAKOTA

A highlight of the annual Ukrainian Festival in Dickinson is the performance of the Stepovi Dity Dancers.

100 Miles
100 Kilometers

The Badlands of North and South Dakota were carved by a huge river that dried up millions of years ago.

 AAA GEMS:
Selected Must-See Points of Interest

FORT ABRAHAM LINCOLN STATE PARK (Mandan) – Lt. Col. George Custer led his troops from this fort to the Battle of Little Bighorn in 1876. Visit the commissary, granary, barracks, and the house where Custer lived. A museum displays military and Native American objects (a Mandan Indian village had been on the site) as well as items from the days of fur traders, railroaders, and homesteaders.

ROOSEVELT PARK AND ZOO (Minot) – The zoo features animals from around the world in a park with flower gardens, duck ponds, a footbridge, a 20-horse carousel, a swimming pool, and water slide. You can board the Magic City Express, a small train and take a ride through the park.

STATE CAPITOL (Bismarck) – This 19-story building is often called the "Skyscraper of the Prairie," and its observation deck on the 18th floor offers panoramic views of the city. The Roughrider Gallery has portraits of famous North Dakotans. There's a statue of Sasakawea (Sacajawea), the young Shoshone woman who was the interpreter for the Lewis and Clark expedition.

THEODORE ROOSEVELT NATIONAL PARK (Medora) – This park is home to American bison, pronghorn antelopes, deer, coyotes, prairie dogs, and other wildlife. Rangers lead daily programs during the summer.

Inside Scoop

THE TWO DAKOTAS were admitted to the Union on the same day. When President Benjamin Harrison signed the statehood bills, he shuffled the papers so that no one knew which is the 39th and 40th states. Officially, North Dakota is first, because its name comes first in the alphabet.

THE GEOGRAPHIC CENTER of the North American continent is near Rugby, 45 miles (72 kilometers) south of the Canadian border.

THE INTERNATIONAL GATEWAY Cities Golf Club is located in both Canada and the United States. A golfer can play eight holes in Saskatchewan, Canada, then cross the border for the final hole in North Dakota.

THE UNITED TRIBES International Powwow, featuring more than 1,500 dancers and drummers from 70 tribes, is held every fall in Bismarck.

A 14-YEAR-OLD from Jud works with puppies that are trained to help people who have disabilities.

1956 The first generator begins to make electricity at Garrison Dam on the Missouri River. The dam is completed four years later.

1883 Former U.S. President Ulysses S. Grant lays the first cornerstone of the Capitol building in Bismarck, and future U.S. President Theodore Roosevelt starts ranching near Medora.

1932 The International Peace Garden that lies partly in North Dakota and partly in Canada honors the peace and friendship between Canada and the United States.

North Dakota is rated by the 1999 Children's Rights Council as one of the top 10 best states in which to raise children.

FRESH FACTS

NAME From the Iroquois word "oheo," meaning "large, or beautiful, river," which described the Ohio River.

ABBREVIATION None

CAPITAL Columbus

NICKNAME Buckeye State

AREA 44,825 square miles (116,096 square kilometers)

POPULATION 11,353,140

STATEHOOD March 1, 1803 (17th state)

HIGHEST POINT Campbell Hill (1,550 feet; 472 meters)

LOWEST POINT Ohio River, Hamilton County (433 feet; 132 meters)

INDUSTRIES Machinery, metal products, rubber products, trade, transportation equipment

AGRICULTURE Cattle, chemicals, chickens, corn, dairy products, food products, hay, hogs, soybeans, wheat, young plants

MOTTO With God, all things are possible.

FLAG Adopted in 1902, it's the only state flag that is not a rectangle. The wide-V at the end is called a swallowtail point. The 17 stars show Ohio as the 17th state to join the Union. The white circle stands for the letter "O" in Ohio, and the red center represents the nut of the buckeye, Ohio's state tree.

BIRD The **cardinal** used to live only in warmer southern states, but now lives in Ohio and other northern states as well. Only the male cardinal is bright red. The female is brown with red on her wings. The cardinal was adopted in 1933.

FLOWER The **scarlet carnation** was adopted in 1904 to honor Ohio-born William McKinley, the 25th president of the United States, who wore a red carnation in his buttonhole for good luck.

TREE The **buckeye tree,** adopted in 1953, got its name from Ohio's American Indians. They thought the tree's large, brown seeds resembled the eyes of a buck, a male deer. The state gets its nickname from this tree, and famous people from Ohio are sometimes called Buckeyes.

SONG "Beautiful Ohio" (words by Ballard MacDonald; music by Mary Earl; special lyrics by Wilbert B. White)

Inside Scoop

SEVEN U.S. PRESIDENTS have hailed from Ohio: James A. Garfield, Ulysses S. Grant, Rutherford B. Hayes, Warren G. Harding, Benjamin Harrison, William McKinley, and William H. Taft.

ROCK 'N' ROLL got its name from Alan Freed when he was starting out as a disc jockey in Cleveland in the 1950s.

HUNDREDS OF BUZZARDS stop in Hinckley every year on the third weekend in March on their way north for the summer.

AWARD-WINNING film director Steven Spielberg was born in Cincinnati. Among his films are "E.T.: The Extra-Terrestrial" and "Raiders of the Lost Ark."

AN 18-YEAR-OLD from Minster became the youngest person elected to the Ohio State Legislature in 2000.

TIMELINE

1763 **France surrenders Ohio land to England under the Treaty of Paris, ending the French and Indian War.**

1788 **Marietta becomes the first permanent settlement in Ohio.**

1832 **The Ohio and Erie Canal opens, connecting Cleveland on Lake Erie to Portsmouth on the Ohio River, greatly increasing trade.**

1833 **The nation's first coeducational college, Oberlin College, is founded in Oberlin.**

1902 **The Ingalls Building, the first reinforced-concrete high-rise office building, is erected in Cincinnati. The skyscraper is six stories high.**

1869 **The Cincinnati Red Stockings (now called the Reds) take the field as the first professional baseball team in the country.**

 Ash Cave in Hocking Hills State Park is 700 feet wide (213 meters), 100 feet (30 meters) deep, and 90 feet (27 meters) high. The huge cave was once used by Indians as a workshop for grinding corn, making arrow and spear points, or skinning and dressing animals killed for food or clothing.

AAA GEMS:
Selected Must-See Points of Interest

CEDAR POINT (Sandusky) – This huge amusement park offers 68 rides, more rides than any other park in the world. There are15 amazing roller coasters. There's also a beach, boardwalk, ice show, musical shows, an IMAX theater, and a fun family area called Camp Snoopy.

GREAT SERPENT MOUND (Locust Grove) – Created by Indians in prehistoric times for religious ceremonies, this earthen mound is topped by the curving form of a snake more than 1,000 feet (305 meters) long. A museum explains how the Indians made the snake with its seven curves.

NATIONAL INVENTORS HALL OF FAME (Akron) – Hands-on exhibits let visitors interact with existing inventions, take gadgets apart, and create their own inventions.

PRO FOOTBALL HALL OF FAME (Canton) – See videos of great moments of professional football history and equipment used by famous players. Special events are scheduled in August during the annual pro football festival.

ROCK AND ROLL HALL OF FAME AND MUSEUM (Cleveland) – Visitors can trace the development of rock 'n' roll from its origins to current trends by listening to recordings, watching music videos, and marveling at instruments, costumes, and other objects used by music's greatest stars, past and present.

Cedar Point's Magnum XI-200 in Sandusky has been voted "Best Steel Roller Coaster in the World." Top speeds reach more than 70 mph (113 kph)!

1911 **In Dayton, Charles Kettering invents** the electric self-starter for cars.

1920 **The National Football League is founded in Canton.**

1962 **John Glenn of New Concord is the first American astronaut to orbit Earth.**

1967 **Carl Stokes is elected mayor of Cleveland and becomes the first black mayor of a major American city.**

1969 **Neil Armstrong of Wapakoneta is the first person to walk on the moon.**

U.S. Sen. John Glenn *1998* **returns to space at 77 years old, the world's oldest astronaut.**

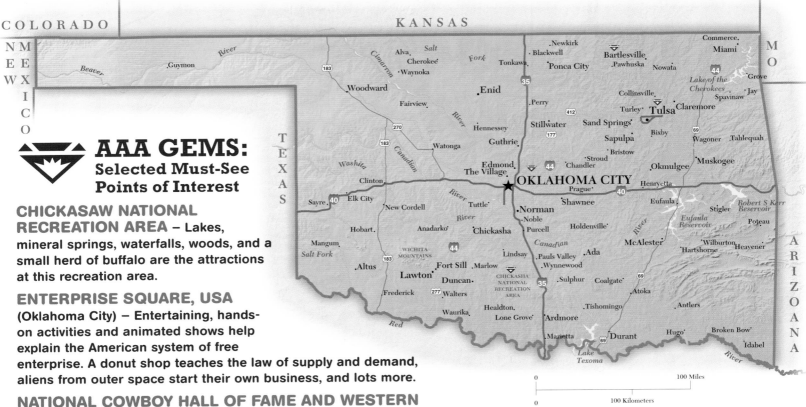

COLORADO   KANSAS

NEW MEXICO   TEXAS   ARIZOANA   MO

◆ AAA GEMS:
Selected Must-See Points of Interest

CHICKASAW NATIONAL RECREATION AREA – Lakes, mineral springs, waterfalls, woods, and a small herd of buffalo are the attractions at this recreation area.

ENTERPRISE SQUARE, USA (Oklahoma City) – Entertaining, hands-on activities and animated shows help explain the American system of free enterprise. A donut shop teaches the law of supply and demand, aliens from outer space start their own business, and lots more.

NATIONAL COWBOY HALL OF FAME AND WESTERN HERITAGE MUSEUM (Oklahoma City) – Exhibits honor the men and women of the West. See displays about American Indian and pioneer life, the Rodeo Hall of Fame, an art collection, and the 33-foot (10-meter) statue of Buffalo Bill.

TULSA ZOO AND LIVING MUSEUM – Explore an Amazon basin, an Arctic tundra, an African savanna, and a coral reef without leaving Oklahoma.

WOOLAROC RANCH, MUSEUM AND WILDLIFE PRESERVE (Bartlesville) – A variety of wild animals live at the preserve. Collections at the museum range from American Indian objects to a 95-million-year-old dinosaur egg.

If you visit Black Mesa State Park in the Oklahoma Panhandle, check out these giant rock formations made of Dakota sandstone. They're known as "The Wedding Party".

Inside Scoop

ANADARKO, home of the National Hall of Fame for Famous American Indians, is host every August to the American Indian Exposition, a festival with parades, war-dance contests, horse races, native arts and crafts, and more.

THE COUNTRY'S FIRST parking meter started clicking in Oklahoma City in 1935.

BASEBALL STAR Mickey Mantle of the New York Yankees was born in Spavinaw in 1931.

OKLAHOMA got its nickname from the homesteaders who raced to claim land "sooner" than the official opening.

A TEEN from Stillwater started a program to provide emergency medical information cards to senior citizens to place on their refrigerators. Over 45,000 cards have been distributed through 4-H clubs in Oklahoma since the program began.

TIMELINE

1682 Explorer René-Robert Cavalier, Sieur de la Salle, claims Oklahoma land for France.

1803 The United States buys Oklahoma land from France as part of the Louisiana Purchase.

1834 Oklahoma land officially becomes Indian Territory.

1842 The Five Civilized Tribes (Chickasaw, Choctaw, Cherokee, Creek, Seminole) complete their forced relocation to Indian Territory from their homes in the Southeast.

1889 The United States opens Indian Territory to white homesteaders, initiating a series of land rushes. Oklahoma City is settled by 10,000 people in one day.

1890 Indian Territory officially becomes Oklahoma Territory.

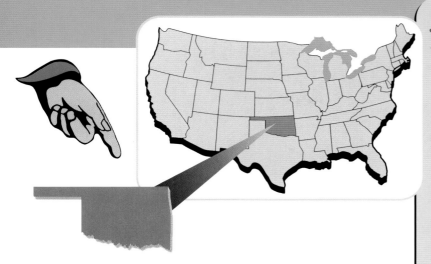

FRESH FACTS

NAME Based on two Choctaw Indian words "'ukla," meaning red and "huma" meaning "human." The two words were joined together by an American Indian missionary who knew the Choctaw language.

ABBREVIATION Okla.

CAPITAL Oklahoma City

NICKNAME Sooner State

AREA 69,898 square miles (181,035 square kilometers)

POPULATION 3,450,654

STATEHOOD Nov. 16, 1907 (46th state)

HIGHEST POINT Black Mesa (4,973 feet; 1,516 meters)

LOWEST POINT Little River, McCurtain County (287 feet; 87 meters)

INDUSTRIES Food products, machinery, metal products, mining, natural gas, oil, transportation equipment

AGRICULTURE Cattle, chickens, corn, cotton, dairy products, hay, peanuts, wheat, young plants

MOTTO Labor conquers all things.

FLAG Adopted in 1925, the flag displays an Osage warrior's shield with seven eagle feathers hanging from it. An olive branch and a peace pipe, symbols of peace, are crisscrossed on the shield.

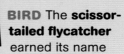

BIRD The **scissor-tailed flycatcher** earned its name because of its long, forked tail, which opens and closes like a scissors when the bird flies. Like other flycatchers, the bird snatches flies and other insects in mid-air. The bird was adopted in 1951.

FLOWER Mistletoe was selected in 1893, when the Chicago World's Fair asked the states to submit a flower. Although Oklahoma was not yet a state, it chose the mistletoe plant, which grows on trees, as its official flower.

TREE The **redbud tree,** adopted in 1971, is named for the clusters of pink-lavender flowers that bloom early in the spring, even before the tree's leaves have unfurled.

SONG "Oklahoma!" (words by Oscar Hammerstein II; music by Richard Rodgers)

Little Sahara State Park, near Waynoka, is the perfect oasis for dune buggy fans.

Hats off to all the competitors at the Oklahoma State Fair's Best-Dressed Cow Contest! The annual fair is held in Oklahoma City.

1912 Jim Thorpe, a Sauk and Fox Indian born near Prague, wins both the pentathlon and decathlon Olympic events.

1933 Oklahoman Wiley Post makes the first successful solo flight around the world.

1970 The Tulsa Port of Catoosa opens; it links Tulsa with the Mississippi River and the Gulf of Mexico.

1897 The first commercial oil well in Oklahoma Territory starts gushing in Bartlesville.

1930 Overplowing and a drought create the Dust Bowl and many farms fail. Farmers then apply water- and soil-conservation techniques to ensure future success.

1995 A terrorist bomb explodes in a U.S. government building in Oklahoma City.

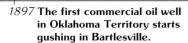

Oregon

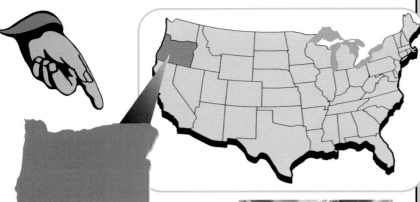

The old Oregon Trail stretches 2,400 miles (3,862 kilometers) from Missouri to Willamette Valley, Oregon. A wagon train pulled by mules moved about 15 miles (24 kilometers) a day, which meant the whole trip took more than six months!

AAA GEMS:
Selected Must-See Points of Interest

CRATER LAKE NATIONAL PARK – The nation's deepest lake is also one of its most beautiful. The lake sits atop a volcano that collapsed inward. Every year, 500,000 visitors marvel at the clear blue water from lookouts along the 33-mile (53-kilometer) Rim Drive.

HIGH DESERT MUSEUM (Bend) – Indoor and outdoor exhibits acquaint you with the people, plants, and animals that live in this dry area, called the High Desert.

OREGON CAVES NATIONAL MONUMENT (near Jacksonville) – Discovered in 1874, these caves are filled with beautiful, strange-looking marble formations. The largest room is called the Ghost Room.

OREGON COAST AQUARIUM (Newport) – View thousands of saltwater and freshwater animals, including exotic jellyfish, a giant octopus, and tuna swimming around a sunken sailing ship. Check out the underwater walkway that lets you pass through shark-filled waters.

OREGON MUSEUM OF SCIENCE AND INDUSTRY – (Portland) At this fun museum, you can travel to outer space, feel the fury of an earthquake, and board a submarine. More than 200 hands-on exhibits and special events are added attractions.

OREGON ZOO (Portland) – The nine major exhibits include more than 1,000 animals, from antelopes to zebras. You can tour an African savanna, Amazon forest, elk meadow, and an insect farm where tarantulas, scorpions, a giant millipede, and an Australian walking stick reside.

FRESH FACTS

NAME Origin of the name is not known. It may come from the French-Canadian word "ouragan" for "storm," or after the Columbia River which was once called "River of Storms," or from the Spanish word "orégano" for "wild sage."

ABBREVIATION Ore.

CAPITAL Salem

NICKNAME Beaver State

AREA 97,073 square miles (251,419 square kilometers)

POPULATION 3,421,399

STATEHOOD Feb. 14, 1859 (33rd state)

HIGHEST POINT Mount Hood (11,239 feet; 3,426 meters)

LOWEST POINT Sea level

INDUSTRIES Construction, electronics, finance, food products, insurance, machinery, paper products, real estate, scientific instruments, trade, wood products

AGRICULTURE Cattle, dairy products, fruits, grass seed, hay, nuts, vegetables, wheat, young plants

MOTTO She flies with her own wings.

FLAG Adopted in 1925, this is the only state flag with a design on both sides. On the front is a heart-shaped seal topped by an eagle that is surrounded by 33 stars, showing that Oregon was the 33rd state to join the Union. The reverse side shows a beaver, the state animal.

BIRD The **Western meadowlark** was chosen by a group of school children and was adopted in 1927. The bird's flute-like song can be heard throughout the state.

FLOWER The **Oregon grape** plant is a shrub whose waxy leaves look like holly and whose dark-blue berries are a favorite among jelly makers and eaters. The flower was adopted in 1899.

TREE Chosen in 1939, **Douglas firs** were a valuable source of lumber in the 1800s. Some trees were so big that a team of 20 oxen was needed to pull one log.

SONG "Oregon, My Oregon" (words by J.A. Buchanan; music by Henry B. Murtagh)

TIMELINE

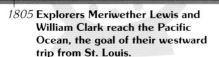

1792 Capt. Robert Gray, an American explorer, sails up the Columbia River, which he names after his ship, the "Columbia."

1834 The first permanent settlement is established in the Willamette Valley.

1805 Explorers Meriwether Lewis and William Clark reach the Pacific Ocean, the goal of their westward trip from St. Louis.

1811 John Jacob Astor builds the headquarters for his fur trading company at Astoria.

1843 The first large wave of pioneers — some 800 settlers, 120 wagons and 5,000 cattle — leave Independence, Mo., and head west on the Oregon Trail.

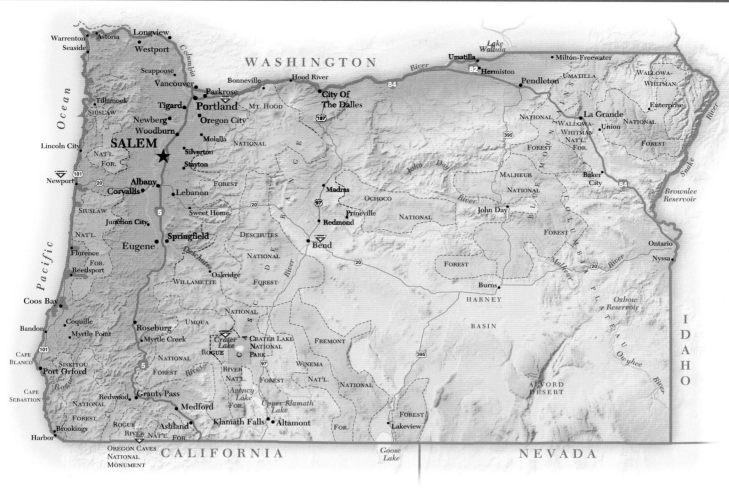

A dog named Ranger is buried at the summit of Oregon's Mount Hood. Ranger, who lived from 1925 to 1939, is said to have climbed the famous 11,235-foot (3,424-meter) mountain 500 times during his life.

0   100 Miles

0   100 Kilometers

Inside Scoop

HELL'S CANYON, carved out by the Snake River, is the country's deepest canyon. It is 8,023 feet (2,445 meters) deep.

WOMEN TRAVELING on the Oregon Trail in the 1840s filled their butter churns with milk in the morning. The ride was so bumpy that the milk turned to butter by the end of the day.

COWBOYS have been competing in the Pendleton Round-Up since 1933. Every September, 50,000 fans watch bronco riding, horse races, American Indian dances, sack races, and fireworks at this popular rodeo.

PORT ORFORD is the westernmost incorporated city in the lower 48 states.

TEEN ATHLETES from the Southern Oregon Special Olympics chapter in Medford chopped wood for families in need.

1868 The first salmon are canned in a factory in Westport.

1937 The Bonneville Dam on the Columbia River begins to generate hydroelectric power.

1850 The Oregon Donation Land Law grants 320 free acres (130 hectares) of land to anyone who has farmed the land for four years.

1883 The Northern Pacific Railroad connects Portland with the East.

1998 National Toy Hall of Fame® is founded in Salem by A. C. Gilbert.

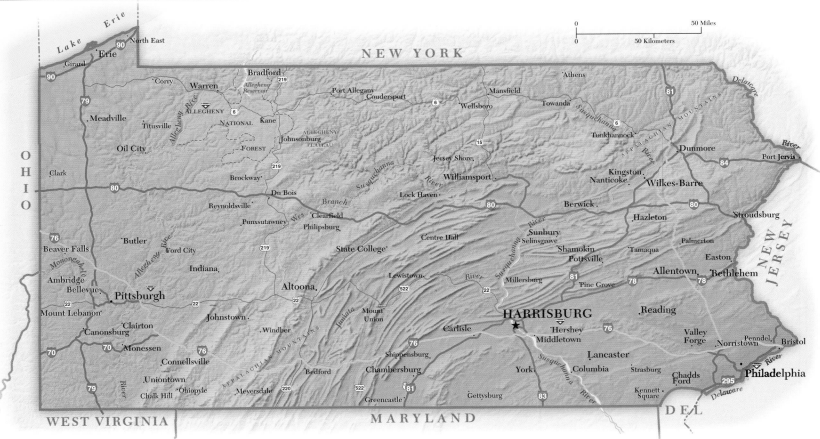

 ## AAA GEMS:
Selected Must-See Points of Interest

CARNEGIE SCIENCE CENTER (Pittsburgh) – More than 250 interactive exhibits make this an "amusement park for the mind." Gaze into outer space in the planetarium, step inside a wind tunnel, feel an earthquake, and check out a tornado in the SciQuest exhibit.

HERSHEY'S CHOCOLATE WORLD (Hershey) – Stroll down Chocolate Street and hop on the automated tour ride to learn how cocoa beans are harvested, processed into chocolate, and then packaged into candy bars and Hershey kisses. A treat awaits you at the end. Visit the Hershey Museum and Hersheypark, where rides offer fun and excitement.

INDEPENDENCE NATIONAL HISTORICAL PARK (Philadelphia) – This park is a treasure-trove of 16 colonial sites where you can investigate the early history of America.

LIBERTY BELL PAVILION (Philadelphia) – Ever since the historic bell rang out the news of American independence, the Liberty Bell has been a symbol of freedom. Park rangers tell the story of the bell, how it had to be hidden in Allentown during the Revolutionary War, and how it cracked in 1835.

PITTSBURGH ZOO & AQUARIUM – You'll have a roaring good time at this zoo and aquarium where thousands of animals, including numerous threatened and endangered species, live.

Amish buggies are common sights in southeastern Pennsylvania. The Amish, a religious group, do not use cars, tractors, electricity, telephones, or other modern machinery.

TIMELINE

1681 William Penn, a Quaker, receives a land grant for Pennsylvania from King Charles II of England.

1777 Gen. George Washington and his troops spend the winter in Valley Forge.

1859 The nation's first commercial oil well is drilled by Edwin Drake near Titusville.

1731 The first circulating library is established by Benjamin Franklin in Philadelphia.

1776 The newly adopted Declaration of Independence is signed in Philadelphia.

1787 The Constitutional Convention, held in Philadelphia, adopts the Constitution of the United States.

1863 Union forces defeat the Confederate army in the Battle of Gettysburg, marking a turning point in the Civil War.

100

FRESH FACTS

NAME Based on the last name of William Penn, founder of the colony, and "sylvania," the Latin word for "woods."

ABBREVIATION Pa.

CAPITAL Harrisburg

NICKNAME Keystone State

AREA 46,055 square miles (119,282 square kilometers)

POPULATION 12,281,054

STATEHOOD Dec. 12, 1787 (2nd state)

HIGHEST POINT Mount Davis (3,213 feet; 979 meters)

LOWEST POINT Delaware River

INDUSTRIES Biotechnology, chemicals, electronic equipment, food products, machinery, medical care, metal products, pharmaceuticals, printed materials, rubber, steel, tourism, transportation equipment, trucking, wood products

AGRICULTURE Apples, cattle, chickens, corn, dairy products, fruit, hay, mushrooms, poultry, young plants

MOTTO Virtue, liberty, and independence.

FLAG When it was adopted in 1907, the flag was standardized so that its blue color would be the same as that of the American flag.

BIRD Sometimes called a partridge, the plump **ruffed grouse** with its feathered legs can be seen in Pennsylvania's woods. It was chosen in 1931.

FLOWER The **mountain laurel** opens its pink and white blossoms in mid-June. It was a favorite plant of members of the state legislature and the wife of the governor who promoted its adoption in 1933.

TREE Pennsylvania's first settlers used wood from **Eastern hemlock** trees to build their sturdy log cabins. The hemlock's tannin proved valuable in making leather. The tree was adopted in 1931.

SONG "Pennsylvania" (words and music by Eddie Khoury and Ronnie Bonner)

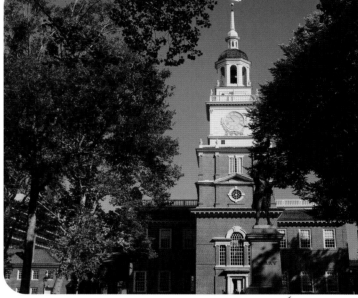

Independence National Historical Park in Philadelphia looks very much the same today as it did in 1776 when representatives from the 13 colonies signed the Declaration of Independence.

Inside Scoop

LITTLE LEAGUE baseball originated in Williamsport in 1939.

THE HERSHEY COMPANY produces some 33 million chocolate kisses each day.

PENNSYLVANIA has a long list of firsts, including the first volunteer fire company, zoo, library, pretzel, root beer, successful daily newspaper, savings bank, and symphony orchestra.

PHILADELPHIA WAS the nation's capital from 1790 to 1800.

IN 2001, 18-year-old Jeffrey Dunkel from Mount Carbon was elected mayor of his district, where some 100 people reside.

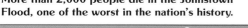

Visitors to Hershey's Chocolate World® learn how chocolate is made by following a cocoa bean from an imaginary tropical jungle to America and then through a model of the Hershey factory. While the factory might not be the real thing, the free chocolate everyone gets at the end of the tour sure is!

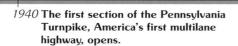

1889 More than 2,000 people die in the Johnstown Flood, one of the worst in the nation's history.

1979 Scientists at the Three-Mile Island nuclear plant near Harrisburg prevent a major disaster after deadly levels of radiation are released.

1874 The nation's first ice cream soda is served up by Robert M. Green in Philadelphia.

1940 The first section of the Pennsylvania Turnpike, America's first multilane highway, opens.

1987 The "We the People 200" bicentennial celebrates the 200th anniversary of the signing of the U.S. Constitution, in Philadelphia.

MASSACHUSETTS

Woonsocket
Cumberland Hill
Pascoag
295
Valley Falls
44
Pawtucket
North Providence
6
★ PROVIDENCE
East Providence
Cranston
Barrington
95
West Warwick
Warwick
Bristol
Tiverton
Portsmouth
Melville
Newport East
Jamestown
Hope Valley
95
Kingston
Newport
Wakefield-Peacedale
Narragansett Pier
Rhode Island Sound
Westerly
1
Watch Hill

C O N N E C T I C U T

Atlantic Ocean

BLOCK ISLAND

0 ————— 20 Miles
0 ————— 20 Kilometers

AAA GEMS:
Selected Must-See Points of Interest

THE BREAKERS (Newport) — Described as the grandest of the Newport mansions, The Breakers was once the summer cottage of Cornelius Vanderbilt II. It has 70 rooms. The great hall is two-stories high with marble columns. Check out the elegant coaches and carriages in the stable.

CHATEAU-SUR-MER (Newport) — This French "Castle by the Sea" features intricate woodwork, a French-style ballroom with sliding mirrored doors, and a stained-glass skylight that illuminates a three-story central hall and grand staircase. The chateau was built in 1852 for William S. Wetmore, a merchant in the China trade.

THE ELMS (Newport) — Highlights of this awesome mansion include a conservatory that mimics the grandeur of the Hall of Mirrors at Versailles in France and a Louis XIV drawing room. The grounds display statues, fountains, and terraces. The mansion was built in 1901 as a summer house for Edward J. Berwind, leader of America's coal industry.

MARBLE HOUSE (Newport) — The most elaborate room of this gold-and-marble palace is the salon, which has a mural on the ceiling, huge chandeliers, and gilded woodwork. It was built in 1892 for William K. Vanderbilt, Cornelius's brother, and is named for the great amount of marble used in the house.

MUSEUM OF ART — RHODE ISLAND SCHOOL OF DESIGN (Providence) — Among the collections are ancient Greek and Roman pieces, European porcelains, American paintings and furniture as well as works from India and China.

Samuel Slater learned how water could power factories as a young man in England in the late 1700s. Although it was against the law for anyone to carry plans for these factories out of England, he memorized how they worked. He then came to Rhode Island, where he built the first water-powered factory in America in 1790.

Inside Scoop

DESPITE ITS NAME, the state of Rhode Island is not an island. The state consists of territory on the mainland and 36 islands.

RHODE ISLAND is America's smallest state. It would take 429 Rhode Islands to fill Alaska, the largest state.

THE FLYING HORSE CAROUSEL, located in Watch Hill, is believed to be America's oldest carousel. It was built around 1879. The hand-carved horses have leather saddles and the manes and tails are made of real horsehair.

SOME 80 TREES and shrubs are shaped into giraffes, camels, and other animals in the sculptured greenery of Alice Brayton's imaginative Green Animals garden in Portsmouth.

IN 2001, a 12-year-old from Hope Valley was nominated for a Grammy Award for Best Male Country Vocal Performance. Johnny Cash won the category for the year.

TIMELINE

1614 Dutch navigator Adriaen Block explores the islands and names one "Roodt Eylandt," which is today called Block Island.

1663 England grants the Charter of Rhode Island and Providence Plantations. This supersedes the colony's first charter, granted in 1644.

1774 Rhode Island is the first American colony to prohibit importing slaves.

1790 America's first water-powered cotton mill starts operating in Pawtucket.

FRESH FACTS

NAME From the Dutch words "roodt eylandt," meaning "red island," for the color of the red clay soil or from the Greek island Rhodes in the Mediterranean Sea. The official name is the State of Rhode Island and Providence Plantations. Providence, the state's first colonial settlement, was named by its founder, Roger Williams, in 1636.

ABBREVIATION R.I.

CAPITAL Providence

NICKNAME Little Rhody (also, Ocean State)

AREA 1,545 square miles (4,001 square kilometers)

POPULATION 1,048,319

STATEHOOD May 29, 1790 (13th state)

HIGHEST POINT Jerimoth Hill (812 feet; 247 meters)

LOWEST POINT Sea level

INDUSTRIES Electronic equipment, jewelry, machinery, metal products, scientific instruments, textiles, tourism, toys

AGRICULTURE Seafood, vegetables, young plants

MOTTO Hope.

FLAG Adopted in 1897, the flag displays a gold anchor, symbolizing hope, which is surrounded by 13 stars representing the nation's original 13 colonies.

BIRD The **Rhode Island Red,** adopted as the state bird in 1954, is a famous breed of chicken that originated in the state in 1854 and became the foundation of the country's poultry industry.

FLOWER Although students elected the **violet** as the state flower in 1897, it wasn't officially adopted until 1968.

TREE The **red maple,** adopted in 1964, is also called scarlet or swamp maple. The tree's flowers and seeds are red and the leaves turn scarlet in the fall.

SONG "Rhode Island It's for Me" (words by Charles Hall; music by Maria Day)

Even though there's no actual "South County" in Rhode Island, locals call the southern shore of Rhode Island by that name. The peaceful resort area is home to sandy beaches where families can do anything from sailing to just catching some sun.

A giant Mr. Potato Head stands outside the original headquarters of toy company Hasbro, Inc.

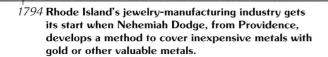

1969 Newport Bridge, linking Jamestown with Newport, opens over Narragansett Bay.

1983 Australia II wins the America's Cup, the first non-American sailboat to do so in 132 years.

1794 Rhode Island's jewelry-manufacturing industry gets its start when Nehemiah Dodge, from Providence, develops a method to cover inexpensive metals with gold or other valuable metals.

1990 Rhode Island celebrates its 200th anniversary as a state.

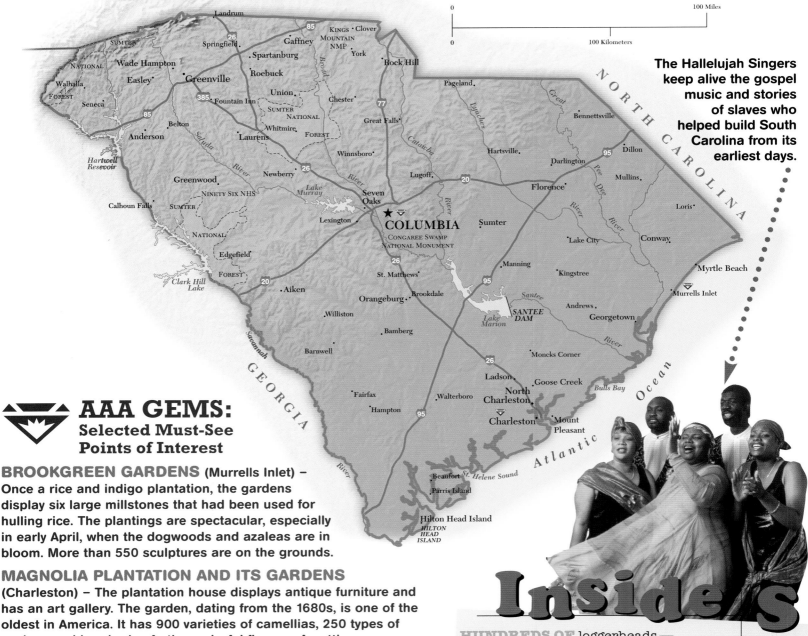

The Hallelujah Singers keep alive the gospel music and stories of slaves who helped build South Carolina from its earliest days.

AAA GEMS:
Selected Must-See Points of Interest

BROOKGREEN GARDENS (Murrells Inlet) – Once a rice and indigo plantation, the gardens display six large millstones that had been used for hulling rice. The plantings are spectacular, especially in early April, when the dogwoods and azaleas are in bloom. More than 550 sculptures are on the grounds.

MAGNOLIA PLANTATION AND ITS GARDENS (Charleston) – The plantation house displays antique furniture and has an art gallery. The garden, dating from the 1680s, is one of the oldest in America. It has 900 varieties of camellias, 250 types of azaleas and hundreds of other colorful flowers. A petting zoo, pre-Civil War cabins, a pasture with sheep and miniature horses, and a maze makes a visit here a most pleasant one.

SOUTH CAROLINA AQUARIUM (Charleston) – This is a good place to learn about the plants, animals, and habitats of the southeastern United States. There's a glass-enclosed aviary, snakes and turtles, a salt marsh, and a two-story tank filled with hundreds of sea animals.

SOUTH CAROLINA STATE MUSEUM (Columbia) – This building was one of the world's first all-electric textile mills. Today you will find exhibits that tell about the state's history and industry as well as science, technology, and natural history. There are hands-on exhibits and a laser show.

Inside Scoop

HUNDREDS OF loggerheads — enormous sea turtles weighing up to 400 pounds (181 kilograms) — crawl onto South Carolina beaches on summer nights. They lay their eggs, cover them with sand and return to the ocean. Eight weeks later, the babies hatch and head for the water.

GEORGE GERSHWIN wrote the music for the folk opera "Porgy and Bess" while he was vacationing in Charleston in 1935. The story's Catfish Row was based on a neighborhood near Charleston's Church Street.

IN 1991 hundreds of volunteers at Myrtle Beach created a sand castle that stretched more than 16 miles (26 kilometers), a record unsurpassed as of 2002.

A 12-YEAR-OLD volunteered her time reading to young children at the library in Rock Hill. She also served on the library's teen advisory board.

TIMELINE

1521 Francisco Gordillo of Spain explores the Carolina coast.

1670 English colonists establish the first permanent settlement at Albemarle Point, near present-day Charleston.

1735 The first opera in America is performed in Charleston.

1780 The British capture Charleston but American troops win the Battle of Kings Mountain, a turning point in the Revolutionary War.

FRESH FACTS

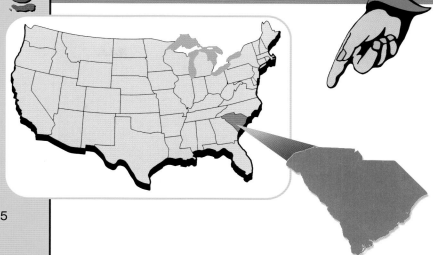

NAME In honor of England's King Charles I, whose Latin name is "Carolus."

ABBREVIATION S.C.

CAPITAL Columbia

NICKNAME Palmetto State

AREA 32,020 square miles (82,932 square kilometers)

POPULATION 4,012,012

STATEHOOD May 23, 1788 (8th state)

HIGHEST POINT Sassafras Mountain (3,560 feet; 1,085 meters)

LOWEST POINT Sea level

INDUSTRIES Chemical products, clothes, machinery, metal products, paper products, plastics, rubber, textiles, tourism

AGRICULTURE Cattle, chickens, corn, cotton, dairy products, peaches, soybeans, tobacco, tomatoes, wheat, young plants

MOTTOES Prepared in mind and resources. While I breathe, I hope.

FLAG In 1775, Col. William Moultrie was asked to design a flag that South Carolina troops could carry in the Revolutionary War. He chose blue to match the color of their uniforms and added a silver crescent like the one on their caps. The palmetto tree was added in 1861, representing Fort Moultrie, which was made of palmetto logs. The fort withstood a British attack in 1780.

BIRD The **Carolina wren's** sweet song can be heard all day long in all kinds of weather. It was adopted in 1948.

FLOWER The fragrant **yellow jessamine** was chosen in 1924 because it was thought to be a symbol of constancy and loyalty.

TREE The **palmetto** helped save Charleston during the Revolutionary War. When British cannon balls bounced off Fort Moultrie's soft wood, the fort and all of Charleston survived the enemy's attack. The tree was adopted in 1939.

SONGS "Carolina" (words by Henry Timrod; music by Anne Custis Burgess). "South Carolina on My Mind" (words and music by Hank Martin and Buzz Arledge)

The South Carolina Low Country on the Atlantic coast south of Charleston is dotted with tidal marshes like this one at Kiawah Island.

1860 **South Carolina is the first state to secede from the Union.**

1861 **The first shots of the Civil War are fired when the South attacks the Union at Fort Sumter.**

1950 **NASCAR'S first 500-mile (805-kilometer) race, the Southern 500, is held at Darlington Raceway.**

1830 **The first steam locomotive to carry passengers, called the "Best Friend of Charleston," begins operation on Christmas Day.**

1865 **Columbia is burned to the ground by Union soldiers.**

1999 **The first female student graduates from The Citadel, a military college in Charleston.**

South Dakota

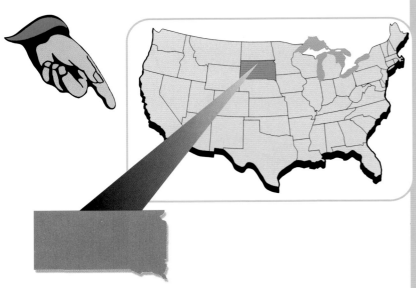

NAME From from the Dakota Indian word "dacotah," meaning "friend or ally."

ABBREVIATION S.D.

CAPITAL Pierre

NICKNAME Mount Rushmore State

AREA 77,116 square miles (199,730 square kilometers)

POPULATION 754,844

STATEHOOD Nov. 2, 1889 (40th state)

HIGHEST POINT Harney Peak (7,242 feet; 2,207 meters)

LOWEST POINT Big Stone Lake (962 feet; 293 meters)

INDUSTRIES Electric and electronic equipment, food products, lumber, machinery, scientific instruments, tourism, wood products,

AGRICULTURE Cattle, corn, hogs, milk, oats, soybeans, sunflowers, wheat

MOTTO Under God, the people rule.

FLAG South Dakota has had two official flags. The first had the state seal on one side and the sun on the other. A new flag was adopted in 1963 and updated in 1992 with South Dakota's name and nickname around the state seal.

BIRD The **ring-necked pheasant,** adopted in 1943, is sometimes called the Chinese pheasant. Judge O.N. Denny, the American consul general of Shanghai, China, brought the bird to the state in the late 1800s. It has thrived in its new home.

FLOWER The **pasqueflower,** chosen in 1903, gets its name from the French word "Pasque," which means "Easter," because the flower blooms in early spring.

TREE The **Black Hills spruce** has been the state tree since 1947. When the trees grow close together, forming thick stands, their blue-green needles look black. The Black Hills of South Dakota are named after this tree.

SONG "Hail! South Dakota" (words and music by Deecort Hammitt)

Based on the sizes of their heads, if each president at Mount Rushmore was carved to his full height, George Washington would be as tall as the Washington Monument, Thomas Jefferson as tall as Seattle's Space Needle, Theodore Roosevelt as tall as the Statue of Liberty, and Abraham Lincoln taller than four space shuttles stacked end to end.

TIMELINE

1743 The Verendrye brothers, French fur traders, explore the region.

1803 The United States buys most of the Dakota region as part of the Louisiana Purchase.

1831 The "Yellowstone" is the first steamboat to go as far north on the Missouri River as present-day Fort Pierre.

1861 The Dakota Territory is created, which includes North and South Dakota as well as parts of Wyoming and Montana.

1874 George Armstrong Custer's expedition discovers gold in the Black Hills.

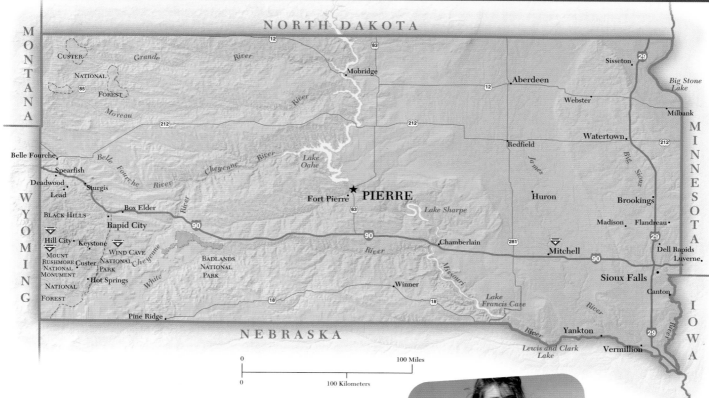

NORTH DAKOTA

MONTANA

Custer
NATIONAL
FOREST

Grande River

Moreau River

Belle Fourche

Spearfish

Deadwood
Lead

Sturgis

Box Elder

BLACK HILLS

Rapid City

Hill City · Keystone

MOUNT
RUSHMORE
NATIONAL
MONUMENT

Custer

WIND CAVE
NATIONAL
PARK

Hot Springs

NATIONAL
FOREST

Belle Fourche River

Cheyenne River

Cheyenne River

White River

Pine Ridge

WYOMING

Mobridge

Lake
Oahe

Fort Pierre · ★ PIERRE

Lake Sharpe

90

BADLANDS
NATIONAL
PARK

River

Chamberlain

Winner

18

Aberdeen

Webster

Redfield

Huron

Missouri River

Lake
Francis Case

Yankton

Lewis and Clark
Lake

NEBRASKA

Sisseton

Big Stone
Lake

Milbank

Watertown

Brookings

Madison · Flandreau ·

Mitchell

Dell Rapids
Luverne ·

Sioux Falls

Canton

Vermillion

MINNESOTA

IOWA

0 ——————— 100 Miles
0 ——————— 100 Kilometers

▲ AAA GEMS:
Selected Must-See Points of Interest

1880 TRAIN (Hill City) — Enjoy a two-hour ride on one of the last steam railroads still running in the United States. As you relax in the luxury of the 19th-century coaches, guides point out places of interest along the route that was used by miners and pioneers.

THE CORN PALACE (Mitchell) — At the risk of sounding corny, the architecture of this building will a-maize you! Parts of the exterior and interior are covered with designs made of ears of corn. Local grasses and grains form the outline of the displays. The decorations change each year.

ENCHANTED WORLD DOLL MUSEUM (Mitchell) — The whole family will enjoy this museum that is housed in a castle with a drawbridge, stained glass windows, and a moat. More than 4,000 antique and modern dolls from around the world are on display in more than 400 scenes.

MOUNT RUSHMORE NATIONAL MEMORIAL — Come face to face with presidents George Washington, Thomas Jefferson, Abraham Lincoln, and Theodore Roosevelt. The memorial is one of the largest pieces of sculpture ever created. The faces of the four presidents are 60 feet (18 meters) high and their noses are about 20 feet (6 meters) long. That makes each nose about the height of three professional basketball players standing on each other's shoulders.

WIND CAVE NATIONAL PARK — Strong winds, which blow alternately in and out, give this cave its name. The walls are covered with unusual formations that resemble boxes, popcorn, and frost. A national park ranger takes you on a tour and explains the highlights.

The fishing's good in South Dakota. This young woman has caught a walleye.

Inside Scoop

CUSTER STATE PARK is home to a herd of 1,500 free-roaming bison. One bison eats 100 acres (40 hectares) of grass each year.

THE BUFFALO NICKEL was designed by James Fraser of Mitchell. It shows a buffalo on one side and the profile of Hollow Horn Bear, a Rosebud tribal chief, on the other. From 1913 to 1938, more than a billion of these coins were minted.

THE HOMESTAKE GOLD MINE in Lead was in operation for 125 years, one of the longest continuously working gold mines in the world.

WORK ON THE Crazy Horse Memorial, near Custer, was begun in 1948. When completed, it will be 563 feet (172 meters) high and 641 feet (195 meters) wide, the world's largest sculpture.

A HIGH SCHOOL SENIOR from Rapid City was the winner of the 2001 Presidential Scholar and Arts Award in the category of instrumental music. He plays the bassoon.

1927 Gutzon Borglum begins work on Mount Rushmore National Memorial.

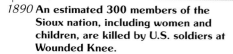

1890 An estimated 300 members of the Sioux nation, including women and children, are killed by U.S. soldiers at Wounded Knee.

1980 The U.S. Supreme Court orders South Dakota to pay millions of dollars to the Sioux nation for land that was seized from them in 1877.

2000 Forest fires devastate thousands of acres in the Black Hills.

Great Smoky Mountains National Park offers more than 800 miles (1,287 kilometers) of hiking trails. The park also has four different riding stables.

AAA GEMS:
Selected Must-See Points of Interest

COUNTRY MUSIC HALL OF FAME AND MUSEUM (Nashville) — See Elvis Presley's "solid gold" Cadillac and his piano as well as treasured items from the Grand Ole Opry and country music stars.

GRAND OLE OPRY (Nashville) — Reserve a ticket for a show at the Grand Ole Opry House, which seats more than 4,000 people and enjoy the foot-stompin' music. The Opry has broadcast its shows over radio since 1925 and has never missed a beat.

GREAT SMOKY MOUNTAINS NATIONAL PARK — The park, divided between North Carolina and Tennessee, gets its name from the blue, smokelike haze that hangs over the mountains. Take a scenic ride, hike, camp, fish, or horseback ride. Check out the "balds," the treeless mountaintops covered with grass and shrubs, and the blaze of colors from blooming azaleas and rhododendrons.

MUSEUM OF APPALACHIA (Norris) — Stroll through the mountain village and working farm and watch blacksmiths, cobblers and others demonstrate pioneer skills. Enjoy the music played from cabin porches and stop at the Appalachian Hall of Fame, which pays tribute to the people who have lived in the area.

SHILOH NATIONAL MILITARY PARK — This park honors the more than 100,000 Union and Confederate soldiers who fought in the fierce Battle of Shiloh in 1862.

WOMEN'S BASKETBALL HALL OF FAME (Knoxville) — In addition to seeing the humongous basketball and photographs of champion players, you can listen to coaches' game strategies, see a video about basketball's history, and admire the stretch station wagon that belonged to the All-American Red Heads, a professional team that played for 50 years (from 1936–86).

TIMELINE

1540 Spanish explorer Hernando de Soto explores the Tennessee region.

1682 René-Robert Cavelier, Sieur de la Salle, claims the region for France.

1763 France surrenders Tennessee land under the Treaty of Paris, ending the French and Indian War.

1775 Pioneer Daniel Boone blazes a trail, called the Wilderness Road, through the Cumberland Gap. Thousands of settlers use it to reach the West.

1827 Famous frontiersman Davy Crockett begins the first of three terms representing Tennessee in the U.S. House of Representatives.

1838 The Cherokee Indians are forced to relocate to Oklahoma Territory. The route they walked is called the Trail of Tears because so many died along the way.

FRESH FACTS

NAME Based on the name of a Cherokee village, "Tanasi."

ABBREVIATION Tenn.

CAPITAL Nashville

NICKNAME The Volunteer State

AREA 42,143 square miles (109,150 square kilometers)

POPULATION 5,689,283

STATEHOOD June 1, 1796 (16th state)

HIGHEST POINT Clingmans Dome (6,643 feet; 2,025 meters)

LOWEST POINT Mississippi River, Shelby County (182 feet; 55 meters)

INDUSTRIES Chemicals, finance, food products, insurance, machinery, metal products, plastic, real estate, rubber, tourism, trade, transportation equipment,

AGRICULTURE Cattle, chickens, corn, cotton, dairy products, grain, hay, hogs, soybeans, tobacco

MOTTO Agriculture and commerce.

FLAG The three stars represent the state's three regions: east, middle, and west. The stars are surrounded by a circle, which symbolizes that the regions are forever bound together. The flag was adopted in 1905.

BIRD The **mockingbird** was adopted in 1933 after the people of the state voted for it over other choices. It is also the state bird for Arkansas, Florida, Mississippi, and Texas.

FLOWER The **iris** was adopted in 1933 after Nashville became known as the "Iris City." The purple iris is the state's official cultivated flower. The passionflower, adopted in 1973, is the state's official wildflower.

TREE The **tulip tree** (also known as yellow poplar) grows throughout the state. Early pioneers used its wood for cabins, barns, and other structures. It was adopted in 1947.

SONGS "My Homeland, Tennessee" (words by Nell Grayson Taylor; music by Roy Lamont Smith). "When It's Iris Time in Tennessee" (words by Willa Waid Newman). "My Tennessee" (words by Francis Hannah Tranum). "The Tennessee Waltz" (words by Pee Wee King; music by Redd Stewart). "Rocky Top" (Boudleaux and Felice Bryant).

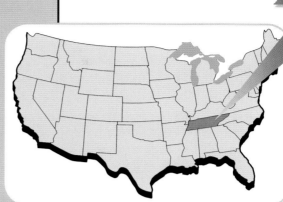

Storytellers from around the country gather to tell their tales at the National Storytelling Festival in Jonesborough. A special performance by young storytellers is always a highlight.

Inside Scoop

GRACELAND, the Memphis mansion of rock 'n' roll star Elvis Presley, is the second-most visited house in the United States (the first is the White House).

TENNESSEE is called the "Mother of Southwestern Statesmen" for the three U.S. presidents who were residents of the state: Andrew Jackson, Andrew Johnson, and James K. Polk.

NASHVILLE is known as the "Country Music Capital of the World."

SEQUOYAH, a Cherokee Indian born near Vonore, developed an alphabet of 86 syllables in 1821, enabling Cherokees to learn to read and write. The giant sequoia tree and a national park are named after him.

A 9-YEAR-OLD Nashville girl started a group devoted to a cleaner environment, which today has hundreds of thousands of members around the world. Among their projects are recycling paper and planting trees.

1960 Wilma Rudolph, born in St. Bethlehem, becomes the world's fastest woman after winning three gold medals in track and field at the Rome Olympics. As a young girl, Rudolph suffered from polio and wore a metal leg brace until she was 9 or 10. She was voted into the Black Athletes Hall of Fame in 1973.

1996 Tennessee celebrates its bicentennial.

1933 The U.S. Congress creates the Tennessee Valley Authority to develop the area's natural resources.

1968 Martin Luther King, Jr. is assassinated at the Lorraine Motel in Memphis. Today, the motel is the home of the National Civil Rights Museum.

1982 Knoxville hosts the World's Fair.

1991 Memphis elects its first African-American mayor.

AAA GEMS:
Selected Must-See Points of Interest

ALAMO (San Antonio) – A symbol of Texas' pride and independent spirit, the Spanish mission that was built in 1718 was used as a fort to defend the city against the Mexican army in 1836. It now houses exhibits from the era of the Texas Revolution. Davy Crockett and Jim Bowie were among the frontiersmen who died there.

BIG BEND NATIONAL PARK – The park derives its name from a U-shaped bend of the Rio Grande bordering the park. This last great wilderness area of Texas offers mountain and desert scenery and a variety of unusual geological structures.

INSTITUTE OF TEXAN CULTURES (San Antonio) – Exhibits illustrate the contributions of more than 25 ethnic groups that helped settle the state.

SIX FLAGS FIESTA TEXAS (San Antonio) – The park is home to The Rattler, reputed to be the world's tallest and fastest wooden roller coaster.

SPACE CENTER HOUSTON – Follow the story of America's manned space flight program through hands-on exhibits, displays, and behind-the-scene tours. Computer simulators let you land a space shuttle and walk on the moon. Don a space helmet and have a blast.

At the Battle of the Alamo in 1836, about 190 Texans held off about 5,000 Mexican soldiers for some 90 minutes. Although the Mexicans finally took the fort and killed all the defenders, stories of what happened turned the battle into a legend.

Texas is a land of wide open spaces and great beauty. This road passes through Big Bend National Park in South Texas.

TIMELINE

1528 Álvar Nuñez Cabeza de Vaca, a Spaniard from Mexico, explores the Texas region.

1682 Yselta, an outgrowth of a Spanish mission and the first permanent European settlement in Texas, is established near present-day El Paso.

1716 The Spanish build a mission named San Antonio de Valero (later called the Alamo) and a fort at present-day San Antonio.

1821 Texas becomes part of Mexico.

1901 Oil is discovered near Beaumont, leading to the huge growth of the state's oil industry.

1836 Sam Houston leads Texas to victory in its fight for independence from Mexico. The Republic of Texas is founded and continues until 1845, when Texas joins the Union as a state.

FRESH FACTS

NAME From the Caddo Indian word "tejas," meaning "friends."

ABBREVIATION None

CAPITAL Austin

NICKNAME Lone Star State

AREA 268,581 square miles
(695,625 square kilometers)

POPULATION 20,851,820

STATEHOOD Dec. 29, 1845 (28th state)

HIGHEST POINT Guadalupe Peak (8,749 feet;
2,667 meters)

LOWEST POINT Sea level

INDUSTRIES Chemical products, clothes, electrical and
electronic equipment, finance, food products, machinery, natural
gas, oil, real estate, tourism, trade, transportation equipment

AGRICULTURE Cattle, chickens, cotton, fruit, peanuts, pecans,
rice, seafood, sheep, sorghum, vegetables, wheat, young plants

MOTTO Friendship.

FLAG Texas gets its nickname, the Lone
Star State, from the flag's single star.
The red band represents bravery, the
white band is for purity, and the blue
symbolizes loyalty. The flag was
adopted in 1876.

BIRD Thousands of children in Texas
voted to help determine which bird
should represent the state. The winner
was the **mockingbird,** and it was
adopted in 1927.

FLOWER The **Texas
bluebonnet** gets its
name from the shape
of its petals, which reminded people of the
bonnets worn by pioneer women living on the
prairie. The flower was adopted in 1901.

TREE The **pecan tree** was
adopted in 1919. It was
probably selected because Gov. James Hogg
requested that one be planted at his
gravesite. The tree's nuts are sweet and a
favorite in such foods as pecan pie and butter
pecan ice cream.

SONG "Texas, Our Texas" (words by William J.
Marsh and Gladys Yoakum Wright; music by William J. Marsh)

Cattle and oil are two reasons that Dallas is one of
the fastest-growing cities in the United States. With
a population of more than one million people, it's
the second biggest city in Texas, after Houston.

Inside Scoop

FOUR U.S. PRESIDENTS have ties to
Texas: Dwight D. Eisenhower, Lyndon B.
Johnson, George H. W. Bush, and George
W. Bush.

TEXAS HAS more farms than any other
state. In the year 2000, 226,000 farms
were counted in Texas.

THE DALLAS COWBOYS were Super Bowl
champions three times during the 1990s—
'93, '94, '96.

TEXAS WAS an independent republic for
10 years before joining the United States
in 1845.

THE STATE CAPITOL in Austin was
modeled after the U.S. Capitol and is made
of pink Texas granite.

A 16-YEAR-OLD Bandera student began a paper-
recycling program in her town that collected
enough paper to save at least 1,000 trees.

1964 **The headquarters of the National Aeronautics and
Space Administration (NASA) Lyndon B. Johnson
Space Center opens at Houston.**

1988 George H.W. Bush of Houston is elected 41st
president of the United States.

1963 U.S. Vice President Lyndon B. Johnson
succeeds to the presidency after President
John F. Kennedy is assassinated in Dallas.

Crawford's George W. Bush, governor of *2001*
Texas and son of former U.S. President
George H.W. Bush, is elected
43rd president of the United States.

Utah

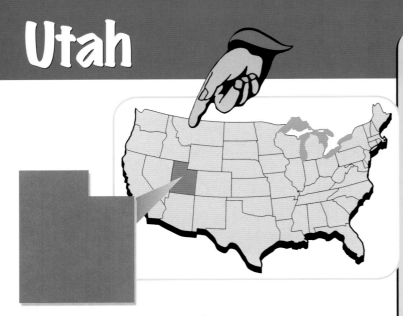

Inside Scoop

THE GREAT SALT LAKE is saltier than the world's oceans.

MORMON SETTLERS called their new homeland "Deseret," the Mormon word for "honeybee," because they worked like bees when they arrived in Utah.

RAINBOW BRIDGE NATIONAL MONUMENT in southern Utah is the world's largest known natural stone arch. It is 290 feet (88 meters) high. Many American Indians consider it a sacred place.

A 12-YEAR-OLD from Parowan rode a lawnmower from Salt Lake City to Washington, D.C., in 1997 to raise money for a neighbor's baby who needed a liver transplant and to bring attention to the importance of organ donations. His trip was successful and so was the baby's operation.

One of the most amazing rock formations at Canyonlands National Park is Mesa Arch. The arch was formed by eroding sandstone. Mesa Arch is in a part of the park known as Island in the Sky.

FRESH FACTS

NAME For the Ute Indians who lived there. "Ute" means "people of the mountains."

ABBREVIATION None

CAPITAL Salt Lake City

NICKNAME Beehive State

AREA 84,899 square miles (219,888 square kilometers)

POPULATION 2,233,169

STATEHOOD Jan. 4, 1896 (45th state)

HIGHEST POINT Kings Peak (13,528 feet; 4,123 meters)

LOWEST POINT Beaverdam Creek (2,000 feet; 610 meters)

INDUSTRIES Electric equipment, food products, medical and other scientific equipment, metals, mining, tourism, trade, transportation equipment

AGRICULTURE Barley, cattle, chickens, dairy products, fruit, hay, wheat

MOTTO Industry.

FLAG The state seal in the center shows a beehive, symbolizing steady, hard work. There are also sego lilies, representing peace, and a bald eagle, which is the U.S. national bird. The year 1847 commemorates the arrival of the Mormons in Utah, and 1896 honors the year Utah joined the Union as a state. The flag was adopted in 1896.

BIRD In 1848 **sea gulls** from the Great Salt Lake fed on millions of grasshoppers that swarmed into the area, thereby saving the new settlers' crops from being destroyed by the insects. Utah honored the sea gull by adopting it as the state bird in 1955.

FLOWER The **sego lily,** which can be found throughout Utah, has been the state flower since 1911. Its bulbs were an important source of food for Utah's native people and the state's first settlers.

TREE The **blue spruce** is an evergreen tree with silvery blue needles that grows high up in the Wasatch and Unita Mountains. It was adopted in 1947.

SONG "Utah We Love Thee" (words and music by Evan Stephens)

TIMELINE

1776 Spanish priests Francisco Atanasio Dominguez and Silvestre Velez de Escalante explore the region.

1824 Fur trapper Jim Bridger discovers the Great Salt Lake.

1847 Mormons led by Brigham Young settle in the Great Salt Lake area.

1848 The United States wins the region after war with Mexico. The first crops are saved by sea gulls.

1861 The nation's first transcontinental telegraph begins operating after lines from Washington, D.C., and San Francisco are joined in Salt Lake City.

1869 The Union Pacific and Central Pacific complete the nation's first transcontinental railroad at Promontory. A golden spike is driven in where the tracks meet.

In 2002, athletes from around the world gathered at Salt Lake City for the Winter Olympic Games.

AAA GEMS:
Selected Must-See Points of Interest

BRYCE CANYON NATIONAL PARK – The park is named after Ebenezer Bryce whose cattle grazed in the maze-like twists of the canyon's stream beds. Bryce is not a true canyon but rather a series of giant amphitheaters. Its walls have some of the Earth's most colorful rocks. Water, ice, and wind have sculpted them into pillars called "hoodoos" and other fantastic forms.

DINOSAUR NATIONAL MONUMENT – This site stretches from Colorado to northeast Utah. You can see fossilized dinosaur bones and fossils of other prehistoric creatures in the same sandstone cliff. Activities include hiking, camping, and fishing and a 31-mile (50-kilometer) drive through the heart of the canyon country.

LAGOON AMUSEMENT PARK (Farmington) – Pioneer Village, a re-created frontier settlement, takes you back to the 1800s. Exhibits and train and stagecoach rides, a wild-animal area, a water park with slides, and roller coasters offer fun and discovery.

ROSENBRUCH WILDLIFE MUSEUM (St. George) – Realistic wildlife habitats have been created to show you how animals live around the world. Animals made from fiberglass or foam forms and covered with real skin and fur look like they have just come in from the wild. On exhibit are wolves, crocodiles, kangaroos, camels, and many others.

ZION NATIONAL PARK – Named Zion by Mormon pioneers, the park is noted for its huge rock formations, canyons, and one of the world's largest free-standing arches called Kolob Arch. The brightly colored rock formations, waterfalls, and hanging gardens amaze visitors from around the world.

Holiday lights cast a beautiful glow over Salt Lake City. The six-spired Mormon Temple can be seen at the left.

1990 Mark Strand of the University of Utah in Salt Lake City is named poet laureate of the United States.

1952 Uranium deposits are discovered near Moab.

1893 The Mormon Temple in Salt Lake City is completed after 40 years of work.

1970 Gary Gavelich sets a world land speed record when he drives his rocket-powered car 622 mph (1,001 kph) at the Bonneville Salt Flats International Speedway.

Salt Lake City hosts the Winter **2002** Olympics. More than 2,000 athletes from 85 nations compete.

Vermont

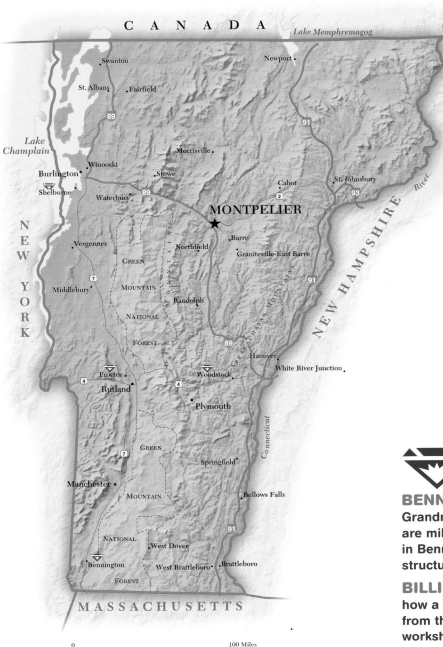

Stowe, one of the most popular ski resorts in the eastern United States, is located at Mount Mansfield, Vermont's highest peak.

The dairy industry is very important to Vermont's economy. Take a tour of the Cabot Creamery to see how cheddar cheese is made.

 ## AAA GEMS:
Selected Must-See Points of Interest

BENNINGTON MUSEUM – The paintings of folk artist Grandma Moses are featured at this museum. Also on exhibit are military uniforms, dolls and toys, and American glass. While in Bennington, stop at the town's Battle Monument, the tallest structure in the state.

BILLINGS FARM AND MUSEUM (Woodstock) – Learn how a modern dairy farm is run and how the daily chores differ from those of farmers in the 1800s. Tools, machinery, a workshop, a kitchen, and a country store are on display.

SHELBURNE MUSEUM – There are 37 buildings and other structures on the museum's grounds related to pioneer life in New England. You can visit a one-room schoolhouse, railroad depot, horseshoe barn, jail, country store, and more. See old-time toys, quilts, duck decoys, and weathervanes. Walk across a covered bridge and check out the Ticonderoga, docked at waterside. It's one of the last steam-powered paddlewheelers.

WILSON CASTLE (Proctor) – Built in 1867, this brick-and-marble castle has a towering turret, 32 rooms, 13 fireplaces, and 84 stained-glass windows. Paintings, photographs, and sculpture are exhibited in the art gallery.

TIMELINE

1609 French explorer Samuel de Champlain claims Vermont for France.

1724 The first permanent European settlement is established at Fort Dummer.

1775 Ethan Allen and the Green Mountain Boys capture Fort Ticonderoga during the Revolutionary War.

1777 Vermont declares itself an independent republic.

1823 The Champlain Canal opens, providing a water route from Vermont to New York City.

1880 Chester Arthur, who was born in Fairfield, is elected the 21st president of the United States.

FRESH FACTS

NAME Based on the French words "verts monts," meaning "green mountains."

ABBREVIATION Vt.

CAPITAL Montpelier

NICKNAME Green Mountain State

AREA 9,615 square miles (24,903 square kilometers)

POPULATION 608,827

STATEHOOD March 4, 1791 (14th state)

HIGHEST POINT Mount Mansfield (4,393 feet; 1,339 meters)

LOWEST POINT Lake Champlain (95 feet; 29 meters)

INDUSTRIES Electrical and electronic equipment, finance, food products, granite, insurance, lumber and wood products, machine tools, marble, printed materials, real estate, tourism

AGRICULTURE Apples, cattle, dairy products, hay, maple products, vegetables, young plants

MOTTO Freedom and unity.

FLAG The coat of arms in the center shows a pine tree, a cow, and three sheaves of wheat, all representing agriculture, with the Green Mountains in the background. The flag was adopted in 1923.

BIRD Many people think the clear flute-like song of the **hermit thrush** is the most beautiful song of all North American birds. It was adopted in 1941.

FLOWER Honeybees convert the nectar of **red clover** into the light, golden honey for which Vermont is famous. It is also a favorite food of grazing cattle. The flower was adopted in 1894.

TREE The **sugar maple,** chosen in 1949, is popular with Vermonters all year long. In the early spring, they collect its sap to make maple syrup, for which Vermont is known. In the fall, Vermonters – and many tourists – marvel at the blazing red and orange foliage.

SONG "These Green Hills" (words and music by Diane B. Martin)

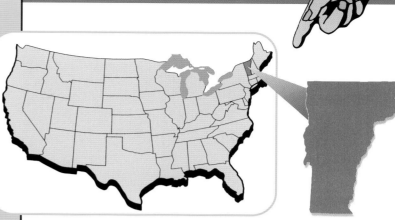

Inside Scoop

VERMONT HAS 114 covered bridges, more than any other state.

VERMONT IS the country's largest producer of maple syrup. About 40 gallons of sap are needed to make one gallon of maple syrup.

BEN AND JERRY'S ICE CREAM factory, near Waterbury, gives its unsold ice cream to local farmers who use it to feed their pigs. The hogs like all the flavors except Mint with Oreo® Cookie.

MORGAN HORSES, one of America's favorite breeds, are named after Justin Morgan, who raised the first Morgan stallion some 200 years ago in Randolph.

MARIA VON TRAPP, made famous by the movie "The Sound of Music," moved to Vermont with her family after escaping from the Nazis in Europe. She started a lodge in Stowe that specializes in cross-country skiing and musical entertainment.

KELLY CLARK, an 18-year-old from West Dover, won the Olympic gold medal in 2002 at Salt Lake City in the women's snowboarding half-pipe competition. It's the first gold for the United States in snowboarding.

Vermont's trees burst with color in the fall. People sometimes call the out-of-staters who tour Vermont to look at the changing colors "Leaf Peepers."

1910 The Green Mountain Club begins to blaze the Long Trail, a **270-mile (435-kilometer)** route between Massachusetts and Canada that is a favorite of hikers.

1923 Calvin Coolidge, of Plymouth Notch, becomes the 30th president of the United States.

1934 The country's first rope tow, powered by a Model T Ford engine, gives skiers a lift in Woodstock.

1970 New laws are passed to protect and preserve the state's environment.

1984 Madeleine Kunin is elected Vermont's first female governor.

Virginia

Sunset casts a glow over the historic James River in this view from the lawn of Shirley Plantation, which was built just six years after English settlers landed at Jamestown.

Some of the trees that George Washington himself planted still stand at his home in Mount Vernon.

AAA GEMS:
Selected Must-See Points of Interest

COLONIAL WILLIAMSBURG HISTORIC AREA – Costumed guides lead you through many reconstructed buildings at Williamsburg, the capital of Virginia from 1699 to 1780. Discover what everyday life was like when you visit the Governor's Palace, the Capitol, the jail, the church, and the shops. Craftsmen demonstrate their trades and skills.

JAMESTOWN SETTLEMENT – The original Jamestown settlement of 1607 was re-created in 1957 with full-scale reproductions of the three ships that brought the first colonists to Jamestown, an Indian village showing how the Powhatan Indians lived, and a reconstructed three-cornered fort, which was the settlers' first home.

LURAY CAVERNS – Deep beneath the Blue Ridge Mountains, this huge cavern has rooms that contain a variety of unusual formations and crystal clear pools. In the Cathedral Room, haunting music can be heard from the "Stalacpipe Organ" whose pipes are specially tuned stalactites.

MONTICELLO (Charlottesville) – Thomas Jefferson designed the mansion he called Monticello, Latin for "little mountain." You can visit 10 of the rooms, which include some of his inventions, such as a dumbwaiter and a polygraph he used to make copies of his letters.

MOUNT VERNON – George Washington's estate includes his mansion, a museum, gardens, the graves of George and Martha (his wife), and 12 outbuildings. A Pioneer Farmer site on the grounds offers hands-on activities and a round barn with horses that thresh wheat.

TIMELINE

1607 The first permanent English settlement in America is founded at Jamestown.

1775 Patrick Henry gives his famous "Give me liberty or give me death" speech in Richmond's St. John's Church.

1789 George Washington of Mount Vernon is elected the first president of the United States.

1619 The House of Burgesses, the first democratically elected legislature in America, sits in Williamsburg. Dutch traders bring the first Africans to Jamestown to be indentured servants.

1781 The Revolutionary War ends when the British surrender at Yorktown.

1861 Richmond becomes the capital of the Confederate States of America.

FRESH FACTS

NAME For Queen Elizabeth I of England, who was often called the "Virgin Queen" because she never married.

ABBREVIATION Va.

CAPITAL Richmond

NICKNAME Old Dominion

AREA 42,774 square miles (110,785 square kilometers)

POPULATION 7,078,515

STATEHOOD June 25, 1788 (10th state)

HIGHEST POINT Mount Rogers (5,729 feet; 1,746 meters.)

LOWEST POINT Sea level

INDUSTRIES Chemicals, electrical and electronic equipment, food products, textiles, tobacco products, trade, tourism, transportation equipment, wood products

AGRICULTURE Cattle, chickens, corn, hogs, milk, peanuts, soybeans, tobacco, wheat

MOTTO Thus always to tyrants.

FLAG The state seal in the center shows two figures acting out the meaning of the state's motto. Virtue, dressed as an Amazon warrior with a spear and sword, stands victoriously over Tyranny. Tyranny's chain is broken and his crown lies on the ground. The flag was adopted in 1931.

BIRD English explorers in the 1700s who had heard the **cardinal** sing called it the "Virginia nightingale." Legend says the bird was named after the cardinals of the Roman Catholic Church who wore crimson robes. The bird was adopted in 1950.

FLOWER The delicate white or pink **dogwood** flowers appear throughout the state each spring. George Washington and Thomas Jefferson planted dogwood trees on their estates. It was adopted in 1918.

TREE In the fall, the leaves of the **dogwood** turn red. It is believed that the color acts as a signal to help birds find the trees' red berries. The tree was adopted in 1956.

SONG None

Inside Scoop

VIRGINIA IS known as the "Mother of Presidents," because it has produced more American presidents than any other state: George Washington, Thomas Jefferson, James Madison, James Monroe, William Harrison, John Tyler, Zachary Taylor, and Woodrow Wilson.

THE PENTAGON, in Arlington, was completed in 1943 and is the headquarters of the U.S. Department of Defense. Although only five stories high, it is the largest office building in the world and has three times as much space as the Empire State Building.

TANGIER ISLAND in Chesapeake Bay can be reached only by boat. Its people led such isolated lives that they spoke Elizabethan English until recently.

IN 1862 at Hampton Roads, the USS "Monitor" and the CSS "Virginia" (formerly the "Merrimac") fought the first battle between metal armored ships, changing the course of naval warfare.

A 16-YEAR-OLD from Charlottesville started an organization in 2000 for kids to raise money to help the thousands of children orphaned by war in Rwanda. One goal is to buy goats, which are a valuable source of milk, cheese, and fertilizer.

Whether you're looking to sail, surf, enjoy the area's natural wildlife, or just to fly a kite, Virginia Beach has it all.

1865 The Civil War ends when Gen. Robert E. Lee surrenders to Gen. Ulysses S. Grant at Appomattox Court House.

1968 Arthur Ashe of Richmond is the first African-American to win the United States Tennis Open.

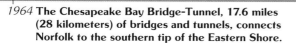

1964 The Chesapeake Bay Bridge-Tunnel, 17.6 miles (28 kilometers) of bridges and tunnels, connects Norfolk to the southern tip of the Eastern Shore.

1990 L. Douglas Wilder becomes the nation's first African-American governor.

Washington

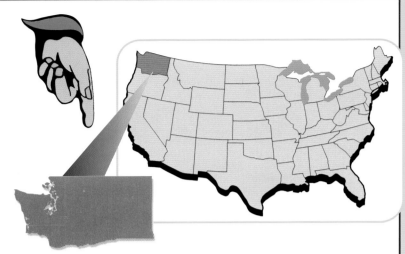

NAME In honor of President George Washington, the nation's first president.

ABBREVIATION Wash.

CAPITAL Olympia

NICKNAME Evergreen State

AREA 71,300 square miles (184,667 square kilometers)

POPULATION 5,894,121

STATEHOOD Nov. 11, 1889 (42nd state)

HIGHEST POINT Mount Rainier (14,410 feet; 4,392 meters.)

LOWEST POINT Sea level

INDUSTRIES Aerospace equipment, biotechnology, chemical products, computer software, food products, lumber, machinery, paper products, tourism, trade, wood products

AGRICULTURE Apples, cattle, dairy products, hay, potatoes, seafood, wheat, young plants

MOTTO By and by.

FLAG This is the only state flag that displays a picture of a U.S. president. George Washington is shown against a green background, which represents the state's extensive forests. The flag was adopted in 1923.

BIRD The **American (willow) goldfinch** has a lively, canary-like song. It was adopted in 1951.

FLOWER The **coast rhododendron,** adopted in 1949, is an evergreen shrub, which blooms in the spring. This variety is usually pink.

TREE State legislator George Adams believed the **Western hemlock** ought to be the state tree. He thought it would prove to be "the backbone of the state's forest industry." The tree was adopted in 1947.

SONG "Washington, My Home" (words and music by Helen Davis)

Inside Scoop

SONORA LOUISE SMART DODD of Spokane was the originator of Father's Day, first celebrated on June 19, 1910.

MORE APPLES are grown in Washington than in any other state.

CAPE ALAVA is the westernmost part of the contiguous United States.

THE PEACE ARCH, built in 1921, marks the border between the United States and Canada. One foot stands in Douglas, British Columbia, the other in Blaine, Wash.

MEGAN QUANN, a 16-year-old from Puyallup, won an Olympic gold medal in 2000 for the 100-meter breast stroke and 400-meter relay, the youngest medalist on the U.S. swim team.

The Hoh Rain Forest in Olympic National Park gets more than 150 inches (381 centimeters) of rain each year. Some of the trees in the forest may be more than 1,000 years old.

TIMELINE

1775 Bruno Heceta and Juan Francisco de la Bodega y Quadra of Spain are the first Europeans to set foot in Washington.

1792 Robert Gray, an American sea captain, discovers the Columbia River. George Vancouver maps Puget Sound.

1846 Canada and the United States draw Washington's boundary at the 49th parallel.

1916 William E. Boeing starts a company in Seattle that is today the world's largest aircraft and spacecraft manufacturer.

1942 Grand Coulee Dam, one of the largest concrete structures in the world, is completed.

AAA GEMS:
Selected Must-See Points of Interest

MOUNT RAINIER NATIONAL PARK (near Ashford) — Mount Rainier is permanently snow-capped and surrounded by 26 glaciers. Farther down, there are dense forests, flowered meadows, streams, and waterfalls. You can hike, fish, camp, climb, ski, and take scenic drives.

OLYMPIC NATIONAL PARK (Olympia) — In this park, you can sample three very different habitats: glacier-clad mountains, the nation's only temperate rain forest, and miles of unspoiled ocean shore. Drive up to Hurricane Ridge to observe deer and marmots and for spectacular views of the Strait of Juan de Fuca, Vancouver Island, and the Olympic Mountains.

POINT DEFIANCE PARK (Tacoma) — One of the nation's largest urban parks offers a zoo and aquarium, a historic fort, a logging museum, hiking trails, and gardens.

SAN JUAN ISLANDS — These 172 picturesque islands are popular getaways due to their moderate climate and tranquil nature.

SEATTLE ART MUSEUM — This collection of Asian, African, and Northwest Coast American Indian art is renowned.

SEATTLE CENTER — A science center, an American popular-music museum, a children's museum, and an amusement park all occupy these landscaped grounds in downtown Seattle. A high point is the observation deck at the Space Needle from which you can survey the city, Puget Sound, and the Cascade and Olympic Mountains.

Did you know that the famous Seattle Space Needle was the headquarters of Dr. Evil in the movie "Austin Powers: The Spy Who Shagged Me"?

1975 Microsoft Corp. in Redmond is founded by Seattle native Bill Gates.

1989 Seattle celebrates its centennial.

1962 Seattle hosts the Century 21 Exposition and inaugurates the nation's first daily-service monorail.

1980 Mount St. Helens erupts, causing much damage. It is the first time this volcano erupted in 123 years. Geologists think it will erupt again in the future.

1996 Seattle native Gary Locke is elected governor, the nation's first Chinese-American governor.

West Virginia

Visitors to the Exhibition Mine in Beckley can ride a guided car through a mine and learn the history of how coal has been mined from West Virginia's hills.

Among the highlights of Pipestem Resort State Park are the scenic views of the Bluestone Gorge. The park also has plenty more to offer including camping, horseback riding, and even golf!

Inside Scoop

MOST OF THE NATION'S glass marbles are produced in Parkersburg.

THE TOWN OF ROMNEY changed sides between the Union and Confederacy at least 56 times during the Civil War.

GRAVE CREEK MOUND, south of Wheeling, is one of the largest Indian burial mounds in the Americas. It is about 2,000 years old and about seven stories high.

DONALD DUNCAN, from Huntington, made yo-yos popular and developed the loop for the end of the string, necessary for doing some advanced yo-yo tricks.

IN 1947 Chuck Yeager, born in Myra, was the first person to break the sound barrier—he piloted a jet that traveled faster than the speed of sound.

A HIGH SCHOOL STUDENT from Frametown organized the first statewide food drive. This helped to bring attention to the problem of hunger and to educate people about practical ways they can help.

TIMELINE

1727 Germans from Pennsylvania establish a settlement at present-day Shepherdstown.

1742 Coal is discovered on the Coal River by John Salling and John Howard.

1836 The first railroad, the B & O (Baltimore and Ohio), reaches Harper's Ferry.

1859 Abolitionist John Brown and a group of his followers are arrested while raiding the federal arsenal at Harper's Ferry, one of the events leading to the Civil War.

1861–62 Western Virginians refuse to secede from the Union and join the Confederacy with other Virginians. West Virginians separate from Virginia and form their own state.

1908 Anna Jarvis establishes the nation's first Mother's Day celebration in a church in Grafton.

FRESH FACTS

NAME For Queen Elizabeth I of England, the "Virgin Queen." The state separated from Virginia in 1861–62 and added West to its name.

ABBREVIATION W.Va.

CAPITAL Charleston

NICKNAME Mountain State

AREA 24,231 square miles (62,758 square kilometers)

POPULATION 1,808,344

STATEHOOD June 20, 1863 (35th state)

HIGHEST POINT Spruce Knob (4,861 feet; 1,482 meters)

LOWEST POINT Potomac River in Jefferson County (240 feet; 73 meters)

INDUSTRIES Chemicals, clay products, coal, glass, machinery, metals, mining, plastic products, salt, steel, stone, tourism, wood products

AGRICULTURE Apples, cattle, chickens, corn, dairy products, peaches, poultry, tobacco, wheat

MOTTO Mountaineers are always free.

FLAG The state seal in the center pictures a farmer and a miner with rifles, showing they are ready to defend their families, freedom, and land. Two wreaths of rhododendrons, the state flower, nearly encircle the seal. The flag was adopted in 1929.

BIRD The **cardinal's** song is loud and clear and sounds like a series of short whistles. Baby cardinals are fed by both their mothers and fathers. The cardinal has been the state bird since 1949.

FLOWER The blossoms of the **rhododendron** can be pink or white. A shrub with dark green leaves that grows throughout the state, it was adopted in 1903 after school children voted for it.

TREE The **sugar maple** is used for making furniture, maple syrup, and maple sugar. A single tree can yield two to three pounds of sugar when it is "sugared off." The sugar maple was adopted in 1949.

SONGS "This Is My West Virginia" (words and music by Iris Bell). "West Virginia My Home Sweet Home" (words and music by Julian G. Hearne, Jr.). "The West Virginia Hills" (words by Rev. David King, although attributed to his wife, Ellen.; music by H.E. Engle).

◆ AAA GEMS:
Selected Must-See Points of Interest

BLACKWATER FALLS STATE PARK (Davis) – Observation points give you spectacular views of the amber waterfalls plunging 65 feet (20 meters) into a deep gorge. Hiking, riding, nature programs, and other outdoor activities are available.

CASS SCENIC RAILROAD (Cass) – Steam locomotives that once hauled logs will take you for a ride through beautiful mountain scenery to the top of Bald Knob. Cass is one of the best-preserved lumber towns in the country.

OGLEBAY PARK (Wheeling) – The park offers a wide variety of activities: you can watch artisans blow glass, observe animals at the zoo, stroll in the formal gardens, and swim, ski, and hike in the appropriate seasons. In the summer, there's a computerized light-and-sound show against a backdrop of cascading waters. In November and December, a million lights decorate the park for the Festival of Lights.

SMOKE HOLE CAVERNS (Petersburg) – The caverns were once used by American Indians to smoke meat. During the Civil War, ammunition was stored here. Today, you can explore the caverns that contain one of the world's longest ribbon stalactites, an underground pool with fish, and helectites that grow sideways!

THEATRE WEST VIRGINIA (Beckley) – This cliff-side amphitheater presents two musical dramas: the story of the feud between families of the Hatfields and McCoys who were good friends until they chose opposite sides in the Civil War; and "The Honey and the Rock," a musical about the history of the state.

1932 Pearl Buck, born in Hillsboro, wins the Pulitzer Prize for her novel, "The Good Earth." Six years later, she is awarded the Nobel Prize for Literature.

1954 The West Virginia Turnpike is opened, linking Princeton in the southeast to Charleston in the northwest.

1959 The National Radio Astronomy Observatory opens in Green Bank. Its huge radio telescopes probe outer space.

1968 Federal mine safety laws are passed after 78 people are killed in a coal mine disaster.

1984 Gymnast Mary Lou Retton, a native of Fairmont, wins five medals at the Olympics. She is the first American female to win an Olympic gold medal at a gymnastic event.

Wisconsin

NAME From the Chippewa Indian word "ouisconsin," meaning "gathering of waters," which referred to the Wisconsin River.

ABBREVIATION Wis.

CAPITAL Madison

NICKNAME Badger State

AREA 65,498 square miles (169,640 square kilometers)

POPULATION 5,363,675

STATEHOOD May 29, 1848 (30th state)

HIGHEST POINT Timms Hill (1,952 feet; 595 meters)

LOWEST POINT Lake Michigan (581 feet; 177 meters)

INDUSTRIES Electrical equipment, food products, lumber, machinery, medical equipment, metal products, paper products, plastics, printed materials, tourism, trade, vehicles

AGRICULTURE Beets, cabbage, cattle, chickens, corn, cranberries, dairy products, hay, oats, peas, potatoes, soybeans

MOTTO Forward.

FLAG The state shield in the center represents agriculture, mining, navigation, and manufacturing. A sailor and a miner stand on either side. A badger, the state animal, is shown above the shield. The flag was adopted in 1913.

BIRD Robins sing their cheerful song at sunrise, as if welcoming the dawn of a new day. The bird was adopted in 1949.

FLOWER School children voted in 1909 for the **wood violet** over the wild rose and other flowers, but it was not officially adopted until 1949.

TREE Adopted in 1949, the **sugar maple** is the best type of maple tree from which to collect sap for maple syrup.

SONG "On, Wisconsin" (words and music by William T. Purdy)

Inside Scoop

WISCONSIN'S NICKNAME comes from the state's early lead miners who burrowed into caves and hillside hollows, like badgers, to keep warm in the winters.

MILWAUKEE IS HOME to the International Clown Hall of Fame that honors outstanding clown performers, sponsors clown shows, and has an exhibit on the history of clowning.

THE COUNTRY'S LARGEST cross-country ski race, called the American Birkebeiner, takes place every February from Hayward to Cable.

WISCONSIN IS KNOWN as America's Dairyland for the milk, butter, and cheese it produces.

A HIGH SCHOOL SENIOR from Milwaukee persuaded his classmates to give up renting tuxedos for the prom, collected the rental money, and donated it to the Cystic Fibrosis Foundation.

The world's largest carousel can be seen at the House on the Rock in Spring Green. The house also has the world's largest collection of working musical organs, mechanical orchestras, and player pianos, as well as the world's largest collections of carousel horses and toy circuses.

TIMELINE

1634 French explorer Jean Nicolet discovers Wisconsin.

1701 The first permanent European settlement is established at Green Bay.

1836 The discovery of lead results in the creation of the territory of Wisconsin.

1673 Father Jacques Marquette, a French missionary, and Louis Jolliet, a French-Canadian explorer, chart the Wisconsin region.

1783 Following the Treaty of Paris, the United States takes ownership of the Wisconsin region.

1856 The first kindergarten in the nation opens in Watertown.

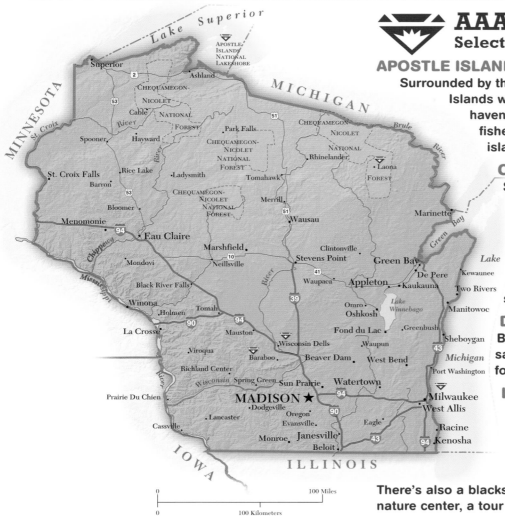

AAA GEMS:
Selected Must-See Points of Interest

APOSTLE ISLANDS NATIONAL LAKESHORE – Surrounded by the waters of Lake Superior, the Apostle Islands were early fur-trading outposts and are now a haven for hikers, sailors, kayakers, campers, and fishermen as well as for wildlife. There are 21 islands. Stockton Island is the largest.

CIRCUS WORLD MUSEUM (Baraboo) – Step right up for big-top circus performances, parades, clowns, rides, and demonstrations in the summer months at the original winter quarters of the Ringling Brothers circus. The museum traces circus history and has a fabulous collection of old circus wagons. The famous magician Harry Houdini had his start here.

DELLS BOAT TOURS (Wisconsin Dells) – Boat tours on the Wisconsin River cruise past sandstone cliffs, canyons, fascinating rock formations, and erosion-carved islands.

LUMBERJACK SPECIAL AND CAMP FIVE MUSEUM COMPLEX TOUR (Laona) – Take a ride on the "Lumberjack Special," a steam-powered train that travels from the historic Laona depot to the museum, which traces the history of logging. There's also a blacksmith at work, a country store, animal corral, nature center, a tour of the forest in a surrey, and a boat ride.

MILWAUKEE COUNTY ZOO – Hop aboard the zoomobile for a close-up tour of the animals that come from five continents. The Oceans of Fun show features sea lions and harbor seals, and the bird show tells you about raptors. A huge Pacific Coast aquarium and a dairy-farm exhibit are fun and informative.

MILWAUKEE PUBLIC MUSEUM – At this museum, you can walk through a Costa Rican rain forest, the streets of Old Milwaukee, and an exhibit called Temples, Tells, and Tombs. The Tribute to Survival exhibit is dedicated to North American Indian history and culture. Don't miss the life-size dinosaurs.

Located on Madeline Island in Lake Superior, Big Bay State Park features a family campground, hiking and nature trails, and a beautiful sand beach.

Visitors to the Wisconsin Dells don't need a boat to explore the area's amazing sandstone rocks. They can also drive right into the water on half-boat, half-car "Ducks"!

1884 The Ringling Brothers circus is founded in Baraboo.

1959 The St. Lawrence Seaway opens, linking the Great Lakes with the Atlantic Ocean.

1997 The Green Bay Packers win their 12th National Football League championship, the most of any team in NFL history.

2000 A dairy farm in Omro successfully starts using robots to milk cows, introducing a new era in dairy farming.

Wyoming

NAME Based on the Delaware Indian words, "meche-weami-ing," meaning "large prairie place" or "big plains."

ABBREVIATION Wyo.

CAPITAL Cheyenne

NICKNAME Equality State (also, Cowboy State)

AREA 97,818 square miles (253,349 square kilometers)

POPULATION 493,782

STATEHOOD July 10, 1890 (44th state)

HIGHEST POINT Gannett Peak (13,804 feet; 4,207 meters)

LOWEST POINT Belle Fourche River Valley (3,100 feet; 945 meters)

INDUSTRIES Aircraft equipment, chemicals, electronic equipment, food products, lumber, mining, natural gas, petroleum products, tourism, wood products

AGRICULTURE Barley, beans, cattle, hay, oats, sheep, sugar beets, wheat

MOTTO Equal rights.

FLAG The red border stands for the blood shed by Indians and pioneers, the white is for purity, and the blue symbolizes justice and faithfulness. The buffalo is branded with the state seal to show the importance of the livestock industry. The flag was adopted in 1917.

BIRD The **Western meadowlark,** adopted in 1927, was first observed by explorers Meriwether Lewis and William Clark on the Missouri River. Its song can be heard in pastures and open grasslands of the West.

FLOWER The **Indian paintbrush,** adopted in 1917, is a source of nectar for hummingbirds.

TREE A giant **cottonwood** more than 50 feet (15 meters) tall once grew on a ranch near Thermopolis. The cottonwood was adopted as the state tree in 1947 in honor of this particular tree.

SONG "Wyoming" (words by Charles E. Winter; music by George E. Knapp)

Inside SCOOP

MEDICINE WHEEL, is a large circle of flat white stones with 28 spokes radiating from its center. Built at least 1,000 years ago atop a mountain crest near Lovell, it may have been a calendar for early American Indians.

DINOSAUR PRINTS 165 million years old (middle Jurassic period) were discovered near Shell in 1997.

GERALD FORD, the 38th president of the United States, worked as a Yellowstone Park ranger in the summer of 1936.

INDEPENDENCE ROCK, near Casper, is a historic landmark rising 193 feet (59 meters) above the Plains. More than 5,000 pioneers traveling westward on the Oregon Trail stopped to carve their names on it.

A SMALL GROUP OF TEENS from Sheridan donated the money they earned from making and selling red-white-and-blue lapel pins to the Red Cross after the 9/11 tragedy in New York City.

A trip on horseback into Wyoming's high country is the highlight of a lifetime for many visitors to the Cowboy State.

TIMELINE

1807 John Colter discovers the hot springs and geysers at Yellowstone.

1834 The trading post at Fort William, later called Fort Laramie, is the first European settlement in the area.

1867 The Union Pacific Railroad reaches Wyoming.

1869 Wyoming women are granted the right to vote.

1872 Yellowstone becomes the country's first national park.

1883 The state's first oil well is drilled.

AAA GEMS:
Selected Must-See Points of Interest

BUFFALO BILL HISTORICAL CENTER (Cody) – Discover what life was like in the American West when you visit the five museums at this complex. On display are Indian art and artifacts, Buffalo Bill's belongings, American firearms, exhibits on the natural history of the region, and paintings of the West by famous artists.

CHEYENNE FRONTIER DAYS OLD WEST MUSEUM – Hold on to your hat when you climb onto a bronco-riding saddle – being a cowboy is harder than it looks. This is a great place to learn all about rodeos and frontier history.

DEVILS TOWER NATIONAL MONUMENT – This unusual volcanic rock with its flat top rises up 867 feet (264 meters) above the prairie. Many American Indians consider it a sacred place. Take time to investigate the prairie dog village near the entrance.

WYOMING TERRITORIAL PARK (Laramie) – At this frontier town, characters from the Old West, such as Calamity Jane, are re-created. See the prison cell where outlaw Butch Cassidy was held, a saloon, a smithy, and a marshal's office. Take the stagecoach and train rides.

YELLOWSTONE NATIONAL PARK – The country's first national park is a wonderland of bubbling mud volcanoes, geysers, colorful mineral springs, and waterfalls. Approximately every 88 minutes, Old Faithful geyser shoots more than 5,000 gallons (18,935 liters) of hot water into the air.

Old Faithful geyser is the most famous attraction at Yellowstone National Park.

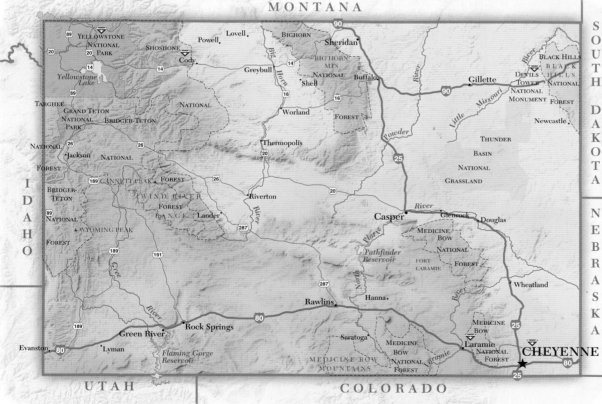

Buffalo, or American bison as they are sometimes called, roam wild in Wyoming's Yellowstone and Grand Teton National Parks. This buffalo lives in Firehole Canyon, Yellowstone.

1906 Devils Tower becomes the first national monument in the United States.

1929 Grand Teton National Park in Moose is established.

1988 One million acres (404,700 hectares) of Yellowstone National Park burn, the area's worst forest fire in 200 years.

1897 The first Cheyenne Frontier Days is held, a festival celebrated every July since. Its famous rodeo attracts both cowboys and tourists.

1925 Nellie Tayloe Ross, from Cheyenne, assumes office as the nation's first woman governor.

1991 Wolves, which nearly disappeared in the early 1900s, are reintroduced into Yellowstone National Park.

México

On Nov. 1 and 2, Méxicans celebrate their most famous holiday, the Day of the Dead. On these days, many Méxicans honor loved ones who have passed away by telling stories, singing songs, and decorating gravestones. One common sight during the celebrations is a skeleton figure known as a calaveras.

One of the most popular attractions in Acapulco is watching the divers at La Quebrada cliff. Men ranging in age from their teens to their mid-40s dive 135 feet (41 meters) into a narrow, rocky cove, hitting the water at 60 mph (102 kph).

El Angel, a monument to Méxican independence, stands still in the middle of México City's busy traffic. México City is North America's most heavily populated city.

TIMELINE

400 B.C.–A.D. 900 **Ancient Indian civilizations flourish at such centers as Teotihuacán, Monte Albán, and the Mayan sites in the Yucatán.**

1519 **Hernán Cortés begins the Spanish conquest of México.**

1821 **México gains its independence from Spain.**

1325–50 **The Aztecs build their capital, Tenochtitlán, the future México City.**

1810 **Father Miguel Hidalgo calls for an uprising against Spanish rule.**

1836 **Texas wins its independence from México.**

FRESH FACTS

NAME United Méxican States

CAPITAL México City, Federal District

ABBREVIATION Méx.

AREA 761,606 square miles (1,972,550 square kilometers)

POPULATION 101,879,171

INDEPENDENCE Sept. 27, 1821 (Independence Day is celebrated on Sept. 16)

HIGHEST POINT Citlaltépetl (Volcán Pico de Orizaba), Veracruz (18,410 feet; 5,610 meters)

LOWEST POINT Laguna Salada (Baja California) (33 feet; 10 meters below sea level)

INDUSTRIES Chemicals, electrical equipment, food products, iron, mining, natural gas, silver, steel, textiles, tourism, transportation equipment

AGRICULTURE Bananas, beans, coffee, corn, cotton, rice, soybeans, sugar cane, tomatoes, wheat

FLAG Adopted in 1821, the Méxican flag has three vertical bands: green for independence, white for religion, and red for unity. The Méxican coat of arms represents the legend about the founding of the Aztec capital, Tenochtitlán (now México City), on the spot where the Aztecs saw an eagle atop a cactus devouring a snake, as had been foretold.

BIRD The **crested caracara,** or **Méxican eagle,** is a member of the falcon family. It is sometimes called king buzzard because it chases vultures away from their catch.

FLOWER The Aztecs called the **dahlia "acocotli"** for "water cane," because the tall plant's hollow stem was used to carry water.

TREE The **ahuehuete tree** (Montezuma cypress) is one of the world's largest and longest-living trees and has been prized since the time of Montezuma. The famous **Tule tree** of Oaxaca (see Inside Scoop, right) is an ahuehuete.

ANTHEM "Méxican National Anthem" (words by Francisco González Bocanegra; music by Jaime Nunó)

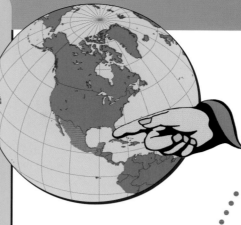

México's most famous music is the sound of a mariachi band. Mariachi band members wear the outfits of charro, or Méxican cowboys, with tight fitting pants, lots of silver spangles, and sometimes wide-brimmed hats called sombreros. One of the best places to see mariachis are in the Plaza Garibaldi in México City.

Inside Scoop

MÉXICO IS the most populous Spanish-speaking country in the world.

AVOCADOS, chili peppers, chocolate, corn, squash, tomatoes, turkeys, pumpkins, and vanilla are among the many foods that originated in México.

ONE OF THE OLDEST and largest trees in the world is the famous Tule tree of Santa Maria del Tule in the state of Oaxaca. It is more than 2,000 years old and its trunk has a circumference of 138 feet (42 meters)!

ADRIANA FERNANDEZ began running as a teenager in México City. In 1999, she won the New York City Marathon, clocking the second-fastest time ever in that race.

1863 At the end of the Méxican-American War, México cedes its northern territories to the United States, including all or part of what are now California, Arizona, New Mexico, Nevada, Utah, and Colorado.

1910 The Méxican Revolution is triggered by a rigged re-election of dictator Porfirio Díaz.

1917 México's new constitution, still in effect today, is approved.

1968 The Summer Olympics are held in México City.

1993 The North American Free Trade Agreement is signed, lowering trade barriers betwen México, Canada, and the United States.

Baja California, Sonora, Sinaloa

CALIFORNIA
Tijuana
MEXICALI
Ensenada

UNITED STATES

ARIZONA

NEW MEXICO

Nogales

BAJA
CALIFORNIA
NORTE

SONORA

C H I H U A H U A

★HERMOSILLO

Pacific Ocean

Ciudad
Obregon

Punta
Chivata

SINALOA

El Rosario

Loreto

BAJA
CALIFORNIA
SUR

Golfo de California

ISLA
FARALLON

CULIACAN★

DURANGO

LA PAZ

Mazatlan

NAYARIT

Cabo San
Lucas

0   100 Miles

0   100 Kilometers

Inside Scoop

BAJA CALIFORNIA is one of the three sunniest places in the world.

DURING THE LATE 1800S, many outlaws from north of the México border sought safety in the Sonoran desert.

A COMMUNITY of sea lions lives on Isla Farallón, near the Sinaloa fishing port of Topolobampo, whose name means "lion's watering place."

Beachcombers at Punta Chivato in Baja California Sur will find miles of sandy beaches. If you like to snorkel, you'll find that nearby tide pools and rocky reefs teem with a rainbow of colors from tropical fish.

TIMELINE

1529 Nuño de Guzmán sets out from México City to conquer the Mexican northwest. He founds the city of Culiacán (Sinaloa) in 1531.

1697 Missionary Father Juan Salvatierra establishes the first permanent European settlement on Baja California at Loreto (Baja California Sur).

1535 Spanish explorer Hernán Cortés arrives in the Bay of Santa Cruz at present-day Baja California Sur.

1687 Spanish explorer and missionary Father Eusebio Kino establishes his first mission among the Sonoran Indians at Nuestra Señora de los Dolores.

1795 Ships from Boston, Mass., begin trading along the coast of Sinaloa.

Must-See Sites

ACUARIO MAZATLÁN (Mazatlán Aquarium, Sinaloa) – More than 150 kinds of colorful fish and other water animals can be viewed here. Highlights include piranhas, a bull shark, sea lion and exotic bird shows, and a crocodile exhibit.

LAGUNA OJO DE LIEBRE (Scammon's Lagoon, Baja California Sur) – This is the best place to observe the thousands of great gray whales that migrate 5,000 miles (8,000 kilometers) every year from Alaska to give birth and spend the winter in warm waters.

MUSEO DE ANTROPOLOGIA E HISTORIA DE BAJA CALIFORNIA SUR (Anthropological and Historical Museum of Baja California Sur) – See re-creations of Indian villages, photographs of ancient cave paintings, copies of documents written in 1535 by Hernán Cortés, exhibits about Spanish missions, Méxican ranch life, the state's plants and animals, and more.

MUSEO DE CIENCIAS DE ENSENADA (Science Museum of Ensenada, Baja California) – Learn about ocean life, endangered species, and marine environments at this museum, which also sponsors guided boat tours of Ensenada Bay.

FRESH FACTS

BAJA CALIFORNIA
NAME Spanish for "Lower California." The name "California" comes from "Califia," an imaginary island rich in gold and pearls described in a Spanish novel written in 1510.
CAPITAL Mexicali
AREA 27,071 square miles (70,113 square kilometers)
POPULATION 2,487,367
STATEHOOD 1952
HIGHEST POINT near Cerros la Botella Azul (10,170 feet; 3,100 meters)
LOWEST POINT Sea level
COAT OF ARMS

BAJA CALIFORNIA SUR
NAME Spanish for "Lower California South." (See Baja California.)
CAPITAL La Paz
AREA 27,578 square miles (71,428 square kilometers)
POPULATION 424,041
STATEHOOD 1974
HIGHEST POINT Sierra la Laguna (6,820 feet; 2,080 meters)
LOWEST POINT Sea level
COAT OF ARMS

SINALOA
NAME Thought to come from the Náhuatl (ancient Aztec) for "place where ears of corn are stored" or from a mixed Cahita-Tarasco-Náhuatl word meaning "place or river of the pitahayas" (a type of cactus).
CAPITAL Culiacán
AREA 22,429 square miles (58,092 square kilometers)
POPULATION 2,538,661
STATEHOOD 1830
HIGHEST POINT Cerro Alto Tapanco (9,580 feet; 2,920 meters)
LOWEST POINT Sea level
COAT OF ARMS

SONORA
NAME Spanish for "sonorous." The name is thought to come from an Indian mispronunciation of the Spanish word "señora," meaning "lady," or from the Opata Indian word "xunuta," meaning "place of the corn."
CAPITAL Hermosillo
AREA 71,403 square miles (184,934 square kilometers)
POPULATION 2,216,969
STATEHOOD 1830
HIGHEST POINT Cerro San José (8,678 feet; 2,920 meters)
LOWEST POINT Sea level
COAT OF ARMS

The Gulf of California, which separates the Baja Peninsula from the Méxican states of Sonora and Sinoloa, is a great place to see humpback whales.

1824 Sinaloa and Sonora become part of the new federal republic of México as a single state, the State of the West. They separate into two states in 1830.

1973 The completion of the Transpeninsula Highway opens up Baja California Sur to development and tourism.

1821 The port of Mazatlán in Sinaloa is opened to international trade.

1848 At the end of the Méxican-American War, Sonora, formerly México's largest state, loses more than one-quarter of its territory to the United States.

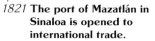

Monterrey, in the state of Nuevo León, was founded in 1596. Today it is one of Mexico's most important industrial cities, producing transportation equipment, electrical appliances, cement, clothing, glass, and more. Home to the largest convention center in all of Latin America, Monterrey is also a major center for trade with the United States.

Inside Scoop

MÉXICO'S LARGEST STATE gave its name to the world's smallest dog breed, the chihuahua.

FOUR OF THE canyons in Chihuahua's Copper Canyon region are deeper than Arizona's Grand Canyon.

FROM THE 1950s through the 1970s, many Hollywood Westerns, some starring John Wayne, were set in Durango's rugged Sierra Madre Occidental range.

"EL CERRO DE MERCADO" (Mercado Hill), just north of Durango city, is one of the largest single iron deposits in the world.

MÉXICO'S TRADITIONAL SHAWLS, called serapes, are a specialty of the weavers of Coahuila's capital, Saltillo.

TIMELINE

1554 Spanish explorer Francisco de Ibarra begins colonizing what is now the state of Durango. He founds the city of Durango in 1563.

1596 Spanish explorer Diego de Montemayor founds Monterrey, Nuevo León.

1762 Postal service begins between Monterrey (now the capital of Nuevo León), the city of San Luis Potosí, and México City.

1709 The town of San Francisco de Cuéllar (the modern city of Chihuahua) is founded.

1821 Mexico wins independence from Spain. Trade routes are established between St. Louis, Mo., and the Mexican cities of Santa Fe and Chihuahua.

1824 Coahuila and Texas become a part of the newly established Mexican republic as a single state. Durango, Chihuahua, and New Mexico also become part of the republic as a single state, but Durango separates later in the year.

FRESH FACTS

Must-See Sites

PARQUE NACIONAL DE BASASEACHIC (National Park of Basaseachic, Chihuahua) – Basaseachic Falls is México's highest waterfall and the fourth highest in North America. The hike to the falls is through forests that are home to deer, wildcats, pumas, tree frogs, woodpeckers and many other kinds of birds.

PARQUE NACIONAL CUMBRES DE MONTERREY (Monterrey Heights National Park, Nuevo León) – The scenic wonders of México's largest park include "Cascada Cola de Caballo" (Horsetail Falls) and Huasteca Canyon, a magnificent rock gorge whose sheer walls reach heights of up to 1,000 feet (305 meters).

PARCQUE NIÑOS HEROES (Heroic Children's Park, Nuevo León) – Named for the brave young cadets who defended Chapultepec Castle in México City during the Méxican-American War, this park encompasses an artificial lake, gardens, a baseball stadium, and the Museum of Fauna and National Sciences.

Many factories in cities like Nuevo Laredo (Tamaulipas) or Ciudad Juárez (Chihuahua) along the U.S.-México border are American-owned and make products for sale in the United States. Many American companies have moved their factories to México since Méxican workers are paid less money than those in the United States.

CHIHUAHUA
NAME From the Tarahumara Indian words for "place where sacks are made" or from the Náhuatl (ancient Atzec) for "dry or sandy place."
CAPITAL Chihuahua
AREA 94,831 square miles (245,612 square kilometers)
POPULATION 3,052,907
STATEHOOD 1824
HIGHEST POINT Cerro Ran Rafael (10,663 feet; 3,300 meters)
LOWEST POINT Not available
COAT OF ARMS

COAHUILA
NAME From the name of the local Coahuilteco Indian tribe or from Náhuatl (ancient Aztec) words meaning either "flying viper," "place where snakes slither," or "place with many trees."
CAPITAL Saltillo
AREA 58,521 square miles (151,571 square kilometers)
POPULATION 2,298,070
STATEHOOD 1864
HIGHEST POINT 12,306 feet (3,700 meters)
LOWEST POINT 328 feet (100 meters)
COAT OF ARMS

DURANGO
NAME After Durango, Spain, the hometown of Francisco de Ibarra, founder of Mexico's Durango.
CAPITAL Durango
AREA 47,560 square miles (123,181 square kilometers)
POPULATION 1,448,661
STATEHOOD 1824
HIGHEST POINT Cerro Gordo (10,991 feet; 3,340 meters)
LOWEST POINT Not available
COAT OF ARMS

NUEVO LEÓN
NAME Spanish for "New León." León (Spanish for "lion") was a kingdom of Spain and is today a province in Spain.
CAPITAL Monterrey
AREA 24,924 square miles (64,555 square kilometers)
POPULATION 3,834,141
STATEHOOD 1824
HIGHEST POINT Cerro el Potosi (12,182 feet; 3,700 meters)
LOWEST POINT Not available
COAT OF ARMS

TAMAULIPAS
NAME From the Huastec Indian word "Tamaholipa," meaning "place of many prayers" or "place of high mountains."
CAPITAL Ciudad Victoria
AREA 30,822 square miles (79,829 square kilometers)
POPULATION 2,753,222
STATEHOOD 1824
HIGHEST POINT 11,000 feet (3,420 meters)
LOWEST POINT Sea level
COAT OF ARMS

Copper Canyon, or Barranca del Cobre, is in the Sierra Tarahumara mountains in southwest Chihuahua. Over 5,000 feet (1,524 meters) deep, it is deeper than the Grand Canyon and is spread out over four times the area.

1836 Texas wins its independence from México.

1897 Construction begins on the Chihuahua-Pacífico Railroad. After many challenges, it is completed in 1961, linking Chihuahua and Los Mochis on the Pacific coast. The train is sometimes called the Chihuahua Choochoo and climbs through the Sierra Madre.

1883 México's first international telephone link is established between Matamoros, Tamaulipas, and Brownsville, Texas, across the Rio Grande.

1913 Francisco ("Pancho") Villa, a key figure in the Mexican revolution of 1910, becomes provisional governor of Chihuahua.

1922 German Mennonites, in search of religious freedom, begin settling in Chihuahua.

1973 Mexico's Baseball Hall of Fame is founded in Monterrey, Nuevo León.

131

Must-See Sites

CERRO DE LA BUFA (Bufa Mountain, Zacatecas) – The views of Zacatecas are breathtaking from the top of Bufa Mountain, site of Francisco ("Pancho") Villa's famous 1914 victory against government forces during the Mexican Revolution. A cable car takes you to the top, where there is a museum commemorating Villa's victory.

SANTUARIO DE LAS MARIPOSAS MONARCA, EL ROSARIO (El Rosario Monarch Butterfly Sanctuary, Michoacán) – Every fall, millions of monarch butterflies from Canada and the United States fly thousands of miles to the highlands in Michoacán and Mexico State to spend the winter. The El Rosario Sanctuary is one of about 12 monarch destinations.

ZOOLOGICO DE GUADALAJARA (Guadalajara Zoo) – If you still have plenty of energy after seeing the animals at this zoo, there's a planetarium and an amusement park next door.

The city of Guanajuato is one of the most historic cities in Mexico. It is also home to Guanajuato University, many art and history museums, and even an underground street built on the bed of an old river!

Inside Scoop

LAKE CHAPALA in Jalisco is Mexico's largest lake.

JALISCO is the birthplace of mariachi bands, the jarabe, or Mexican hat dance, and the flashy horsemanship seen at charreadas, Mexican rodeos.

THE CITY OF Aguascalientes is the site of Mexico's oldest state fair, held every spring since 1604. Visitors to the San Marcos fair enjoy fireworks, rides, craft shows, parades, bullfights, and the crowning of the festival queen.

HUNDREDS OF FANTASTIC ceremonial masks made by Mexico's native peoples are displayed at the National Mask Museum in the city of San Luis Potosí.

BUILT BY the Spanish more than 200 years ago, Querétaro's aqueduct still brings fresh water into the city today. The aqueduct is 6 miles (9.7 kilometers) long and 50 feet (15 meters) high.

THE CANDY MARKET in Morelia, Michoacán, is a wonderland of Mexican sweets. The market is especially busy on the Day of the Dead (Nov.1-2), when Mexicans buy great quantities of sugar skulls, skeletons, and other ghostly treats.

TIMELINE

1522 Spanish soldiers reach the Pacific coast territory of Colima. The city of Colima is founded in 1523.

1530 Guadalajara in Jalisco is founded. It is now Mexico's second largest city.

1575 The town of Aguascalientes is founded.

1546 Juan de Tolosa discovers the vast silver mines of Zacatecas. The precious metal helps fund Spanish colonial expansion and foreign wars into the next century.

1810 Father Miguel Hidalgo delivers his famous "Cry of Dolores"— a call to arms that triggers Mexico's 11-year struggle for independence from Spain— in the Guanajuato town of Dolores Hidalgo.

1848 The Treaty of Guadalupe Hidalgo, ending the Mexican-American War, is approved by the Mexican Congress in Querétaro, the nation's temporary capital. Mexico loses more than half its land to the United States.

Jalisco, Michoacan, Nayarit, Zacatecas

AGUASCALIENTES
NAME Spanish for "hot waters," referring to the state's many thermal springs.
CAPITAL Aguascalientes
AREA 2,158 square miles (5,589 square kilometers)
POPULATION 943,506
STATEHOOD 1835
HIGHEST POINT Sierra Fría (10,006 feet; 3,050 meters)
LOWEST POINT Calvillo Valley (5,250 feet; 1,600 meters)
COAT OF ARMS

COLIMA
NAME From the Náhuatl (ancient Aztec) word "coliman," thought to mean "place conquered by our ancestors."
CAPITAL Colima
AREA 2,106 square miles (5,455 square kilometers)
POPULATION 540,679
STATEHOOD 1856
HIGHEST POINT Volcán Fuego de Colima (12,989 feet; 3,959 meters)
LOWEST POINT Sea level
COAT OF ARMS

GUANAJUATO
NAME From the Tarascan Indian word meaning "frog mountain."
CAPITAL Guanajuato
AREA 11,880 square miles (30,769 square kilometers)
POPULATION 4,656,761
STATEHOOD 1824
HIGHEST POINT Cerro Los Rosillos (10,433 feet; 3,180 meters)
LOWEST POINT Cañón del río Santa María (2,625 feet; 800 meters)
COAT OF ARMS

JALISCO
NAME From the Náhuatl (ancient Aztec) word "xalisco," meaning "on sand."
CAPITAL Guadalajara
AREA 31,211 square miles (80,836 square kilometers)
POPULATION 6,322,002
STATEHOOD 1824
HIGHEST POINT Volcán Nevado de Colima 14,365 feet; 4,378 meters)
LOWEST POINT Sea level
COAT OF ARMS

MICHOACAN
NAME From the Náhuatl (ancient Aztec) word "michihuacán," meaning "place of the fishermen."
ABBREVIATION Mich.
CAPITAL Morelia
AREA 22,471 square miles (58,200 square kilometers)
POPULATION 3,979,177
STATEHOOD 1824
HIGHEST POINT Pico de Tancítaro (12,598 feet; 3,840 meters)
LOWEST POINT Sea level
COAT OF ARMS

NAYARIT
NAME From the Cora Indian word meaning "place of the god of battles."
CAPITAL Tepic
AREA 10,417 square miles (26,979 square kilometers)
POPULATION 920,185
STATEHOOD 1917
HIGHEST POINT Cerro El Vigía (9,055 feet; 2,760 meters)
LOWEST POINT Sea level
COAT OF ARMS

QUERETARO
NAME From the Otomí or Purépecha Indian words meaning "place of the stone" or "place of the great ball game."
CAPITAL Querétaro
AREA 4,420 square miles (11,978 square kilometers)
POPULATION 1,404,306
STATEHOOD 1824
HIGHEST POINT Cerro El Zamorano (3360 meters)
LOWEST POINT Near Jalapa (500 meters)
COAT OF ARMS

SAN LUIS POTOSI
NAME A combination of St. Louis (king of France) and Potosí, the name of the fabulous silver mountain in Bolivia, referring to the rich silver and gold deposits near San Luis.
CAPITAL San Luis Potosí
AREA 24,351 square miles (63,068 square kilometers)
POPULATION 2,299,360
Statehood 1853
HIGHEST POINT Cerro Grande (10,433 feet; 3,180 meters)
LOWEST POINT The meeting place of the Tampaon and Moctezuma rivers (328 feet; 100 meters)
COAT OF ARMS

ZACATECAS
NAME From the Náhuatl (ancient Aztec) word "zacatecatl," meaning "people of the pastures."
CAPITAL Zacatecas
AREA 28,973 square miles (75,040 square kilometers)
POPULATION 1,353,610
STATEHOOD 1824
HIGHEST POINT Sierra de Mazapil (9,974 feet; 3,040 meters)
LOWEST POINT Cañón de Juchipila
COAT OF ARMS

The tiny village of Yelapa on the southern coast of Banderas Bay in Jalisco can only be reached by boat and has no electricity. Even so, Yelapa has attracted many artists from elsewhere in North America who live there year round.

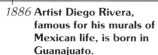

1886 Artist Diego Rivera, famous for his murals of Mexican life, is born in Guanajuato.

1888 The railroad joining Mexico City and Guadalajara, Jalisco, is completed.

1960–65 The University of Aguascalientes is established.

1982 Colima-born Miguel de la Madrid becomes president of Mexico.

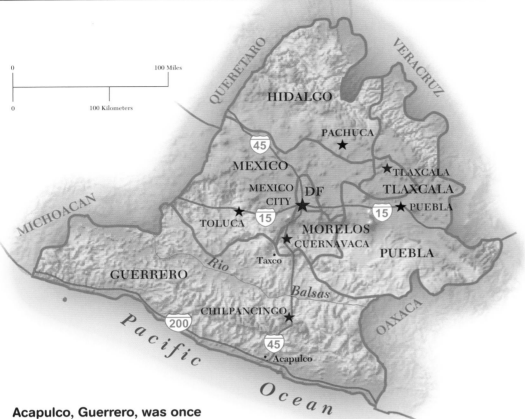

0 100 Miles
0 100 Kilometers

QUERETARO

VERACRUZ

HIDALGO

PACHUCA ★

45

MEXICO

MICHOACAN

MEXICO CITY ★ DF

TOLUCA ★

15

★ TLAXCALA

TLAXCALA

★ PUEBLA

15

MORELOS

CUERNAVACA ★

Taxco •

Rio

Balsas

PUEBLA

GUERRERO

OAXACA

CHILPANCINGO ★

200

Pacific

45

Acapulco •

Ocean

The Church of San Francisco in Puebla is well known for its colorful tiles. Although the church was damaged during a 1999 earthquake, it is being restored.

Acapulco, Guerrero, was once the place where Spanish treasure ships came ashore carrying riches from Asia for almost 300 years. After a new road was cut through the surrounding mountains in 1927, connecting Acapulco to Mexico City, Acapulco's beaches started to attract visitors from around the world. By the 1950s, Acapulco had became the most famous resort in México, attracting the rich and famous.

Inside Scoop

THE LA QUEBRADA CLIFFS in Acapulco (Guerrero) are famous for the daredevil divers who plunge 135 feet (41 meters) into a narrow cove, hitting the water at about 60 mph (97 kph).

PUEBLA'S most famous dish is turkey (or chicken) in mole poblano, or "Puebla-style sauce," a rich, dark blend of chili peppers, spices, almonds, and chocolate.

ACCORDING TO LEGEND, Quetzalcóatl, the "plumed serpent" god widely worshipped in pre-Spanish México, was born in the ancient Toltec capital of Tula. Tula's ruins are Hidalgo's most-visited attraction.

THE CITY OF TAXCO (Guerrero) is one of North America's oldest mining towns, and its mines still supply many silver shops.

TIMELINE

1325 Tenochtitlán, the capital of the Aztec empire, is founded in what is today México City.

1519 The Tlaxcalan people ally themselves with Hernán Cortés, and go on to play an important role in his conquest of the Aztec capital of Tenochtitlan, today's México City.

1813 México's first Congress meets in Chilpancingo (capital of Guerrero).

1523 Spanish Friar Pedro de Gante establishes México's first school for Indians in Texcoco (México State).

1862 On May 5, poorly armed and outnumbered Méxican soldiers defeat French invasion forces at Puebla, a great victory that is still celebrated by Méxicans as Cinco de Mayo.

1824 The new Federal Constitution of the United Méxican States establishes a Federal District, encompassing México City as the seat of the federal government.

DISTRITO FEDERAL
NAME Spanish for "Federal District."
CAPITAL México City
AREA 579 square miles
(1,499 square kilometers)
POPULATION 8,605,239
STATEHOOD Created in 1824,
incorporating the nation's capital.
HIGHEST POINT Volcan Ajusco
(12,890 feet; 3,930 meters)
LOWEST POINT Not available
COAT OF ARMS

Must-See Sites

IZTACCÍHUATL-POPOCATÉPETL NATIONAL PARK (México, Puebla and Morelos) –
In this park are the two snowcapped volcanoes that tower over the Valley of México, and straddle three states. Popocatépetl (Nahuatl for "smoking mountain") is still active but Iztaccíhuatl ("white lady") is not. They are México's second and third highest peaks.

PLAZA DE LA CONSTITUCION (Constitution Plaza, Distrito Federal) –
México City's Zócalo (main square) is the center of Méxican national life and one of the world's great public squares. It is surrounded by the 16th century Metropolitan Cathedral, City Hall, and the National Palace, which contains the offices of the nation's president and cabinet. The Zócalo was the main plaza of Tenochtitlán, the capital of the Aztec empire.

TEOTIHUACÁN ARCHEOLOGICAL SITE (México) –
Teotihuacán (Náhuatl for "place where men become gods") was one of the world's largest cities and a major religious center about A.D. 500. And then mysteriously, some time after A.D. 650, it was abandoned. Its ruins include the great Pyramid of the Sun, Pyramid of the Moon, palaces, temples, and many other fascinating structures.

GUERRERO
NAME In honor of Vicente Guerrero, a hero in México's struggle for independence.
CAPITAL Chilpancingo
AREA 24,818 square miles (64,281 square kilometers)
POPULATION 3,075,083
STATEHOOD 1849
HIGHEST POINT Cerro Teotepec (11,647 feet; 3,550 meters)
LOWEST POINT Sea level
COAT OF ARMS

HIDALGO
NAME In honor of Father Miguel Hidalgo, the Catholic priest known as the "Father of Méxican Independence."
CAPITAL Pachuca
AREA 8,071 square miles (20,905 square kilometers)
POPULATION 2,235,591
STATEHOOD 1869
HIGHEST POINT Cerro El Rosario (11,290 feet; 3,440 meters)
LOWEST POINT Not available
COAT OF ARMS

MÉXICO
NAME From "Méxica" (pronounced "Meshica"), the name of a group of nomadic native peoples, among them the Aztecs, who founded a city they called México around 1325.
CAPITAL Toluca
AREA 8,245 square miles (21,355 square kilometers)
POPULATION 13,096,686
STATEHOOD 1824
HIGHEST POINT Popocatépetl (17, 887 feet; 5, 452 meters)
LOWEST POINT Near Vicente Guerrero Dam in the Balsas River basin
COAT OF ARMS

MORELOS
NAME In honor of José María Morelos, a hero in the Méxican War of Independence.
CAPITAL Cuernavaca
AREA 1,911 square miles (4,950 square kilometers)
POPULATION 1,555,296
STATEHOOD 1869
HIGHEST POINT Volcan Popocatépetl (17,887 feet; 5,452 meters)
LOWEST POINT Cuernavaca Valley (4,921 feet; 1,500 meters)
COAT OF ARMS

PUEBLA
NAME Spanish for "town" (from the original Spanish name of the state capital, Puebla de los Angeles, or "Town of the Angels").
CAPITAL Puebla
AREA 13,096 square miles (33919 square kilometers)
POPULATION 5,076,686
STATEHOOD 1824
HIGHEST POINT Volcan Pico de Orizaba (18,410 feet; 5,600 meters)
LOWEST POINT Not available
COAT OF ARMS

TLAXCALA
NAME From the Náhuatl (ancient Aztec) word "tlaxcalla," meaning "place of the tortilla."
CAPITAL Tlaxcala
AREA 1,568 square miles (4,061 square kilometers
POPULATION 962,646
STATEHOOD 1857
HIGHEST POINT Malinche (14,640 feet; 4,420 meters)
LOWEST POINT Not available
COAT OF ARMS

1869 **The states of Hidalgo and Morelos are carved out of the State of México.**

1890 Telephone service begins in Tlaxcala.

1910 **The Méxican Revolution begins throughout the country. Emiliano Zapata, from Morelos State, leads a people's army that helps topple México's dictator, Porfirio Díaz.**

1950 Acapulco becomes one of the world's most popular tourist destinations.

1968 México City hosts the Summer Olympic Games.

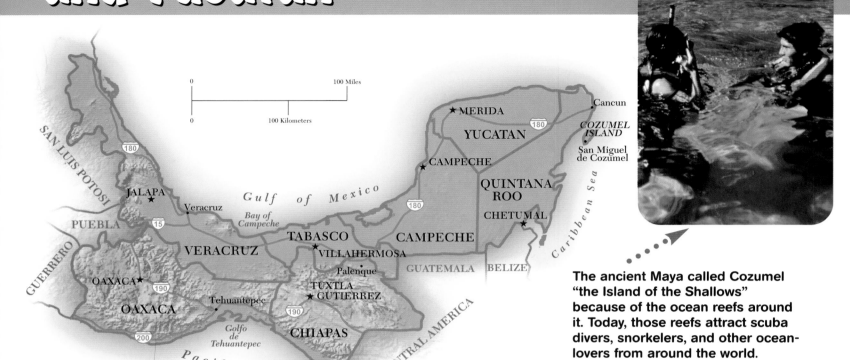

The ancient Maya called Cozumel "the Island of the Shallows" because of the ocean reefs around it. Today, those reefs attract scuba divers, snorkelers, and other ocean-lovers from around the world.

Originally built in about the year 500 by the Maya people, Chichen Itza (Yucatán) is the best known and one of the oldest ruins in México. By about the year 1000, it was occupied by the warlike people called the Toltec. The Temple of 1000 Warriors, seen here, was probably built by the Toltec. It is guarded by Chac Mool, Toltec god of rain.

Inside Scoop

ONE OF THE WORLD'S OLDEST and largest trees is the Tule tree of Santa Maria del Tule in the state of Oaxaca. It is more than 2,000 years old and the circumference of its trunk measures 138 feet (42 meters).

CHEWING GUM is made with a sticky substance called chicle that comes from sapodilla trees in Quintana Roo and other southern states of México. Historians believe the ancient Mayans chewed it more than 1,000 years ago.

COZUMEL ISLAND, off Quintana Roo's Caribbean coast, is a superb place from which to snorkel or scuba dive and see coral reefs swarming with thousands of brilliantly colored fish.

RITUAL BALL GAMES were an important part of the religious and social life of many cultures in pre-Spanish México.

TIMELINE

400 B.C.–A.D. 900 The Mayan Indians build in Yucatan and the Zapotec Indians build in Oaxaca.

1519 Spanish conquistador Hernán Cortés lands on Cozumel Island (Quintana Roo) and goes on to found the city of Veracruz, from which he begins his conquest of México.

1806 Benito Juárez, México's first president of Indian descent, is born in Oaxaca.

1568 Spanish and Méxican forces in Veracruz defeat the English pirate John Hawkins and his famous explorer-nephew, Francis Drake.

c.1888 Henequen, a thorny plant from whose fibers twine and burlap are made, creates an economic boom in Mérida (Yucatán).

1839 Englishman Frederick Catherwood and American John Stephens rediscover the Mayan city of Palenque in present-day Chiapas.

FRESH FACTS

CAMPECHE
NAME From the Maya word "canpech," meaning "place of serpents and ticks."
CAPITAL Campeche
AREA 21,953 square miles (56,858 square kilometers)
POPULATION 731,336
STATEHOOD 1863
HIGHEST POINT near Laguna Champerico (1,280 feet; 390 meters)
LOWEST POINT Sea level
COAT OF ARMS

Must-See Sites

CHICHEN ITZA ARCHEOLOGICAL ZONE
(Yucatán)—Chichen Itza, the sacred city of the Mayas, was founded about the year 500 and includes the largest pre-Spanish ball-court in the Americas, an astronomical observatory, and the great "El Castillo" ("The Castle") pyramid, whose design was based on the Mayan solar calendar.

MONTE ALBÁN ARCHEOLOGICAL ZONE
(Oaxaca) — The Zapotec capital of Monte Albán ("white mountain") was founded about 500 B.C. on a leveled hill overlooking Oaxaca. A palace, a ball-court, and ceremonial platforms border the city's great central plaza.

PALENQUE NATIONAL PARK
(Chiapas)—People from around the world marvel at the ancient Maya city of Palenque, with its magnificent palaces, towers, tombs, and ball-courts — all surrounded by a lush rain forest filled with birds, monkeys, and other wildlife.

CHIAPAS
NAME Thought to come from the Náhuatl (ancient Aztec) word "chiapan," meaning "where the chía grows" (chía is a type of sage, an herb).
CAPITAL Tuxtla Gutiérrez
AREA 28,653 square miles (74,211 square kilometers)
POPULATION 3,920,892
STATEHOOD 1824
HIGHEST POINT Volcan Tacana (13,428 feet; 4,080 meters)
LOWEST POINT Sea level
COAT OF ARMS

OAXACA
NAME From the Náhuatl (ancient Aztec) word "huaxyacac," meaning "place where the guaje (wild tamarind) begin."
CAPITAL Oaxaca
AREA 36,820 square miles (95,364 square kilometers)
POPULATION 3,438,765
STATEHOOD 1824
HIGHEST POINT Cerro el Nacimiento (12,300 feet; 3,700 meters)
LOWEST POINT Sea level
COAT OF ARMS

QUINTANA ROO
NAME In honor of Andrés Quintana Roo, noted Yucatán poet, philosopher, and political leader, who fought for Mexico's independence from Spain.
CAPITAL Chetumal
AREA 19,631 square miles (50,844 square kilometers)
POPULATION 874,963
STATEHOOD 1974
HIGHEST POINT near Tres Garantias (790 feet; 240 meters)
LOWEST POINT Sea level
COAT OF ARMS

TABASCO
NAME Thought to come from the Náhautl (ancient Aztec) for "place that has an owner" or "place where the earth is damp," a reference to the state's many lagoons and swamps and abundant rainfall.
CAPITAL Villahermosa
AREA 9,756 square miles (24,578 square kilometers)
POPULATION 1,891,829
STATEHOOD 1824
HIGHEST POINT near Raya Zaragoza (3,940 feet; 1,200 meters)
LOWEST POINT Sea level
COAT OF ARMS

VERACRUZ
NAME From the Latin words "vera crux," meaning "true cross."
CAPITAL Jalapa
AREA 27,961 square miles (72,420 square kilometers)
POPULATION 6,908,975
STATEHOOD 1824
HIGHEST POINT Not available
LOWEST POINT Sea level
COAT OF ARMS

YUCATÁN
NAME According to legend, when asked by the first Spanish explorers what the name of the region was, local Mayans replied, "Yucatan," Mayan for "I don't understand."
CAPITAL Mérida
AREA 16,748 square miles (43,379 square kilometers)
POPULATION 1,658,210
STATEHOOD 1843
HIGHEST POINT 19 unnamed points (690 feet; 210 meters)
LOWEST POINT Sea level
COAT OF ARMS

1899 The world-renowned painter Rufino Tamayo is born in Oaxaca.

1914 The United States intervenes in the Méxican Revolution, which began in 1910. U.S. naval forces seize Veracruz in April and withdraw in November.

1972 New oil deposits are discovered in Chiapas.

1974 Cancun, in the state of Quintana Roo, becomes a major tourist resort. Computers help plan and design it.

Central America

The Garífuna people, who are descendants of Africans brought to the New World as slaves, live along the Caribbean coast in Belize, Nicaragua, Guatemala and Honduras. The Garífuna have a unique form of music, with bands composed of three large drums, a turtle shell, maracas, and a large conch shell.

QUINTANA ROO

CAMPECHE

TABASCO

BELIZE

GUATEMALA

BELMOPAN

MEXICO

CHIAPAS

Gulf of Honduras

Caribbean Sea

2

9

HONDURAS

GUATEMALA CITY

TEGUCIGALPA

1

SAN SALVADOR

EL SALVADOR

NICARAGUA

Lago de Managua

MANAGUA

2

Lago de Nicaragua

The Guatemalan town of Chichicastenago is famous for its Sunday and Thursday markets that attract tourists from around the world. Local merchants, wearing their colorful traditional costumes, sell all [kind]s of crafts, including masks, [ham]mocks, blankets and other textiles, [as] well as basic necessities like socks.

COSTA RICA

SAN JOSE

Pacific

PANAMA

Ocean

0   100 Miles

0   100 Kilometers

TIMELINE

400 B.C. to A.D. 900 Mayan Indians are the ruling culture in Central America. No one knows why they abandon their cities around A.D. 900.

1502 Christopher Columbus, sailing for Spain, explores the Caribbean coast of Central America, from Honduras to Panama.

1570 Spain sets up an administrative center (Audiencia) in Guatemala, which rules over all of Central America except Panama.

1501 Spanish explorers Rodrigo de Bastidas and Juan de la Cosa are the first Europeans to visit the coast of Central America.

1525 Spanish conquistadors control the region.

1821 Costa Rica, El Salvador, Guatemala, Honduras, and Nicaragua become independent from Spain.

AREA 201,000 square miles
(521,000 square kilometers)

POPULATION 37 million

HIGHEST POINT Volcán Tajumulco,
Guatemala (13,845 feet; 4,220 meters)

LOWEST POINT Sea level

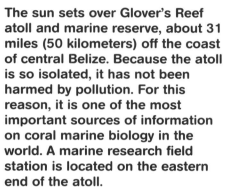

The sun sets over Glover's Reef atoll and marine reserve, about 31 miles (50 kilometers) off the coast of central Belize. Because the atoll is so isolated, it has not been harmed by pollution. For this reason, it is one of the most important sources of information on coral marine biology in the world. A marine research field station is located on the eastern end of the atoll.

Scarlet macaws are native to both Guatemala and Belize, as well as to México and some parts of South America. Scarlet macaws form a life-long bonds with their mates. Sadly, because forests are being cleared for human beings and because macaws are being hunted for their feathers or to be sold as pets, they have become endangered.

Inside Scoop

ALTHOUGH CENTRAL AMERICA is in the tropics, it is a mountainous region and there is snow at high elevations.

THE COUNTRIES OF Central America are subject to severe earthquakes, hurricanes, and volcanic eruptions that can, and have, caused extensive damage and loss of life.

BELIZE is the only English-speaking country in Central America.

THE COUNTRIES OF Central America produce about 10 percent of the world's coffee and bananas.

PANAMA
CITY

Gulf
of
Panama

COLOMBIA

1903 Panama, which has been united with Colombia, becomes an independent nation.

1940s–1950s Military dictatorships take over a number of Central American countries.

1990s Peace agreements are signed after civil wars have been waged in several Central American countries.

1823–38 Costa Rica, El Salvador, Guatemala, Honduras, and Nicaragua form a united federation.

1914 The Panama Canal is completed.

1981 Belize gains independence from the United Kingdom.

Must-See Sites

LAKE ATITLAN (Guatemala) – The lake's pure blue waters and bordering volcanoes attract many tourists. The area's exotic flowers, birds and other animals add to the beauty of the place.

MONTECRISTO NATIONAL PARK (El Salvador) – Montecristo is the country's largest tropical mountain forest. It has a great variety of plants, 230 species of birds including quetzals (brilliant green tropical birds), and endangered animals, such as spider monkeys.

PULHAPANZAK (Honduras) – Waterfalls cascade more than 300 feet (91 meters) over a cliff into a jungle canyon. Many tourists come here to hike, swim, and visit the nearby Mayan ceremonial center.

Inside Scoop

BELIZE HAS the world's second longest barrier reef, which lies just off the country's Atlantic coast.

CHRISTOPHER COLUMBUS, or perhaps a later explorer, named the land "Honduras," the Spanish word for "depths," after the deep waters off its northern coast.

EL SALVADOR'S IZALCO VOLCANO sprang up suddenly in 1770 and grew for 187 years. It was nicknamed "Lighthouse of the Pacific," because its molten lava could be seen at night for miles out at sea.

MORE THAN 880 KINDS of animals live in Guatemala, including armadillos, macaws, and quetzals, the brightly colored birds with long, flowing tail feathers.

A traditional dance troupe in Yuscaran, Honduras, performs with the aid of large puppets.

TIMELINE

400 B.C.–A.D. 900 Mayan civilizations flourish in present-day Belize, El Salvador, Guatemala, and Honduras.

1638 Shipwrecked British sailors start the first English settlement in present-day Belize. More English colonists settle there over the next two centuries.

1821 Costa Rica, El Salvador, Guatemala, Honduras, and Nicaragua declare independence from Spain, forming a Central American federation that lasts until 1838.

1502 Christopher Columbus claims Honduras for Spain.

1520s Spain conquers what is now Belize, El Salvador, and Guatemala.

1862 Present-day Belize becomes a British colony and is named British Honduras.

Guatemala

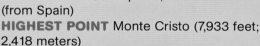

FRESH FACTS

BELIZE
CAPITAL Belmopan
AREA 8,763 square miles
(22,696 square kilometers)
POPULATION 251,000
INDEPENDENCE Sept. 21, 1981
(from the United Kingdom)
HIGHEST POINT Victoria Peak (3,680 feet;
1,122 meters)
LOWEST POINT Sea level

EL SALVADOR
CAPITAL San Salvador
AREA 8,124 square miles
(21,041 square kilometers)
POPULATION 507,000
INDEPENDENCE Sept. 15, 1821
(from Spain)
HIGHEST POINT Monte Cristo (7,933 feet;
2,418 meters)
LOWEST POINT Sea level

GUATEMALA
CAPITAL Guatemala City
AREA. 42,042 square miles
(108,889 square meters)
POPULATION. 11,980,000
INDEPENDENCE Sept. 15, 1821
(from Spain)
HIGHEST POINT Volcán Tajumulco (13,845 feet;
4,220 meters)
LOWEST POINT Sea level

HONDURAS
CAPITAL Tegucigalpa
AREA 43,277 square miles
(112,088 square kilometers)
POPULATION 6,812,000
INDEPENDENCE Sept. 15, 1821
(from Spain)
HIGHEST POINT Cerro Las Minas
(9,347 feet; 2,849 meters)
LOWEST POINT Sea level

Most Guatemalans (and most people throughout Latin America) belong to the Catholic Church. To celebrate Good Friday, a beautiful "carpet" made entirely of colored sawdust is laid in the street. Villagers dress in biblical clothing and watch as a flower-draped float is pulled down the street along the carpet.

1973 **British Honduras is renamed Belize.**

1983 **El Salvador adopts a new constitution and restores democracy after more than 50 years of dictatorships and military governments.**

1992 **Government and guerrilla forces in El Salvador end 12 years of civil war.**

2000 **El Salvador, Guatemala, and Honduras sign a free trade agreement with Mexico to increase economic activity.**

1969 **Honduras and El Salvador fight a brief border war.**

1981 **Honduras elects a civil government after nearly a century of military rule, revolutions, and violence.**

1996 **Guatemalan rebels and government forces sign a peace agreement, ending more than 30 years of conflict.**

Must-See Sites

CAHUITA NATIONAL PARK (Costa Rica) — Fascinating coral reefs just offshore are the park's main attraction. The white sandy beaches, coconut trees, and clear seawater make it a wonderful place to snorkel and swim. A glass-bottom boat gives you a good view of blue parrotfish, angelfish, and other tropical marine life in this aquatic garden.

COMMANDANTE EDGARD LANG SACASA ZOO (Nicaragua) — The zoo is the home to many animals, including some from the tropical rain forests. Among the 50 species here are monkeys, crocodiles, peccaries (wild pigs), pumas, and parrots.

TORTUGUERO NATIONAL PARK (Costa Rica) — "Tortuga" means "turtle" and this park was set up to protect green sea turtles that nest here by the thousands. The beaches are great for walking, but swimming is not advised because of riptides and sharks.

Costa Rica's Arenal Volcano is an active cone-shaped volcano. During the daytime, you can see clouds of smoke flowing from Arenal's crater. At night, spectators can sometimes see lava and burning rocks flying through the air!

TIMELINE

1502 Christopher Columbus claims present-day Costa Rica, Nicaragua, and Panama for Spain.

1513 Spanish explorer Vasco Núñez de Balboa is the first European to cross the Isthmus of Panama and see the east coast of the Pacific Ocean.

1564 Juan Vásquez de Coronado, Spanish conquistador, sets up the first permanent European settlement at present-day Cartago, Costa Rica.

1821 Panama breaks ties with Spain and becomes a province of Colombia.

1912 U.S. Marines arrive in Nicaragua to protect American economic interests and remain for more than 20 years.

1914 The Panama Canal, which crosses the Isthmus, is completed, linking the Caribbean Sea and the Pacific Ocean.

Large freighters like this one can sail from the Atlantic to the Pacific through the 51-mile (82 kilometer) Panama Canal in just eight hours. Before the canal opened in 1914, boats had to sail around the southern tip of South America.

Inside Scoop

PERFECTLY ROUND BALLS, some more than 6 feet (2 meters) high, are scattered over the Diquis region in southwest Costa Rica. Made of hard granite, they are thought to be about 1,000 years old. No one knows why they were carved by ancient people.

A SPANISH SHIP CARRYING 700 tons of treasure from Peru sank in 1631 and was found off the coast of Panama in 2002. The value of the treasure, including gold and silver ingots, was estimated at $50 million.

PANAMA IS AN ISTHMUS, the link between North and South America.

IT TOOK 10 YEARS to dig the Panama Canal, which is 51 miles (82 kilometers) long. Thousands of workers from 40 countries helped build it.

FRESH FACTS

COSTA RICA
CAPITAL San Jose
AREA 19,730 square miles (51,100 square kilometers)
POPULATION 4,188,000
INDEPENDENCE Sept. 15, 1821 (from Spain)
HIGHEST POINT Chirripo Grande (12,530 feet, 3,819 meters)
LOWEST POINT Sea level

NICARAGUA
CAPITAL Managua
AREA 50,193 square miles (130,000 square kilometers)
POPULATION 5,350,000
INDEPENDENCE Sept. 15, 1821 (from Spain)
HIGHEST POINT Pico Mogoton (6,913 feet; 2,107 meters)
LOWEST POINT Sea level

PANAMA
CAPITAL Panama City
AREA 29,157 square miles (75,517 square kilometers)
POPULATION 2,938,000
INDEPENDENCE Nov. 3, 1903 (from Colombia)
HIGHEST POINT Vocán Baru (11,401 feet; 3,475 meters)
LOWEST POINT Sea level

1948–49 Costa Rica disbands its army and replaces it with a civilian guard. It is the only nation in the Western Hemisphere without an army.

1987 Costa Rica President Oscar Arias Sanchez wins the Nobel Peace Prize for his efforts to establish peace in Central America.

1990 Free elections defeat the Sandinistas in Nicaragua.

2000 Costa Rica and Nicaragua settle a border dispute over use of the San Juan River.

1937–79 The Somoza family rules Nicaragua.

1979 Sandinista rebels rule Nicaragua.

1999 Mireya Moscoso is elected president of Panama, the country's first female leader.

The Caribbean

UNITED STATES

FLORIDA

Gulf of Mexico

MEXICO

★ HAVANA

CUBA

CAYMAN ISLANDS
★ GEORGE TOWN

JAMAICA ★ KINGSTON

THE BAHAMAS

★ NASSAU

A T L A N T I C

CAICOS ISLANDS

COCKBURN TOWN ★ TURKS ISLANDS

DOMINICAN REPUBLIC

PORT-AU-PRINCE ★

HAITI ★ SANTO DOMINGO

C a r i b b e a n   S e a

ARUBA   BONAIR

CURAÇAO

S O U T

0 ——— 500 Miles
0 ——— 500 Kilometers

Originally settled by the Spanish in 1521, the seven-square-block area of Old San Juan in Puerto Rico is partly enclosed by walls built to protect from invasion. Even today, some streets are paved with bricks that were once used for ballast in Spanish treasure ships!

One of the most popular sounds of the Caribbean is that of the steel drum. Neville York, a native of St. Maarten, is one of the top 10 steel drum players in the world. Although he often travels the world performing with symphony orchestras, he always makes time for concerts back home.

TIMELINE

500 B.C. – A.D. 600 Ancestors of the Taino Indians migrate from northern South America up the Lesser Antilles to Puerto Rico and Hispaniola. Taino culture reaches its peak in the Greater Antilles from A.D.1200–1500.

1510 The first African slaves arrive in Hispaniola to work the gold mines.

1600s The French, British, Dutch, and Danes establish colonies in the Caribbean. Slaves are brought to work the sugar plantations.

1492–1504 Christopher Columbus discovers the islands he names the West Indies.

1496 The Spanish establish the first permanent European settlement in the Caribbean at what is now Santo Domingo on Hispaniola.

c. 1530 French, British, and Dutch pirates begin attacking Spanish ships and ports in the Caribbean.

FRESH FACTS

NAME Also called the West Indies because Christopher Columbus thought he had discovered parts of India.

AREA 90,618 square miles (234,700 square kilometers)

POPULATION 36,026,000

HIGHEST POINT Duarte Peak, Dominican Republic (10,417 feet; 3,175 meters)

LOWEST POINT Lake Enriquillo, Dominican Republic (151 feet; 46 meters below sea level)

GREATER ANTILLES Cuba, Hispaniola (shared by Haiti and the Dominican Republic), Jamaica, Puerto Rico

LESSER ANTILLES Anguilla, Antigua and Barbuda, Aruba, Barbados, Bonaire, British Virgin Islands, Curaçao, Dominica, Grenada, Guadeloupe, Martinique, Montserrat, Saba, Saint Barthélemy, Saint Eustatius, Saint Kitts and Saint Nevis, Saint Lucia, Saint Martin/Sint Maarten, St. Vincent and the Grenadines, Trinidad and Tobago, U.S. Virgin Islands

OCEAN

PUERTO RICO
SAN JUAN
ST. THOMAS TORTOLA
ST. JOHN ANGUILLA
ST. CROIX
ST. KITTS BARBUDA
ST. MARTIN ANTIGUA
NEVIS ST. JOHNS
GUADELOUPE
MONSERRAT BASSE-TERRE
DOMINICA
ROSEAU
MARTINIQUE
FORT-DE-FRANCE
CASTRIES
ST. LUCIA
BARBADOS
ST. VINCENT
KINGSTOWN
BRIDGETOWN
ST GEORGE'S GRENADA
TORTUGA TOBAGO
PORT-OF-SPAIN
TRINIDAD

AMERICA

Inside Scoop

THE ISLANDS OF the Caribbean are divided into three groups: 1) the Bahamas, the Cayman Islands, and the Turks and Caicos; 2) the Greater Antilles: Cuba, Jamaica, Hispaniola (shared by Haiti and the Dominican Republic) and Puerto Rico; and 3) the Lesser Antilles, which include the arc of smaller islands from the U.S. Virgin Islands south to Trinidad and Tobago, off the northeastern coast of South America.

THE INDIANS Christopher Columbus met in the Caribbean consisted of three groups: the Lucayans of the Bahamas, the peaceful Tainos of the Greater Antilles, and the fierce Caribs of the Lesser Antilles.

"CANOE," "hurricane," "hammock," and "tobacco" are a few of the Taino Indian words that have become part of the English language.

THE CARIBBEAN is famous for its rhythmic music: reggae from Jamaica, calypso from Trinidad, merengue from the Dominican Republic, and salsa from Puerto Rico and Cuba.

BLACK SAND BEACHES are made of volcanic rock ground up fine like baby powder. White sand beaches are made mostly of ground-up coral, limestone, or chalk.

The scuba diving in the waters off Turks and Caicos Islands is thought to be some of the best in the world. One reason is "the Wall", a 7,000 foot (2,100 meter) offshore trench that attracts experienced divers from around the world.

1833 Britain grants freedom to slaves throughout its empire. France does so in 1848, and the Netherlands in 1863.

1917 The United States buys the Virgin Islands from Denmark.

1968 The Caribbean Free Trade Area is established. In 1973 it becomes the Caribbean Common Market, or CARICOM.

1804 After a 13-year struggle, Haiti wins its independence from France, becoming the first black-ruled nation in the modern world and the first independent nation in the Caribbean.

1898 Spain is defeated in the Spanish-American War and cedes its last New World colonies, Cuba and Puerto Rico, to the United States.

1962 The Cuban missile crisis brings the United States and the Soviet Union to the brink of war.

The Bahamas, Cayman Islands,

Founded in 1519, Havana is one of the oldest cities in North America. In 1896, the USS Maine blew up in Havana harbor. The explosion started the Spanish-American War, which led to Cuba winning its independence. The remains of the USS Maine can still be seen at the bottom of Havana harbor.

Every year, residents of the Bahamas celebrate a festival called the Junkanoo Fest. Junkanoo dates back to 1600 when African slaves were given a special holiday at Christmas time, when they could leave the plantations to be with their families and celebrate with African dance, music, and costumes.

Inside Scoop

THE CAYMAN ISLANDS' name comes from the Carib Indian word for the marine crocodile once found on the islands. Christopher Columbus had named the islands "Las Tortugas" for all the large turtles he saw in the waters.

CUBA IS the largest of the Caribbean islands.

ERNEST HEMINGWAY'S fishing trips off the Bimini Islands in The Bahamas inspired him to write his famous story "The Old Man and the Sea."

TIMELINE

1492 On Oct.12, Christopher Columbus lands in the Bahamas, his first stop in the New World.

1647 Religious freedom-seekers from England and Bermuda establish the first European colony in the Bahamas.

1503 Christopher Columbus sights the Cayman Islands during his fourth and last voyage to the New World.

1511 Spanish forces under Diego Velázquez conquer Cuba and establish settlements.

1670 The Cayman Islands are ceded to Britain by the Treaty of Madrid.

146

and Cuba

THE BAHAMAS
ISLANDS About 20 of the 3,000 islands, cays, and reefs are inhabited. Most people live on the islands of New Providence and Grand Bahama.
CAPITAL Nassau, New Providence
AREA 5,380 square miles (13,934 square kilometers)
POPULATION 297,852
INDEPENDENCE July 10, 1973 (from the United Kingdom)
HIGHEST POINT Mount Alvernia, Cat Island (206 feet; 63 meters)
LOWEST POINT Sea level
FLAG

CAYMAN ISLANDS
ISLANDS Grand Cayman, Little Cayman, Cayman Brac
CAPITAL George Town, Grand Cayman
AREA 100 square miles (259 square kilometers)
POPULATION 35,527 (estimate)
INDEPENDENCE None (overseas territory of the United Kingdom)
HIGHEST POINT The Bluff (141 feet; 43 meters)
LOWEST POINT Sea level
FLAG

CUBA
CAPITAL Havana
AREA 42,804 square miles (110,862 square kilometers)
POPULATION 11,184,023
INDEPENDENCE May 20, 1902 (from the United States)
HIGHEST POINT Pico Turquino (6,578 feet; 2,005 meters)
LOWEST POINT Sea level
FLAG

The Cayman Islands are one of the world's most famous places for scuba diving. You'll find an amazing variety of fish, coral, and other sea life!

Must-See Sites
ATLANTIS SUBMARINE (Grand Cayman) – Sailing out of George Town harbor, this 48-passenger underwater vessel provides great views of coral reefs and sea creatures at a depth of up to 100 feet (30 meters).

CRYSTAL CAY MARINE PARK (New Providence, The Bahamas) – You can get up close to the shark tank, sea turtle pool, stingray pool, and 24 separate aquariums at this park in Nassau. Touch underwater creatures at the Marine Encounter Pool and view the underwater coral reef from above and below at the offshore observation tower.

PIRATES OF NASSAU (New Providence, The Bahamas) – Learn all about local pirates and their adventures from taped commentaries, sound effects, and costumed interpreters. Climb aboard a full-scale replica of Blackbeard's boat, named "Revenge."

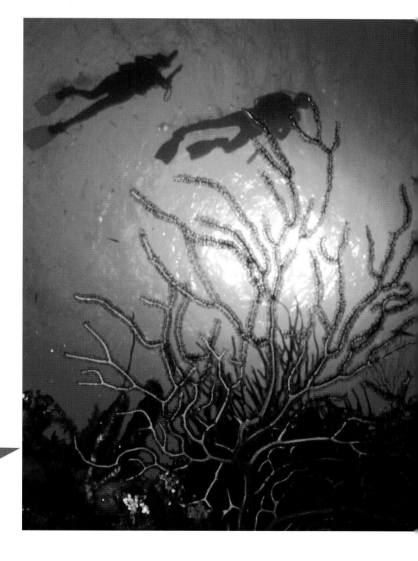

1898 The United States defeats Spain in the Spanish-American War. Spain cedes Cuban to the United States and it is ruled by a U.S. military governor.

1959 Fidel Castro and his revolutionary forces take control of Cuba.

1962 The Cayman Islands are separated politically from Jamaica and vote to remain a British dependency.

1895 Writer José Martí launches a war for Cuban independence from Spain.

1902 Cuba becomes independent, and its first president is sworn in.

1973 The Bahamas achieve independence from the United Kingdom.

The sun sets over Grand Caicos Island. The earliest shipwreck ever discovered in the Americas was found in these waters. The ship can now be seen in the Turks and Caicos National Museum.

CAICOS

COCKBURN TOWN   TURKS

Atlantic Ocean

0 ——————————— 100 Miles

0 ——————————— 100 Kilometers

Santiago

HAITI

DOMINICAN REPUBLIC

PORT-AU-PRINCE

SANTO DOMINGO

Montego Bay

Caribbean Sea

JAMAICA

KINGSTON

Jamaica's Blue Mountains get their name from the greenish-blue color of the thick plants and trees that cover their slopes.

Inside Scoop

THE DOMINICAN CAPITAL of Santo Domingo is home to the first paved street, stone house, cathedral, hospital, university, and fortress in the New World.

DOMINICANS ARE wild about baseball. The country has produced such major league stars as Juan Marichal, the Alou brothers, Juan Samuel, Tony Perez, Tony Fernandez, Pedro Martinez, Mariano Duncan, and Sammy Sosa.

JAMAICA IS famous for its reggae music, especially the songs of the late, great star Bob Marley. His birthday on Feb. 6 is celebrated by fans as Bob Marley Day.

AMERICAN ASTRONAUT John Glenn splashed down near Grand Turk after his historic space flight in 1962.

TIMELINE

1492 On Christmas Day, Christopher Columbus founds a settlement, La Navidad ("The Nativity"), on Hispaniola, in what is now Haiti.

1509 The first Spanish settlements in Jamaica are established.

1512 Juan Ponce de León discovers the Turks and Caicos Islands.

1494 Christopher Columbus claims Jamaica for Spain.

1496 Christopher Columbus' brother Bartolomé establishes a town in southeastern Hispaniola, in what is now the Dominican Republic. This becomes Santo Domingo.

1655 The British capture Jamaica from the Spanish.

FRESH FACTS

DOMINICAN REPUBLIC
CAPITAL Santo Domingo
AREA 18,815 square miles (48,730 square kilometers)
POPULATION 8,581,477
INDEPENDENCE Feb. 27, 1844 (from Haiti)
HIGHEST POINT Duarte Peak (10,417 feet; 3,175 meters)
LOWEST POINT Lake Enriquillo (151 feet [46 meters] below sea level)
FLAG

HAITI
CAPITAL Port-au-Prince
AREA 10,714 square miles (27,750 square kilometers)
POPULATION 6,964,549
INDEPENDENCE Jan.1, 1804 (from France)
HIGHEST POINT La Selle Peak (8,793 feet; 2,680 meters)
LOWEST POINT Sea level
FLAG

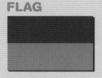

JAMAICA
CAPITAL Kingston
AREA 4,243 square miles (10,990 square kilometers)
POPULATION 2,665,636
INDEPENDENCE Aug. 6, 1962 (from the UK)
HIGHEST POINT Blue Mountain Peak (7,402 feet; 2,256 meters)
LOWEST POINT Sea level
FLAG

TURKS and CAICOS ISLANDS
ISLANDS About 30 islands. The major ones are: Grand Turk and Salt Cay (Turks); North, Middle (also known as Grand), South, East, and West Caicos, and Providenciales (Caicos).
CAPITAL Cockburn Town
AREA 166 square miles (430 square kilometers)
POPULATION 18,122
INDEPENDENCE None (overseas territory of the United Kingdom)
HIGHEST POINT Blue Hills (161 feet; 49 meters)
LOWEST POINT Sea level
FLAG

Must-See Sites

COLUMBUS LIGHTHOUSE (Dominican Republic) — This massive seven-story cross-shaped lighthouse was opened in 1992 to house what are thought to be the remains of Christopher Columbus.

PROSPECT PLANTATION (Jamaica) — Jitney tours take visitors behind the scenes of a large working Jamaican plantation near Ocho Rios. Guides identify and describe the crops and other plants that grow on the estate.

RIO GRANDE RAFTING (Jamaica) — Rafting is popular on several Jamaican rivers. One of the most exciting rides is the 2.5-hour trip down the Rio Grande near Port Antonio on a bamboo raft.

Merengue is the most popular dance and the favorite type of music in the Dominican Republic.

1697 Spain recognizes French rule over the western third of Hispaniola, today's Haiti.

1822 Haiti conquers the newly declared republic on the Spanish side of Hispaniola.

1962 Jamaica becomes a member of the United Nations.

1991 Turks and Caicos National Museum opens on Grand Turk.

1670 Jamaica is ceded to Britain by the Treaty of Madrid.

1804 Haiti wins its independence from France.

1844 Juan Pablo Duarte leads a successful revolt against Haitian rule in Spanish Hispaniola and establishes the Dominican Republic.

1994 Haitian president Jean-Bertrand Aristide resumes office after being toppled by a military coup and is re-elected in 2000.

Must-See Sites

ARCHAEOLOGICAL MUSEUM (St. Martin) – Learn about the island's first inhabitants at this collection of pre-Columbian pottery and objects, called "On the Trail of the Arawaks."

ARECIBO OBSERVATORY (Puerto Rico) – View the world's largest and most sensitive radio-radar telescope close up and sample the observatory's interactive exhibits and video displays.

BUCK ISLAND REEF NATIONAL MONUMENT (St. Croix) – Underwater trails along the offshore barrier reef offer great snorkeling and sightseeing, and markers identify the reef's plants and animals.

FORT SAN FELIPE DEL MORRO (Puerto Rico) – A symbol of Old San Juan, El Morro Fort was the most strategic part of San Juan's colonial defense system. Begun in 1539, El Morro has withstood attacks by British, Dutch, and French invaders.

Because Puerto Rico is an overseas commonwealth of the United States, these young girls and all Puerto Ricans are U.S. citizens.

Visitors to Anguilla can splash along the shore of white, sandy beaches on horseback.

Inside Scoop

PUERTO RICO'S Caribbean National Forest, or El Yunque, is the only tropical rain forest that is part of the United States. Annual rainfall at the highest elevations is more than 200 inches (508 centimeters).

THE VIRGIN ISLANDS National Park covers about two-thirds of St. John and includes offshore waters.

THE FIRST MONDAY in August is the start of Carnival week in Anguilla, featuring sailboat races, calypso contests, street dancing, and the coronation of the Carnival Queen.

TIMELINE

1493 Columbus discovers Anguilla, Puerto Rico, Saba, St. Barthélemy, St. Martin/St. Maarten, Saint Eustatius, and the Virgin Islands.

1508 Juan Ponce de León founds Caperra, the start of Spanish settlement of Puerto Rico.

1636 The Dutch gain control of St. Eustatius.

1648 France and the Netherlands agree to share the island of St. Martin/St. Maarten.

1649 Anguilla becomes a British colony.

1816 Saba becomes a Dutch possession.

FRESH FACTS

ANGUILLA
CAPITAL The Valley
AREA 37 square miles
(96 square kilometers)
POPULATION 12,132
INDEPENDENCE None (overseas territory of the United Kingdom)
HIGHEST POINT Crocus Hill
(213 feet; 65 meters)
LOWEST POINT Sea level
FLAG

BRITISH VIRGIN ISLANDS
ISLANDS Anegada, Jost van Dyke, Tortola, Virgin Gorda Islands (largest)
CAPITAL Road Town, Tortola
AREA 59 square miles
(153 square kilometers)
POPULATION 20,812
INDEPENDENCE None (overseas territory of the United Kingdom)
HIGHEST POINT Mount Sage
(1,709 feet; 521 meters)
LOWEST POINT Sea level
FLAG

PUERTO RICO
CAPITAL San Juan
AREA 3,515 square miles
(9,104 square kilometers)
POPULATION 3,937,316
INDEPENDENCE None (commonwealth associated with the U.S.)
HIGHEST POINT Cerro de Punta
(4,390 feet; 1,338 meters)
LOWEST POINT Sea level
FLAG

SABA
CAPITAL The Bottom
AREA 5 square miles
(13 square kilometers)
POPULATION 1,500
INDEPENDENCE None (part of the Netherlands Antilles)
HIGHEST POINT Mount Scenery
(2,920 feet; 890 meters)
LOWEST POINT Sea level
FLAG

ST. BARTHÉLEMY
CAPITAL Gustavia
AREA 8 square miles
(21 square kilometers)
POPULATION 5,800
INDEPENDENCE None (overseas department of Guadeloupe)
HIGHEST POINT Morne Vitet (922 feet; 281 meters)
LOWEST POINT Sea Level
FLAG

ST. EUSTATIUS (STATIA)
CAPITAL Oranjestad
AREA 8 square miles
(21 square kilometers)
POPULATION 2,300
INDEPENDENCE None (part of the Netherlands Antilles)
HIGHEST POINT Mount Mazinga
(1,968 feet; 600 meters)
LOWEST POINT Sea level
FLAG

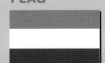

ST. MARTIN
CAPITAL Marigot
AREA 21 square miles
(54 square kilometers)
POPULATION 32,900
INDEPENDENCE None (French overseas department of Guadeloupe)
HIGHEST POINT Paradise Peak
(1,391 feet; 424 meters)
LOWEST POINT Sea level
FLAG

ST. MAARTEN
CAPITAL Philipsburg
AREA 13 square miles (34 square kilometers)
POPULATION 47,400
INDEPENDENCE None (part of the Netherlands Antilles)
HIGHEST POINT Paradise Peak
(1,391 feet; 422 meters)
LOWEST POINT Sea level
FLAG

UNITED STATES VIRGIN ISLANDS
ISLANDS Saint Croix, Saint John, Saint Thomas
CAPITAL Charlotte Amalie, St. Thomas
AREA 132 square miles
(342 square kilometers)
POPULATION 122,211 (estimated)
INDEPENDENCE None (territory of the United States)
HIGHEST POINT Crown Mountain, St. Thomas (1,556 feet; 474 meters)
LOWEST POINT Sea level
FLAG

1898 Spain cedes Puerto Rico to the United States after the Spanish-American War.

1917 Puerto Ricans become U.S. citizens. Denmark sells St. Croix, St. John, and St. Thomas to the United States.

1952 Puerto Rico becomes a commonwealth of the United States.

1980 Anguilla becomes a British territory separate from St. Kitts and St. Nevis.

Antigua and Barbuda, Dominica, Monserrat, St. Kitts and Nevis, St. Vincent and the Grenadines

On Nevis, hikers will enjoy climbing through forest that encircles the slopes of Nevis Peak, the island's highest mountain.

Must-See Sites

BRIMSTONE HILL FORTRESS NATIONAL PARK (near Basseterre, St. Kitts) – The British commissioned this fort to be built in the late 1600s and thought it was invincible. The French proved them wrong in 1782. Tour the fort and find out how the British and the French struggled for control in the 1700s. Enjoy the scenic views from the top of the hill.

MORNE TROIS PITONS NATIONAL PARK (Dominica) – The park is the first natural heritage site in the eastern Caribbean and only the second in the Caribbean to be listed as a UNESCO World Heritage Site. It includes a rain forest, river pools, and thousands of tropical flowers.

VOLCANO AND SULPHUR SPRINGS (St. Lucia) – La Soufrière has been called the world's only drive-in volcano, because a road goes right there. A path winds around the crater past bubbling pools of grayish mud and smoldering hot springs that emit sulphuric gases.

ST. KITTS

BASSETERRE
NEVIS

BARBUDA

ST. JOHNS

ANTIGUA

MONSERRAT

PLYMOUTH

GUADALOUPE

BASSE-TERRE

DOMINICA

ROSEAU

MARTINIQUE

FORT-DE-FRANCE

LESSER ANTILLES

CASTRIES
ST. LUCIA

ST. VINCENT

KINGSTOWN

0   100 Miles

0   100 Kilometers

Climb a palm tree on Grand Anse des Salines beach to watch the sun set over Martinique.

TIMELINE

1493 Christopher Columbus discovers Antigua, Dominica, Guadeloupe, Martinique, St. Kitts and Nevis, and St. Lucia.

1632 The British establish a colony on Antigua.

1814 France cedes St. Lucia to the United Kingdom.

1623 The British establish a settlement on St. Kitts.

1635 France colonizes Martinique and Guadeloupe.

1783 The British gain control of St. Vincent and the Grenadines from the French and native Caribs.

Guadeloupe, Martinique, St. Lucia,

Few challenges compare to reeling in a fish as big as a marlin. This one was caught off the coast of Dominica.

Inside Scoop

DOMINICA'S BOILING LAKE is the world's second largest boiling lake. Gases from underground molten lava keep the water percolating at nearly 200° F (93° C) and the steamy vapors rising.

NAPOLEON BONAPARTE'S WIFE, Empress Josephine, was born on Martinique, the daughter of a French planter.

ST. LUCIA'S TWO VOLCANIC PEAKS, Petit Piton and Gros Piton, are among the Caribbean's most well-known natural landmarks.

ANTIGUA AND BARBUDA
CAPITAL St. John's, Antigua
AREA 171 square miles (443 square kilometers)
POPULATION 66,970
INDEPENDENCE Nov. 1,1981 (from the United Kingdom)
HIGHEST POINT Boggy Peak (1,319 feet; 402 meters)
LOWEST POINT Sea level
FLAG

DOMINICA
CAPITAL Roseau
AREA 290 square miles (751 square kilometers)
POPULATION 70,786
INDEPENDENCE Nov. 3,1978 (from the United Kingdom)
HIGHEST POINT Morne Diablatins (4,747 feet; 1,447 meters)
LOWEST POINT Sea level
FLAG

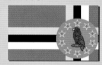

GUADELOUPE
CAPITAL Basse-Terre
AREA 687 square miles (1,779 square kilometers)
POPULATION 431,170
INDEPENDENCE None (overseas department of France)
HIGHEST POINT Soufrière (4,813 feet; 1,467 meters)
LOWEST POINT Sea level
FLAG

MARTINIQUE
CAPITAL Fort-de-France
AREA 424 square miles (1,100 square kilometers)
POPULATION 418,454
INDEPENDENCE None (overseas department of France)
HIGHEST POINT Montagne Pelée (4,583 feet; 1,397 meters)
LOWEST POINT Sea level
FLAG

MONSERRAT
CAPITAL Plymouth
AREA 39 square miles (101 square kilometers)
POPULATION 5,000
INDEPENDENCE None (overseas territory of the United Kingdom)
HIGHEST POINT Chances Peak (2,999 feet; 914 meters)
LOWEST POINT Sea level
FLAG

ST. KITTS AND NEVIS
CAPITAL Basseterre, St. Kitts
AREA 101 square miles (262 square kilometers)
POPULATION 38,756
INDEPENDENCE Sept. 19, 1983 (from the United Kingdom)
HIGHEST POINT Mount Liamuiga (3,792 feet; 1,156 meters)
LOWEST POINT Sea level
FLAG

ST. LUCIA
CAPITAL Castries
AREA 240 square miles (622 square kilometers)
POPULATION 158,178
INDEPENDENCE Feb. 22, 1979 (from the United Kingdom)
HIGHEST POINT Mount Gimie (3,117 feet; 950 meters)
LOWEST POINT Sea level
FLAG

ST. VINCENT AND THE GRENADINES
CAPITAL Kingston
AREA 150 square miles (389 square kilometers)
POPULATION 115,942
INDEPENDENCE Oct. 27,1979 (from the United Kingdom)
HIGHEST POINT La Soufrière (4,049 feet; 1,234 meters)
LOWEST POINT Sea level
FLAG

1967 St. Kitts, St. Nevis, St. Lucia are granted self-government.

1980 Mary Eugenia Charles becomes Dominica's prime minister, the first female to hold that position in the Caribbean.

1995 Soufrière Hills' volcano erupts on Monserrat for the first time.

Aruba, Bonaire, Barbados, and Tobago

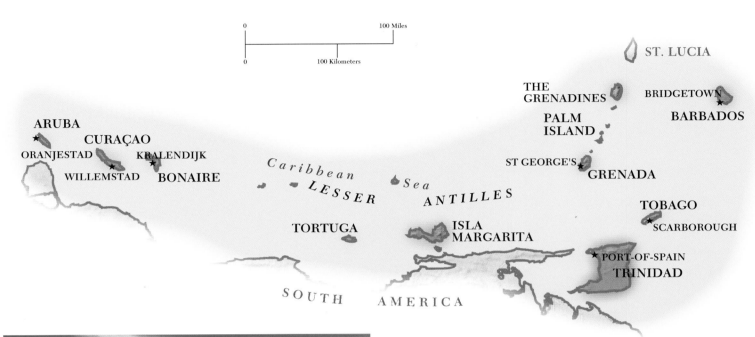

ST. LUCIA

THE GRENADINES
BRIDGETOWN
PALM ISLAND
BARBADOS

ARUBA
CURAÇAO
ORANJESTAD
KRALENDIJK
WILLEMSTAD
BONAIRE

Caribbean Sea
LESSER ANTILLES

ST GEORGE'S
GRENADA

TOBAGO
SCARBOROUGH

TORTUGA
ISLA MARGARITA

PORT-OF-SPAIN
TRINIDAD

SOUTH AMERICA

0   100 Miles
0   100 Kilometers

A cactus in the Caribbean? It's true. This scene on the island of Curaçao is just one of the deserts found in Aruba and Dutch territories of Bonaire and Curaçao.

Inside Scoop

CURAÇAO'S GUILDER COINS are the only square-shaped coins in the world and are prized as souvenirs.

GRENADA IS KNOWN as the Spice Island of the Caribbean because of all the spices that grow there, including nutmeg, cinnamon, cloves, bay leaves, ginger, saffron, and others.

THE ISLAND on which the fictional character Robinson Crusoe was stranded is believed to have been modeled after Tobago.

Wild iguanas are common sights in Curaçao. In fact, barbecued iguana and iguana soup are both local delicacies.

TIMELINE

1498 Christopher Columbus discovers Grenada and Trinidad.

1627 The British begin to colonize Barbados.

1889 Trinidad and Tobago are united as a single British colony.

1634 The Dutch take control of Aruba and neighboring islands over the next 15 years, creating the Netherlands Antilles.

1797 The British take over Trinidad from Spain, ruling for the next 165 years.

1783 The British take over Grenada from the French.

Curaçao, Grenada, Trinidad

Must-See Sites

GOTO MEER LAKE (Bonaire) – Great numbers of pink flamingos gather at this inland lake. The best time to view the graceful birds is early in the morning.

NATURAL BRIDGE (Aruba) – The 100-foot (30-meter) coral bridge was shaped by the continuous pounding of the sea against the coral cliffs, which wore the rock away over centuries of time. The bridge arches 25 feet (8 meters) above the sea.

NATIONAL UNDERWATER PARK (Curaçao) – Snorklers and scuba divers can follow the marked underwater trails past sunken ships, tropical fish, coral reefs, sponges, anemones, and other marine life. Before or after, visit the aquarium and observe sea lions, sharks, stingrays, and other sea animals.

Riding the waves on a banana boat like these teens are doing is just one of the activities you can find in Aruba.

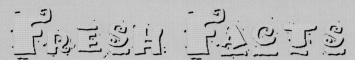

ARUBA
CAPITAL Oranjestad
AREA 75 square miles (194 square kilometers)
POPULATION 70,007
INDEPENDENCE Jan.1,1986 (from the Netherlands Antilles)
HIGHEST POINT Mount Jamanota (617 feet; 188 meters)
LOWEST POINT Sea level
FLAG

BONAIRE
CAPITA Kralendijk
AREA 111 square miles (287 square kilometers)
POPULATION 17,500
INDEPENDENCE None (part of Netherlands Antilles)
HIGHEST POINT Brandaris (787 feet; 240 meters)
LOWEST POINT Sea level
FLAG

BARBADOS
CAPITAL Bridgetown
AREA 166 square miles (430 square kilometers)
POPULATION 275,330
INDEPENDENCE Nov. 30, 1966 (from the United Kingdom)
HIGHEST POINT Mount Hillaby (1,102 feet; 336 meters)
LOWEST POINT Sea level
FLAG

CURAÇAO
CAPITAL Willemstad
AREA 171 square miles (443 square kilometers)
POPULATION 186,300
INDEPENDENCE None (part of Netherlands Antilles)
HIGHEST POINT St. Christoffelberg (1,220 feet; 372 meters)
LOWEST POINT Sea level
FLAG

GRENADA
CAPITAL St. George's
AREA 133 square miles (344 square kilometers)
POPULATION 89,227
INDEPENDENCE Feb. 7, 1974 (from the United Kingdom)
HIGHEST POINT Mount St. Catherine (2,755 feet; 846 meters)
LOWEST POINT Sea level
FLAG

TRINIDAD AND TOBAGO
CAPITAL Port-of-Spain
AREA 1,980 square miles (5,128 square kilometers)
POPULATION 1,169,682
INDEPENDENCE Aug. 31,1962 (from the United Kingdom)
HIGHEST POINT El Cerro del Aripo (3,084 feet; 940 meters)
LOWEST POINT Sea level
FLAG

Grenada's colorful food market is at its busiest on Saturdays, as vendors sell all types of fruits, vegetables, seafood, and spices.

1962 Trinidad and Tobago become an independent nation.

1966 Barbados gains independence from Britain.

1983 Rebels take over Grenada. U.S. and Caribbean armed forces arrive and restore the government. Elections resume in 1984.

1958 Barbados, Grenada, and Trinidad and Tobago, along with seven other British colonies, form the Federation of the West Indies.

1974 Grenada gains independence from Britain.

1986 Aruba separates from the Netherlands Antilles.

1995 Basdeo Panday becomes prime minister of Trinidad and Tobago, the first person of Indian heritage to do so.

Index

All place names listed in the AAA GEM sections, timelines, Fresh Facts, Inside Scoops, and captions are indexed here.

Photo Credits

PEOPLE

North American country with largest population: United States of America – 281,421,906 (see p. 22)

North American country with smallest population: St. Kitts and Nevis – 38,756 (see p. 153)

North American country with highest percentage of children: Mexico, with over one-third of its total population under 14.

North American country or territory with lowest population density in North America (and the world): Greenland, with one person per 10 square miles (0.3 square kilometers)

U.S. state with largest population: California – 33,871,648 (see p. 33)

U.S. state with smallest population: Wyoming – 493,782 (see p. 124)

Mexican state with largest population: Mexico State – 13,096,686 (see p. 135)

Mexican state with smallest population: Baja California Sur – 424,041 (see p. 129)

Canadian province or territory with largest population: Ontario – 11,410,046 (see p. 17)

Canadian province with smallest population: Nunavut – 26,745 (see p. 15)

Canadian city with largest population: Toronto: 2,481,494

Central American nation with largest population: Guatemala – 11,980,000 (see p. 141)

Central American nation with the smallest population: Belize – 251,000 (see p. 141)

Caribbean nation with largest population: Cuba – 11,184,023 (see p. 147)

Caribbean country with smallest population: St. Kitts and Nevis – 38,756 (see p. 153)

PLACES

Largest North American country: Canada – 3,556,000 square miles (9,220,970 square kilometers) (see p. 9)

Smallest North American country: St. Kitts and Nevis – 101 square miles (261 square kilometers) (see p. 153)

Largest U.S. state: Alaska – 663,267 square miles (1,717,861 square kilometers) (see p. 27)

Smallest U.S. state: Rhode Island – 1,545 square miles (4,001 square kilometers) (see p. 103)

Largest Mexican state: Chihuahua – 94,831 square miles (245,612 square kilometers) (see p. 131)

Smallest Mexican state or district: Distrito Federal – 579 square miles (1,499 square kilometers) (see p. 135)

Largest Canadian province or territory: Northwest Territories – 1,322,910 square miles (3,426,337 square kilometers) (see p. 15)

Smallest Canadian province or territory: Prince Edward Island – 2,185 square miles (5,560 square kilometers) (see p.18)

Largest Central American nation: Nicaragua – 50,193 square miles (130,000 square kilometers) (see p. 143)

Smallest Central American nation: El Salvador – 8,124 square miles (21,041 square kilometers) (see p. 141)

Largest Caribbean nation: Cuba – 42,804 square miles (110,861 square kilometers) (see p. 147)

Smallest Caribbean nation: St. Kitts and Nevis – 101 square miles (261 square kilometers) (see p. 153)

Longest river in North America: Mississippi/Missouri river system – 3,740 miles (6,020 kilometers).

Shortest river in North America: The D River, Lincoln City, Oregon – 120 feet (37 meters), connecting Devil's Lake and the Pacific Ocean

Deepest lake in North America: Great Slave Lake, Northwest Territories – 2,015 feet (614 meters)

Largest lake in North America: Lake Superior, 31,700 square miles (82,103 square kilometers)

Highest point in North America: Mount McKinley, Alaska – 20,320 feet (6,194 meters) (see p. 27)

Lowest point in North America: Death Valley, Calif. – 282 feet below sea level (86 meters below sea level) (see p. 33)

Highest tides in North America: Bay of Fundy, Nova Scotia – 56 feet (17 meters) (see p. 16)

Northernmost occupied area in North America (and the world): Thule, Greenland – 800 people, 76° north latitude (see p. 6)

Highest temperature in North America: Death Valley, Calif. on July 10, 1913: 134°F (56.7°C) (see p. 33)

Lowest temperature in North America: Northice, Greenland, on Jan. 9, 1954: -87°F (-66°C) (see p. 6)

First British colony to ratify the U.S. Constitution and become a state: Delaware, in 1787 (see p. 39)

Oldest continuously occupied settlement in North America: St. Augustine, Fla., inhabited since 1565

Newest Canadian province or territory: Nunavut Territory in 1999 (see p. 15)

Newest U.S. state: Hawaii, admitted to the United States in 1959 (see p. 46)

THINGS

Biggest living thing in North America: the honey mushroom, which grows underground at Malheur National Forest, John Day, Ore.: 2,200 acres (736 hectares)

Oldest living thing in North America: Bacillus bacteria from a salt mine in Carlsbad, N.M.: 250 million years old

Largest discovery of dinosaur bones in North America: Dinosaur National Monument, Dinosaur, Colo.: over 2,000 bones from the Jurassic Period (see p. 34)

Tallest building in North America (by highest occupied floor): Sears Tower, Chicago, Ill.: 1,450 feet (442 meters) (see p. 51)

Tallest building in North America (including TV and radio antennas): CN Tower, Toronto, Ontario: 1,815 feet (553.33 meters) (see p. 17)

Biggest roller coaster in North America: Millennium Force at Cedar Point, Sandusky, Ohio: 310 feet high, 92 mph, 6,595 feet of track (94.5 meters high, 148 kph, 2,010 meters of track) (see p. 95)

Biggest mall in North America: West Edmonton Mall, Edmonton, Alberta: 5.3 million square feet (493,000 square meters) (see p. 10)

Biggest mall in the United States: The Mall of America, Bloomington, Minn.: 4.2 million square feet (390,194 square meters)